PERSONAL REMINISCENCES

BY

BARHAM, HARNESS, AND HODDER.

Bric-a-Brac Series

PERSONAL REMINISCENCES

BY

BARHAM, HARNESS, AND HODDER.

EDITED BY

RICHARD HENRY STODDARD

NEW YORK
SCRIBNER, ARMSTRONG, AND COMPANY
1875

RIVERSIDE, CAMBRIDGE:
STEREOTYPED AND PRINTED BY
H. O. HOUGHTON AND COMPANY.

CONTENTS.

PREFACE.

IF reasons for the existence of some books are occasionally sought by their readers, the class of books to which this volume belongs generally presents "its own excuse for being." The world demands it. "The world," says stalwart *Christopher North*, "would seem to have a natural right to know much of the mind, morals, and manners of the chosen few — as they exhibited themselves in private life, — whose genius may have delighted or enlightened it, — to know more than in general can have been revealed in their works. It desires this, not from a paltry and prying curiosity, but in a spirit of love, or admiration, or gratitude, or reverence. It is something to the reader of a great poet, but to have seen him, to be able to say '*Virgilium tantum vidi.*' How deeply interesting to hear a few characteristic anecdotes related of him by some favored friend! To have some glimpses, at least, if not full and broad lights, given to us into his domestic privacy and the inner on-goings beneath what, to our imaginations, is a hallowed roof! We cannot bear to think that our knowledge of our benefactors — for such they are — should be limited to the few and scanty personal notices that may be scattered under the impulse of peculiar emotions here and there, over their writings; we cannot bear to think that, when the grave closes upon them, their memory must survive only in their works; but the same earnest and devout spirit that gazes upon the shadows of their countenances on the limner's canvas, yearns to hear it told, in pious biography, what manner of men they were at the frugal or the festal board, by the fire-side, in the social or the family circle, in the discharge of those duties that solemnize the relations of kindred, and that support the roof-tree of domestic life."

The personal reminiscences which follow concern a number of illustrious names, most of whom belong to the England of the present century. They are drawn from the works of those men of letters, who, if not great themselves, were frequently in contact with greatness, — Barham, Harness, and Hodder. A few pages concerning them may not be unacceptable here.

Richard Harris Barham was born December 6, 1788, at Canterbury. He was the only son of Richard Harris Barham, a gentleman of good family, and a *bon-vivant* who died in 1795, leaving a moderate fortune somewhat encumbered. In consequence of the feeble health of his mother, the fatherless boy of seven was left to the three-fold guardianship of Mr. Morris Robinson, afterwards Lord Rokeby, a Mr. Morris, and a rascally attorney, whose name has not been handed down. Young Barham was sent at the age of nine to St. Paul's School, where he made rapid progress in the classics. In his fourteenth year he was nearly killed by the upsetting of the Dover mail, in which he was travelling on his way to town. He thrust his hand from the window for the purpose of opening the door just as the vehicle turned over upon its side, pinning his exposed limb to the ground, and dragging it some distance along a recently repaved road. He recovered from his injuries after a long illness, and without suffering amputation, and continuing for two years at St. Paul's he entered as a gentleman commoner Brazenose College, where he made the acquaintance of Theodore Hook, and where, after passing his examination, he took a Bachelor's degree. He intended originally to study for the bar, and went so far as to enter the office of Chitty, the eminent conveyancer; but he changed his mind, and entering holy orders was admitted to the curacy of Ashford, in Kent, in 1813.

He was married shortly afterward, and in 1817 was promoted by the Archbishop of Canterbury to the rectory of Snargate. Two years later he was overturned in his gig with his two children, breaking his right leg. He was confined to the house for several weeks, which he turned to account by writing a work entitled, "Baldwin." After his recovery he made a visit to London, where he learned that a minor canonry in St. Paul's was vacant. He resolved to relinquish his curacy and canvass for it. He succeeded in obtaining it, and in the summer of 1821 took up his abode permanently in London. His family having increased, a larger income than he had hitherto enjoyed was necessary, and he set to work resolutely to procure it by literature. He edited the "London Chronicle," a journal originally conducted by Dr. Johnson; he wrote light articles in prose and verse on the topics of the day, with an occasional review in "John Bull," the "Globe and Traveller," the "Literary Gazette," "Blackwood," and other periodicals, besides assisting in the production of a Biographical Dictionary.

The success which attended Barham in his literary labors attended him in his clerical career. In 1824 he received the appointment of priest in ordinary of His Majesty's Chapels Royal, and was presented to the incumbency of St. Mary Magdalen and St. Gregory by St. Paul's, which he held for about eighteen years. In 1842 he was elected to the presidency of Sion College, and in the same year his long services at St. Paul's were rewarded with the Divinity lectureship, and by being allowed to exchange his living for that of St. Faith.

Barham's last days were darkened by illness, which appears to have been brought on by his own imprudence. The Queen visited London in state in the autumn of 1844, for the purpose of presiding at the ceremony of opening the new Royal Exchange, and Barham, wishing to witness the pageant, accepted seats for himself and his family at the house of one of his parishioners. The weather was bleak; a strong east wind whistled through the open windows, and he caught a severe cold. His case became so alarming in the following winter that he was ordered to Bath, where his health improved. He returned to London imprudently to attend a meeting of the Archælogical Association, caught cold again, and had a relapse. He recovered sufficiently in May to undertake a journey to Clifton with his wife, who was ill. The journey benefited neither. A temporary convalescence enabled them to return to town, where, on the morning of June 17, 1845, Barham expired, in the fifty-seventh year of his age.

The life of Barham was in a certain sense typical of the class to which he belonged. He enjoyed life, loved his friends, was fond of a good dinner and a good story, a right-minded, jovial English parson. Literature was as much his amusement as his employment, the work by which he is best known, "The Ingoldsby Legends," ranking high among the drolleries of English humorous verse. They originally appeared in the pages of "Bentley's Miscellany," where they attracted as much attention as the fictions of its young editor, Charles Dickens.

The life of William Harness was simple and uneventful. He was born on March 14, 1790, near the village of Wickham, where his father, Dr. Harness, resided until 1796, when, on the breaking out of war, he accompanied Lord Hook to the Mediterranean as physician to the fleet. He was afterwards sent to Lisbon, whither his family followed him. When they returned to England, young Harness, who was then in his twelfth year, was placed at Harrow, where he had Lord Byron for his schoolfellow. From Harrow he proceeded to Christ's College, Cambridge, where he took his degree. Shortly after he was graduated he was ordained to the curacy of Kilmeston, near Abresford. He soon received an appointment to St. Pancras, London, where he entered the list of Shakespearian editors by an edition of his favorite poet. It was published in 1825. A second edition, with plates, appeared in 1830; and a third, with illustrations by Heath and others, in 1833. Other editions, in different forms, were issued in 1836, 1840, and 1842. In 1837 he published a little story, "Reverses," in "Blackwood," which his friend and early playfellow, Mary Russell Mitford, pronounced delightful. He published also four volumes of an edition of Massinger, and wrote a dramatic poem, "The Wife of Antwerp," which he printed for private circulation.

After Harness's removal to London he was made private chaplain to the Dowager Countess of Delaware, and became successively morning preacher at Trinity Chapel, and minister and evening lecturer at St. Ann's, Soho.

A note, jotted down incidentally, on the back of one of his sermon cases in commemoration of some country visitors, bears incidental testimony that he commanded the confidence of the most eminent clergymen in the metropolis: "September 7th, 1823. I preached to-day at St. George's, St. Pancras, and the Magdalen, and was heard at each place by the same party from the country, who went to St. George's to hear the Dean of Carlisle, to St. Pancras to hear Moore, and to the Magdalen to hear Pitman! Poor creatures! they were ignorant that the great preachers are away in September!" In 1825 he was appointed Minister of Regent Square Chapel, an important and arduous post, which he occupied for nearly twenty years. His success in the pulpit was the principal cause of his being selected for it; and during his time the chapel was densely crowded, not only by parishioners, but by members of other congregations. At a later period a church was built for him at Knightsbridge. His last literary labor was to edit the Letters and write the "Life of Miss Mitford."

The end of Harness was a tragical one. In November, 1869, he made a visit into the country at the Deanery of an old friend. He was well when he arrived, and spent the greater portion of two days in reading Shakespeare. The next day he walked for a considerable time up and down the garden, and returning to the house by some new stairs, remarked to the Dean, "When you are an old man you'll repent having placed those stairs there!" His last hour was approaching. "Later in the day some friends called, and a lady observed that he seemed in unusually good spirits, and that, but for his slight deafness, no one would have thought him an old man. He talked with animation, and seemed to take as much interest as ever in the affairs of life, although he observed, somewhat sadly, that he had survived all his contemporary friends. They left at six o'clock, and, the Dean having by this time started to keep an engagement in St. Leonards, Mr. Harness was left quite alone. At half-past six his servant came to the study to inform him that it was time to prepare for dinner, when, to his consternation, he found the room vacant; and almost at the same time the butler, who was going across the hall, was horrified at finding Mr. Harness's body lying head-foremost at the bottom of the stone stairs. He saw at once that he was dead; his head was lying in a pool of blood; but his expression was so peaceful and benign, the man said, that, although he knew he was dead, he could almost have imagined he was asleep.

"It seems probable that Mr. Harness left the study when the light was uncertain, just before the lamps were lit, and in the dusk did not observe the staircase. On examination, it was found that the skull was severely fractured." He died on the 11th of November, 1869, in his eightieth year.

Of George Hodder I know only what he has chosen to tell regarding himself, which is next to nothing. Sensible, modest, hard-working, he does not appear to have been fortunate in his profession. His chief claim to remembrance is that he was the amanuensis of Thackeray, when that great writer was composing his "Four Georges."

From the recollections of this unknown man of letters, and these well known English clergymen, the materials of the present volume are drawn. Mr. Hodder's rambling autobiography is entitled "Memoirs of my Time, including Personal Reminiscences of Eminent Men" (London,

1870). The biography of Byron's schoolfellow, "The Literary Life of the Rev. William Harness" (London 1871), was written by the Rev. A. G. L'Estrange, a trusted friend, who assisted him in collecting and arranging the letters of Miss Mitford. The biography of the creator of Ingoldsby, "The Life and Letters of the Rev. Richard Harris Barham" (London 1870), was written by his son, R. H. D. Barham. The substance of these volumes is here presented, and I trust it will prove entertaining.

R. H. S.

RICHARD HARRIS BARHAM.

RICHARD HARRIS BARHAM.

Theodore Hook.

BOUT this time (1827) Mr. Barham found opportunities of renewing his acquaintance with one, who, in many respects, was to be ranked among the most extraordinary men of his age — Mr. Theodore Hook. To say nothing of this gentleman's unequaled happiness in impromptu versification, conveying, as he not unfrequently did, a perfect epigram in every stanza — a talent, by the way, which sundry rivals have affected to consider mere knack, and one of whom long bore in his side the *lethalis arundo* of James Smith, for his bungling effort at imitation ; to pass by those practical jokes with which his name is so commonly associated, and in the devising and perpetration of which he was *facile princeps*, Mr. Hook possessed depth and originality of mind, little dreamed of, probably, by those who were content to bask in the sunshine of his wit, and to gaze with wonder at the superficial talents which he exhibited at table, but sufficient, nevertheless, to place him far beyond the position of a mere sayer of good things, or " diner-out of the first water." To those, indeed, who have never been fortunate enough to witness those extraordinary displays, no description can convey even a faint idea of the brilliancy of his conversational powers, of the inexhaustible prodigality with which he showered around puns, bon mots, apt quotations, and every variety of anecdote ; throwing life and humor into all by the exquisite adaptation of eye, tone, and gesture to his subject. His writings, admirable as they are, fail to impress one in any way commensurate with his society.

Of the few sketches of him that have been given in works of fiction, not one can claim the merit of being more than a most shadowy resemblance. It needs a graphic skill surpassing his own to draw his portrait with any approach to correctness. Nowhere, perhaps, is failure more conspicuous than in the miserable and meagre attempt in "Coningsby." Not the faintest glow of humor, not one flash of wit, not an ebullition of merriment breaks forth from first to last; the author, apparently in utter incapacity for the task, contents himself with simply observing, "Here Mr. Lucian Gay (the name under which Hook is introduced) was vastly amusing," "there he made the table roar," etc., much in the manner of the provident artist, who, to obviate mistake, affixed the notice to his painting, — "This is the lion — this is the dog!" Of the moral portraiture I will venture to say that it is as unjust as the intellectual is weak. As regards the great calamity — the defalcation at the Mauritius — which befell him in his youth, and which darkened the remainder of his career, shutting out hope, paralyzing his best energies, and by consequence inducing much of that recklessness of living which served to embitter his privacy and hasten his end, it may almost be unnecessary to say, that one who continued to regard him with the feelings of affection which Mr. Barham entertained to the last, must have had full reason for believing him free from every imputation save that of carelessness, not wholly inexcusable in one so young, so inexperienced, and so constitutionally light-hearted.

Of what appears to have been his first interview with his old companion after their separation at college, my father gives a somewhat detailed account: —

"*November* 6, 1827. — Passed one of the pleasantest evenings I ever spent at Lord William Lennox's. The company, besides the host and hostess, consisted of Mr. Cannon, Mr. C. Walpole, Mr. Hill, generally known as 'Tom Hill,' Theodore Hook, and myself. It was Hook's first visit there, and none of the party but myself, Cannon, and Hill, who were old friends of his, had ever seen him before. While at dinner, he began to be excessively amusing. The subject of conversation was an absurdly bombastic prologue, which had been given to Cooper of D. L. T., to get by heart, as a hoax, beginning :—

"'When first the Drama's muse, by Freedom reared,
In Grecian splendor unadorned appeared,
Her eagle glance, high poised in buoyant hope
O'er realms restricted by no partial scope,
Saw one vast desert horrify the scene;
No bright oasis showed its mingling green,
But all around, in colors darkly rude,
Scowled forth the intellectual solitude!
And vain her heart till Time's translucent tide,
Like some sweet stream that scarcely seems to glide,
The heaven-engendered embers fanned to flame,
The ray burst forth! Immortal Shakespeare came!
'T was his with renovated warmth to glow,
To feel that fire within "that passeth show,"
And nobly daring in a dastard age
To raise, reform, and dignify the stage!
To force from lids unsullied by a tear
The pensive drops that bathe fond Juliet's bier,
Bow the duped Moor o'er Desdemona's corse,
Or bid the blood-stained tyrant cry "A horse!"
Waft the rapt soul with more than seraph flight
From fair Italia's realms of soft delight,
To mourn with Imogen her murdered lord,
Or bare the patriot stoic's vengeful sword,
To raise the poet's noblest cry "Be free!"
To breathe the tocsin blast of "Liberty!"' etc.

"Gattie, whose vanity is proverbial, was included in the joke. Wallack, the stage-manager, who had the arranging of it, produced some equally ridiculous lines, which he said Poole, the author of the new comedy ('The Wealthy Widow'), had written for him, but that he had not sufficient nerve to deliver them.

"'No man on the stage has such nerve as I,' interrupted Gattie.

"'Then it must be spoken in five characters; the dresses to be thrown off one after the other.'

"'No performer can change his dress so quickly as I can,' quoth Gattie.

"'Then I am afraid of the French dialect and the Irish brogue.'

"'I'm the only Frenchman and Irishman on the stage,' roared Gattie.

"The hoax was complete, and poor Gattie sat up the whole night to learn the epilogue; went through three rehearsals with five dresses on, one over the other, as a Lady, a Dutchman, a Highlander, a Teague, and lastly as 'Monsieur Tonson come again.' All sorts of impediments were thrown in his way, such as sticking his breeches to his kilt, etc. The time at length arrived, when the stage-manager informed him with a long face, that Coleman, the licenser, instigated no doubt by Mathews, who trembled for his reputation, had refused to license the epilogue; and poor Gattie, after waiting during the whole of the interlude in hopes that the license might yet come down, was obliged to retire most reluctantly and disrobe.

"Hook took occasion from this story to repeat part of a prologue which he once spoke as an amateur before a country audience, without one word being intelligible from the beginning to the end. He afterwards preached part of a sermon in the style of the Rev. Mr. Fisher of Norwich, of whom he gave a very humorous account. Not one sentence of the harangue could be understood, and yet you could not help, all through, straining your attention to catch the meaning. He then gave us many absurd particulars of the Berners Street hoax, which he admitted was contrived by himself and Henry H——, who was formerly contemporary with me at Brasenose and whom I knew there, now a popular preacher at Poplar. He also mentioned another of a similar character, but previous in point of time, of which he had been the sole originator. The object of it was a Mr. William Griffiths, a Quaker who lived in Henrietta Street, Covent Garden. Among other things brought to his house were the dresses of a Punch and nine blue devils, and the body of a man from Lambeth bone-house, who had the day before been drowned in the Thames.

"In the evening, after Lady William had sung 'I've been roaming,' Hook placed himself at the pianoforte, and gave a most extraordinary display of his powers both as a musician and an improvisatore. His assumed object was to give a specimen of the burlettas formerly produced at Sadler's Wells, and he went through the whole of one which he composed upon the spot. He commenced with the tuning of the instruments, the prompter's bell, the rapping of the fiddlestick by the leader of the band, and the overture, till, the curtain being supposed to rise, he proceeded to describe —

"The first scene. — A country village — cottage (O. P.) — church (P. S.) — large tree near wing — bridge over a river occupying the centre of the background. *Music.* — Little men in red coats seen riding over bridge. *Enter* Gaffer from cottage, to the symphony usually played on introducing old folks on such occasions. Gaffer, in recitative, intimates that he is aware that the purpose of the Squire in thus early

> A crossing over the water,
> Is to hunt, not the stag, but my lovely daughter.

Sings a song and retires, to observe Squire's motions, expressing a determination to balk his intentions;

> For a peasant's a man, and a Squire 's no more,
> And a father has feelings, though never so poor.

"*Enter* Squire with his train. — Grand chorus of huntsmen — 'Merry-toned horn — Blithe is the morn — Hark, forward, away! — Glorious Day,' 'Bright Phœbus,' 'Aurora,' etc., etc.

"The Squire dismisses all save his confidant, to whom, in recitative, he avows his design of carrying off the old man's daughter, then sings under her window. The casement up one pair of stairs opens. Susan appears at it, and sings — asking whether the voice which has been serenading her is that of her

> True blue William, who, on the seas,
> Is blown about by every breeze?

"The Squire hiding behind the tree, she descends to satisfy herself; is accosted by him, and refuses his offer; he attempts force. The old man interferes, lectures the Squire, locks up his daughter, and *exit* (P. S.). Squire sings a song expressive ot rage and his determination to obtain the girl, and *exit* (P. S.).

"*Whistle* — Scene changes with a slap. — Public-house door; sailors carousing, with long pig-tails, checked shirts, glazed hats, and blue trousers. *Chorus* — 'Jolly tars — Plough the main — Kiss the girls — Sea again.' William, in recitative, states that he has been 'With brave Rodney,' and has got 'gold galore;' tells his messmates he has heard a land-lubber means to run away with his sweetheart, and asks their assistance. They promise it: —

> Tip us your fin! We 'll stick t' ye, my hearty,
> And beat him! Hav' n't we beat Boneyparty?

Solo, by William, 'Girl of my heart — Never part.' *Chorus* of sailors — 'Shiver my timbers,' 'Smoke and fire — D—n the Squire,' etc., etc. (*Whistle* — Scene closes — slap.)

"Scene — the village as before. Enter Squire; reconnoitres in recitative; beckons on Gypsies, headed by confidant in red. *Chorus* of Gypsies entering — 'Hark? hark? — Butchers' dogs bark! — Bow, wow, wow — Not now, not now.' 'Silence, hush! — Behind the bush — Hush! hush! hush!' — 'Bow, wow, wow.' — 'Hush! hush! — Bow, wow.' — 'Hush! hush! hush! *Enter* Susan from cottage. *Recitative* —

> What can keep father so long at market?
> The sun has set, altho' it 's not quite dark yet.
> — Butter and eggs,
> — Weary legs.

"Gypsies rush on and seize her; she screams; Squire comes forward. *Recitative Affettuoso* — She, scornful, imploring, furious, frightened! Squire offers to seize her; True Blue rushes down and interposes; Music *agitato;* Sailors in pig-tails beat off Gypsies; Confidant runs up the tree; True Blue collars Squire. *Enter* Gaffer: —

> Hey-day! what 's all this clatter;
> William ashore — why, what 's the matter?

"William releases Squire; turns to Sue; she screams and runs to him; embrace; 'Lovely Sue — Own True Blue.'

She faints; Gaffer goes for gin; she recovers and refuses it; Gaffer winks, and drinks it himself; Squire, *Recitative*— 'Never knew — About True Blue — Constant Sue.' 'Devilish glad — Here, my lad — What says dad?' William, *recitative* — 'Thank ye, Squire — Heart's desire — Roam no more — Moored ashore.' Squire joins lovers — 'Take her hand — house, and bit of land, my own ground —

'And for a portion here 's two hundred pound!'

Grand chorus; huntsmen, gypsies, and sailors with pig-tails; *Solo,* Susan — 'Constant Sue — Own True Blue.' *Chorus; Solo,* William — 'Dearest wife — laid up for life.' *Chorus; Solo,* Squire — 'Happy lovers — truth discovers.' *Chorus; Solo,* Gaffer — 'Curtain draws — your applause.' *Grand chorus;* huntsmen, gypsies, sailors in pig-tails; William and Susan in centre; Gaffer (O. P.), Squire (P. S.), retire singing —

Blithe and gay — Hark away!
Merry, merry May;
Bill and Susan's wedding day."

Such is a brief sketch of one of those extemporaneous melodramas with which Hook, when in the vein, would keep his audience in convulsions for the best part of an hour. Perhaps, had his improvising powers been restricted to that particular class of composition, the impromptu might have been questioned; but he more generally took for subjects of his drollery the company present, never succeeding better than when he had been kept in ignorance of the names of those he was about to meet. But, at all times, the facility with which he wrought in what had occurred at table, and the points he made bearing upon circumstances impossible to have been foreseen, afforded sufficient proof that the whole was unpremeditated. Neither in this, nor in any other of his conversational displays, was there anything of trickery or effort. No abruptness was apparent in the introduction of an anecdote; there was no eager looking for an opportunity to fire off a pun, and no anxiety touching the fate of what he had said. In fact, he had none of the artifice of the professional wit about him, and none of that assumption and caprice which minor "lions" exhibit so liberally to their admirers. It may be fairly said, as he knew no rival, so he has left no successor.

"Natura lo fece, e poi ruppe la stampa."

A kindred spirit and a similarity of style have been found by critics in the writings — that is to say, in the poetical compositions of Theodore Hook and Thomas Ingoldsby. And here the latter would probably have had little to fear from a comparison. Even in point of facility he was hardly, if at all, inferior to his friend. I am not aware indeed that my father, with a single exception,[1] ever attempted any extempore effusion, but pen in hand he would have hit off a dozen lively stanzas on a given subject, with a rapidity equal to that of any writer of the day. In conversation, dismissing all notion of equality between the powers of the two, it may be observed that, with some points of resemblance, a much greater diversity of manner separated them than when their pleasantries were expressed in rhyme. Mr. Barham uttered scarcely a dozen puns in the course of his life. He loved rather to play with a subject something after the manner of Charles Lamb; and his humor, always genial, was displayed in an agreeable irony (in the stricter and inoffensive sense of the term) which sometimes strangely perplexed matter-of-fact folks. Ready and fluent in conversation, and having at command an uncommon fund of anecdote, upon which he would draw largely, he possessed in addition one very valuable qualification — he was an excellent listener. In English literature he was well read, and moreover displayed just enough of that old-fashioned love of classical allusion and quotation to give a seasoning to his discourse, and a certain refinement to his wit, which, without exposing him to the charge of pedantry, bespoke the scholar and the man of taste.

"*March* 13, 1828. — Lord W. Lennox, Sir Andrew Barnard, Theodore Hook, Mr. Price, Capt. E. Smart, and Cannon dined

[1] Once in the company of a few intimate friends, he was induced to improvise a song which, with very little correction, was afterwards published as *Mr. Barney Maguire's Account of the Coronation.*

here. The last told a story of a manager at a country theatre who, having given out the play of 'Douglas,' found the whole entertainment nearly put to a stop by the arrest of Young Norval as he was entering the theatre. In this dilemma, no other performer of the company being able to take the part, he dressed up a tall, gawky lad who snuffed the candles, in a plaid and philabeg, and pushing him on the stage, advanced himself to the footlights with the book in his hand, and addressed the audience with, 'Ladies and Gentlemen, —

> 'This young gentleman's name is Norval. On the Grampian hills
> His father feeds his flock, a frugal swain,
> Whose constant care was to increase his store,
> And keep his only son (this young gentleman) at home.
> For this young gentleman had heard of battles, and he longed
> To follow to the field some warlike lord;
> And Heaven soon granted what — this young gentleman's — sire denied.
> The moon which rose last night, round as this gentleman's shield,
> Had not yet filled her horns,' etc.

And so on through the whole of the play, much to the delectation of the audience.[1]

"In the evening Hook went to the piano, and played and sang a long extempore song, principally leveled against Cannon, who had gone up earlier than the rest, and fallen asleep on the sofa in the drawing-room. Sir Andrew Barnard, who now met the former for the first time, expressed a wish to witness more of his talent as an improvisatore, and gave him Sir Christopher Wren as a subject, on which he immediately commenced, and sang, without a moment's hesitation, twenty or thirty stanzas to a different air, all replete with humor."

"*March* 23, 1828. — Dined at Sir Andrew Barnard's in the Albany. The party consisted of Theodore Hook, Price, Cannon, Lord Graves, Lord W. Lennox, Col. Armstrong, Walpole, and myself. Sir Andrew was called away to attend the King, but returned before ten. In the mean time an unpleasant alter-

[1] In this anecdote, which rests on the authority of a celebrated singer who told it to Cannon as having been herself present at the representation, will be recognized the subject of one of the elder Mathews's most successful *scenas*; it was repeated by Mr. Barham to Mr. Peake, who introduced it in *Mathews's Comic Annual for* 1831.

cation took place between Cannon and Hook, owing to an allusion, somewhat ill-timed, made by the former to 'treasury defaulters.' This circumstance interrupted the harmony of the evening, and threw a damp upon the party. Hook made but one pun; on Walpole's remarking that, of two paintings mentioned, one was 'a shade above the other in point of merit,' he replied, 'I presume you mean to say it was a *shade over* (*chef d'œuvre*).' "

"*September* 6, 1828. — Called at Hook's on my return from the Isle of Thanet. Mr. Powell there; then came in a Mr. E——, an Irish barrister, rich and stingy, from whom Hook afterwards told me he had taken his character of Gervase Skinner, in the third series of 'Sayings and Doings.' He mentioned, in proof of the saving propensities of this gentleman, that on a visit to Dover Castle with the Crokers he was about to leave without offering anything to the sergeant who had attended them, when Mrs. Croker, observing the omission, borrowed half a crown from her friend, in the absence of her husband, for the purpose of rewarding the man. This she repaid at the hotel before going down to dinner. But Mr. E——, making many excuses, affected to be half-affronted at her insisting on discharging the debt, and with becoming indignation threw the coin upon the table, There it lay till the waiter announced dinner, when offering his left arm to the lady, he contrived in passing to slip the piece of money — unobserved as he thought — off the table with his right hand, and deposit it in his breeches pocket.

"Hook told us an amusing story of his going down to Worcester, to see his brother the dean, with Henry Higginson (his companion in many of his frolics). They arrived separately at the coach, and taking their places in the inside, opposite to each other, pretended to be strangers. After some time they begin to hoax their fellow-travellers — the one affecting to see a great many things not to be seen, the other confirming it and admiring them.

"'What a beautiful house that on the hill!' cried Higginson, when no house was near the spot; 'it must command a most magnificent prospect from the elevation on which it stands.'

"'Why, yes,' returned Hook, 'the view must be extensive enough, but I cannot think these windows in good taste; to run out bay windows in a gothic front, in my opinion, ruins the effect of the whole building.'

"'Ah! that is the new proprietor's doings,' was the reply, 'they were not there when the marquis had possession.' Here one of their companions interfered; he had been stretching his neck for some time, in the vain hope of getting a glimpse of the mansion in question, and now asked,—

"'Pray, sir, what house do you mean? I don't see any house.'

"'That, sir, with the turrets and large bay windows on the hill,' said Hook, with profound gravity, pointing to a thick wood.'

"'Dear me,' returned the old gentleman, bobbing about to catch the desired object, 'I can't see it for those confounded trees.'

"The old gentleman, luckily for them, proved an indefatigable asker of questions, and the answers he received of course added much to his stock of authentic information.

"'Pray, sir, do you happen to know to whom that house belongs?' inquired he, pointing to a magnificent mansion and handsome park in the distance.

"'That, sir,' replied Hook, 'is Womberly Hall, the seat of Sir Abraham Hume, which he won at billiards from the Bishop of Bath and Wells.'

"'You don't say so!' cried the old gentleman, in pious horror, and taking out his pocket-book begged his informant to repeat the name of the seat, which he readily did, and it was entered accordingly — the old gentleman shaking his head gravely the while, and bewailing the profligacy of an age in which dignitaries of the church practiced gambling to so alarming an extent.

"The frequency of the remarks, however, made by the associates on objects which the eyesight of no one else was good enough to take in began at length to excite some suspicion, and Hook's breaking suddenly into a raptuous exclamation at 'the magnificent burst of the ocean!' in the midst of an inland country, a Wiltshire farmer, who had been for some time staring alternately at them and the window, thrust out his head, and after reconnoitring for a couple of minutes drew it in again, and looking full in the face of the sea-gazer, exclaimed with considerable emphasis, —

"'Well, now then, I 'm d—d if I think you can see the ocean, as you call it, for all you pretends' — and continued very sulky the rest of the way."

"'*December* 8, 1828. — Called on Hook. In the course of conversation he gave me an account of his going to Lord Melville's trial with a friend. They went early, and were engaged in conversation when the peers began to enter. At this moment a country-looking lady, whom he afterwards found to be a resident at Rye, in Sussex, touched his arm, and said, —

"'I beg your pardon, sir, but pray who are those gentlemen in red now coming in?'

"'Those, ma'am,' returned Theodore, 'are the Barons of England; in these cases the junior peers always come first.'

"'Thank you, sir; much obliged to you. Louisa, my dear! (turning to a girl about fourteen), tell Jane (about ten) those are the Barons of England, and the juniors (that 's the youngest, you know) always goes first. Tell her to be sure and remember that when we get home.'

"'Dear me, Ma," said Louisa, 'can that gentleman be one of the *youngest?* I am sure he looks very old.'

"'Human nature, added Hook, 'could not stand this; any one, though with no more mischief in him than a dove, must have been excited to a hoax.

"'And pray, sir,' continued the lady, 'what gentlemen are these?' pointing to the Bishops, who came next in order, in the dress which they wear on state occasions, namely the rochet and lawn sleeves over their doctor's robes.

"'Gentlemen, madam!" said Hook, "these are not gentlemen : these are ladies — elderly ladies — the dowager peeresses in their own right."

"'The fair inquirer fixed a penetrating glance upon his countenance, saying, as plainly as an eye can say, "Are you quizzing me or no?" Not a muscle moved ; till at last, tolerably well satisfied with her scrutiny, she turned round and whispered, —

"'Louisa, dear, the gentleman *says* that these are elderly ladies, and dowager peeresses in their own right ; tell Jane not to forget that.'

"All went on smoothly till the Speaker of the House of Commons attracted her attention by the rich embroidery of his robes.

"'Pray, sir,' said she, 'and who is that fine-looking person opposite?'

"'That, madam,' was the answer, is Cardinal Wolsey!"

"'Now, sir!' cried the lady, drawing herself up, and casting at her informant a look of angry disdain, 'we knows a little better than that; Cardinal Wolsey has been dead a good year!'

"'No such thing, my dear madam, I assure you,' replied Hook, with a gravity that must have been almost preternatural; 'it has been, I know, so reported in the country, but without the least foundation ; in fact, those rascally newspapers will say anything.'

"The good old gentlewoman appeared thunderstruck, opened her eyes to their full extent, and gasped like a dying carp ; *vox faucibus hæsit* — seizing a daughter with each hand, she hurried without another word from the spot."

Mr. Hook has been accused of a tolerably strong leaning to superstition ; one instance in particular is given by Mrs. Mathews, in the memoirs of her husband, of the ludicrous advantage taken by the latter of this weakness, to turn the tables on his fomer tormentor. His biographer in "The Quarterly" also alludes to indications of a similar feeling apparent in the diary to which he had access ; but for these concurrent testimonies, one might be apt to refer the following statement to that love of mystification in which this singular being was so profound an adept. Mr. Barham, however, always believed him to have spoken in perfect good faith ; and certainly the circumstances of the story in question, supported, as they are, by most respectable authority, have more than common claims on the attention of the skeptical.

The date of the interview is not given, but it must have been between September 6th and December 8th of this year.

"Met Hook in the Burlington Arcade ; walked with him to the British Museum. As we passed down Great Russell Street, Hook paused on arriving at Charlotte Street, Bedford Square, and, pointing to the northwest corner, nearly opposite the house (the second from the corner) in which he himself was born, observed, —

"'There, by that lamp-post, stood Martha the gypsy!'[1]

"'Yes,' I replied, 'I know that is the spot on which you *make* her stand.'

"'It is the spot,' rejoined Hook, seriously, 'on which she actually did stand ;' and he went on to say that he entertained no doubt whatever as to the truth of the story ; that he had simply given the narrative as he had heard it from one (Major Darby) who was an eye-witness of the catastrophe, and was present when the extraordinary noise was heard on the evening previous to the gentleman's decease. He added, that he was intimately acquainted with the individual who had experienced the effects of Martha's malediction, and whose name was Hough. He said, further, that he had merely heightened the first accident, which had been but a simple fracture of the leg, occasioned by his starting at the sight of the gypsy, and so slipping off the curb-stone ; but that in all other main incidents he had adhered strictly to fact."

"*Diary : August* 18, 1835. — Took young Tom Haffenden over with me to Captain Williams's at Strand-on-Green, and went with him and Theodore Hook to Twickenham, fishing ; caught little or nothing. Hook observed that as we often had fish without *roe*, now we must be content with *row* without fish. Gave excellent imitation of the Duke of Cumberland and Colonel Quentin.

[1] *Vide* First Series of *Sayings and Doings*.

"Story of Lord Middleton, out hunting, calling to Gunter, the confectioner, to 'hold hard' and not ride over the hounds. 'My horse is so hot, my lord, that I don't know what to do with him.' 'Ice him, Gunter; ice him.'

"Dined at Williams's afterwards. Hook in high spirits, and full of anecdote. Stories of Grattan, C. Fox, and Marquis of Hertford. The latter said after all his expenses were paid he had 95,000*l.* per annum he did not know what to do with; yet Hook said he questioned much whether, intimate as they were, and kind as he always was to him, he would lend him or any other friend a thousand pounds. At his *fêtes* the dinners always ordered at two guineas and a half a head, exclusive of wine. Duke of Buccleugh, on the other hand, with a yearly income of 172,000*l.*, not a rich man; his property consumed by his houses; can go to Scotland by easy stages, stopping always to sleep at some place of his own.

"The house in which I used to visit F. Gosling, the banker, at Twickenham, namely, that with the octagon room once occupied by Louis Phillppe, the one alluded to in 'Gilbert Gurney.' The wealthy citizen described as at Hill's dinner in the same, an imaginary character; the others, Dubois and Mathews.

"Hook assured me with the greatest seriousness that on his return from the Mauritius he and six or seven more on board had seen the 'Flying Dutchman;' that is, that at a time when they could scarce keep up a rag of canvas for the hurricane, a large ship bore down on the opposite tack, seemingly in the wind's eye, with all her sails set, and apparently at the distance of not more than half a mile. He told a story of a gentleman driving his Irish servant in his cab, and saying to him, half jocularly, half in anger, —

"'If the gallows had it's due, you rascal, where would you be now?'

"'Faith, then, your honor, it's riding in this cab I 'd be, all alone by myself may be!'

"He also mentioned that last week an old Irishwoman came to St. George's Hospital to fetch away the body of her husband, who had recently died. Not expecting it to be claimed, the surgeons had been to work and had cut off the head, as well as those of half a dozen more, for phrenological investigation. Some confusion was occasioned by the old woman's demand, as they did not know precisely which head belonged to any specific corpse.

"'Had your husband any mark you would know him by?' was asked.

"'Oh! then sure he had; he had a scar on his right arrum.'

"The body, of course, was identified at once; but to find the right head was not so easy, especially as most of them had been a good deal disfigured. At last one was found that seemed to fit better than the others, and it was carefully sewn on. When the woman was admitted she at once recognized the scar, which was rather a remarkable one; but when she looked at the face, 'Oh! murder,' she cried, 'and it 's death that alters one entirely, it is! My poor Dennis had carroty hair, and now the head of him is as black as a tom-cat!' This Hook said he had from Keate the surgeon, who declared it to be true."

"*Diary: Wednesday, August* 21, 1839.—Hook drove me down to Thames Ditton, from his house at Fulham. Fished all day, and dined *tête-à-tête* at the Swan. He felt but poorly, and complained much of a cough which he said they told him proceeded from the deranged state of his liver, and drank only a tumbler of sherry and water, our dinner consisting of a dish of eels and a duck. Though not in health, his spirits were as good as ever. We caught eight dozen and a half of gudgeons, and he repeated to me almost as many anecdotes. Among the rest, one of a trick he played when a boy behind the scenes of the Haymarket. He was there one evening, during the heat of the Westminster election, at the representation of 'The Wood Demon,' and observing the prompter with the large speaking trumpet in his hand, used to produce the supernatural voices incidental to the piece, he watched him for some time, and saw him go through the business more than once. As the effect was to be repeated, he requested of the man to be allowed to make the noise for him ; the prompter incautiously trusted him with the instrument, when, just at the moment the 'Fiend' rose from the trap, and the usual roar was to accompany his appearance, 'SHERIDAN FOR EVER ! ! !' was bawled out in the deepest tones that could be produced — not more to the astonishment of the audience, than to the confusion of the involuntary partisan himself, from whom they seemed to proceed.

"He mentioned also a reply that he made to the Duke of Rutland, who, observing him looking about the hall, as they were leaving the Marquis of Hertford's, asked him what he had lost?

"'My hat; if I had as good a beaver (Belvoir), as your Grace, I should have taken better care of it."

"Close to the Swan, the house at which we had dined, is Boyle Farm, the residence of Sir Edward Sugden, whose father was a hairdresser. The place is splendidly fitted up, and in the hall is a beautiful vase of very rich workmanship. Hook said that when he and Croker went to dine there one day by invitation from Sir Edward, their host happened to meet them in the hall, and on their stopping for a moment to admire this fine specimen of art, he told them that it was a fac-simile of the celebrated one known as the Warwick vase. 'Aye,' returned Croker, 'it is very handsome; but don't you think a copy of the Barberini one would be more appropriate?' — a question the wit of which will hardly atone for its ill-nature.

"The Chartists had visited St. Paul's on the preceding Sunday in a body, to show 'a strong demonstration of physical force;' I had mentioned that the Marquis of Westminster was present, on which Hook said that nobleman had recently received an invitation from a particular friend, couched in the following terms : —

"'DEAR WESTMINSTER,— Come and dine with me to-morrow. You will meet London, Chelsea, and the two Parks.

"'Yours, etc.'"

Whether Theodore Hook and his great rival, Mr. Sydney Smith, ever met in society, I do not know; if they did, it must have been towards the close of their career, when the habitual caution of acknowledged wits in the presence of one another, would probably have prevented any unusual display on either side. An arrangement was made for the purpose of bringing them together at the table of a common friend, but, alas! a tailor, —

'What dire mishaps from trivial causes spring!'

one to whom Hook owed a considerable sum, having failed in the interval, the latter was unable, or indisposed, to keep the appointment. The circumstance served to elicit one of those happy strokes of sarcasm which the Canon dealt so adroitly.

Mr. H——, the host, not aware of the cause of his expected guest's detention, delayed dinner for some time, observing that 'he was sure Hook would come, as he had seen him in the course of the afternoon, at the Anthenæum, evidently winding himself up for the encounter with tumblers of cold brandy and water.'

"That's hardly fair," said Smith, "I can't be expected to be a match for him, unless wound up too, so when your servant ushers in Mr. Hook, let Mr. H——'s *Punch* be announced at the same time."

It was, I believe, at the breaking up of the same party, that one of the company having said he was about to 'drop in' at Lady Blessington's, a young gentleman, a perfect stranger to him, said, with the most "gallant modesty," —

"Oh! then you can take me with you; I want very much to know her, and you can introduce me."

While the other was standing aghast at the impudence of the proposal, and muttering something about being "but a slight acquaintance himself," and "not knowing very well how he could take such a liberty," etc., Sydney Smith observed,—

"Pray oblige our young friend; you can do it easily enough by introducing him in a capacity very desirable at this close season of the year — say you are bringing with you the *cool* of the evening."

"*Diary: November* 21, 1840. — The Queen was this day brought to bed of the Princess Royal, and I carried the news down to Fulham, where I dined with Hook, Francis Broderip, and Major Shadwell Clarke. The latter expressed himself much annoyed at the infant's being a girl, as there would be no brevet.

"Hook mentioned several anecdotes of his early life; among others, he said that the day on which he was first sent down to Harrow school, Lord Byron, who was there at the time, took him into the square, showed him a window at which Mrs. Drury was undressing, gave him a stone, and bid him 'knock her eye out with it.' Hook threw the stone, and broke the window. Next morning there was a great 'row' about it, and Byron, coming up to him, said, —

"'Well, my fine fellow, you 've done it! She had but one eye (the truth), and it 's gone!' Hook's *funk* was indescribable.

"He said that my old friend Cecil Tattersall, whom I knew at Canterbury and at Christ Church, was at that time there; he was very intimate with Byron, and had the *sobriquet* of 'Punch Tattersall.'

"He spoke in the course of the evening of his two eldest daughters, of whom Mary, the senior, had just turned twenty-one; the name of the second was Louisa, and he designated them accordingly as 'Vingt-un' and 'Loo!' He read us a letter also from his eldest son in India, who had just got his commission there, at the age of seventeen. It was full of fun, and showed much of his father's talent, together with a great deal of good feeling.

"Another of his stories was of Sir George Warrender, who was once obliged to put off a dinner party in consequence of the death of a relative, and sat down to a haunch of venison by himself. While eating, he said to his butler: —

"'John, this will make a capital hash to-morrow.'

"'Yes, Sir George, if you leave off *now!*'"

The following entry is without date. The dinner, however, which it commemorates, must have been given in the course of the year 1840. Its main object was to make known Hook and Haliburton, the author of "Sam Slick," to each other.

"Dined at Bentley's. There were present, Hook, Haliburton, Jerdan, Moran, and my son. Hook told us several anecdotes, among others one of Sir George Warrender, and said that on one occasion that worthy baronet, wishing to go to Plymouth, inquired of John Wilson Croker, the Secretary to the Admiralty, of which Sir George was one of the lords, —

"'Come, Mr. Secretary, you understand these things — which is my best route?'

"Croker described the line, mentioning the towns he recommended him to pass through; 'and then,' said he, 'not to return like a dog by the same round you went, you can come home through Wiltshire, and see Stonehenge on your way.'

"'Oh, no,' said the baronet, 'I have no patience with the man. Ever since he tacked on that name to his own, for the sake of the estate, he has become so insufferably conceited that I never wish to see him again!'

"It is supposed that Sir George here alluded to Mr. Heneage, M. P. for Devizes, whose name he was confounding with that of the ancient Druidical monument.

"In the course of the evening, Hook, looking at my son, said to me, 'How old these young fellows make us feel! It was but the other day that chap was standing at my knee, listening to my stories with ears, eyes, and mouth wide open, and now he is a man, I suppose?'

"'Yes,' I said, 'he is three or four and twenty.'

"'Ah, I see, — *Vingt-un* overdrawn.'"

"*May* 5, 1841. — Dinner party here: Lord Nugent, Fitzroy Stanhope, Sergeant Talfourd, John Adolphus, Theodore Hook, Dr. White, Frank Fladgate, George Raymond, and Dick. Anecdote told of the marriage of the Hon. Mr. D——, son of Lord G——: 'As the happy pair were starting on their wedding tour, the lady's maid was for putting a huge bandbox into the carriage. Mr. D—— was about to make room for it, at some little inconvenience, when an old French valet who had long lived in the family touched his young master's elbow and said softly, "No, no, sare! turn him out; bandbox to-day, bandbox all your life!"'"

This was the last time that Theodoore Hook dined at Amen Corner; he was unusually late, and dinner was served before he made his appearance. Mr. Barham apologized for having sat down without him, observing that he had quite given him up, and had supposed "that the weather had deterred him."

"Oh!" replied Hook, "I had determined to come *weather* or no."

He eat literally nothing but one large slice of cucumber, but seemed in tolerable spirits; and towards the end of the evening, the slight indications of effort which were at first visible had completely disappeared. Lord Nugent, who had never met him before, was exceedingly desirous of hearing one of his extempore songs, but my father, certain that he was ill, interfered and saved him that exertion. From this time his disease made rapid progress, and he dined from home but twice afterwards, once at Lord Harrington's, and once, I believe, with his friend Major Clarke. Mr. Barham saw him but once again; on July 29, about a month before his decease, the former spent the morning with him at Fulham.

To Richard Bentley, Esq.

"MARGATE, *August* 26, 1841.

"MY DEAR BENTLEY,— Dick's letter and yours had but too well prepared me for the melancholy event announced in your last. Poor fellow! I little thought when I shook his hand at parting that it was the last time I should ever grasp it. The whole thing, indeed, has quite upset me. All my oldest and best friends seem dropping off one by one. Poor Cannon was the first to go, James Smith, Bacon, Tom Hill, and now Hook, the one whom I had known the longest and spent the most pleasant hours with of them all! In our college days, 't is true, I saw comparatively little of him (for he was only two terms at St. Mary's Hall), and then his voyage to the Mauritius separated us; but since his return, about twenty years ago, we have ever been on the most friendly terms of intimacy and, I believe, mutual regard. The world believes him older than he was; his birth took place in September, 1789, consequently he would have been fifty-three had he lived a month longer. Independent of the loss to his private friends, I consider his death just at this juncture a public calamity. Barnes gone! and Hook gone! the two ablest, beyond all comparison, of the advocates of civil order and all that is valuable in our institutions. For myself the shadow of a shade never intervened during our long intercourse to cloud our friendship for a moment. I have seen him at times irritable, and sometimes, though rarely and only when other circumstances had combined to ruffle him, disposed to take offense with others; with myself *never!* and it is a source of sincere satisfaction to me at this moment that I cannot recall even an expression of momentary petulance that ever escaped either to the other. Among all his numerous acquaintance and friends there are none who will regret him more sincerely. Most faithfully yours,

"R. H. BARHAM."

To Richard Bentley, Esq.

"MARGATE, *August* 29, 1841.

"MY DEAR BENTLEY, — Since my return from the business which so exclusively occupied my attention this morning, I have thought much and anxiously as to the best mode of proceeding in this business of poor Hook's, so as at once to secure your object of not being anticipated and at the same time avoid anything that may be premature or indelicate. If you were a stranger to Mr. B——, the step I should recommend would be a different one from that which, after mature consideration, I would now suggest; but you have already been in negotiation with him on Mathews's account, which seems to me to make the interference, in the first instance, of a third party between you, strange and inexpedient. I would, first of all, write him immediately some such letter as that of which I inclose a draft. As I have before observed, B—— is not a man to do anything in a hurry, and Mr. Shackell will in all probability, or Mrs. Hook herself, have broken ground for you and led him to expect some application on your part. Your letter will, of course, produce an immediate reply, and act, I have no doubt, as a preventive against any movement of the kind you seem to anticipate from that or any other quarter. If you think my interference would be of the slightest use afterwards, I would either write, or, what would be I think a better way of going to work, see B—— immediately on my return; but I do not think he is a man likely to yield to influence of any kind in a matter of this sort. Before you see him you should, if possible, make up your mind as to whose hands you would confide the task, so as to be able to submit the name or names, if you like to give him a choice of them, to him, for depend upon it this is a question he would be sure to ask. If you decide upon Croker there can be no question that the two names would insure a very large sale; and Croker's regard to his friend, if, in order to keep his memory out of inefficient or injudicious hands, he would be induced to undertake the work at all, would insure its being done rather more with a view to the credit of Hook himself and benefit of his children than to personal profit. If you can't get Croker, what think you of Jerdan? He was intimate with him for a great number of years, would handle the subject with tact and good-nature, and would I think do it well. It should certainly be some one personally acquainted with Hook's humors and peculiarities, and be at the same time a practiced hand. Of course all the assistance I can give you you may command, both in furnishing you with what matter recollection may supply, and in any general supervision, as in the Mathews case, you may think worth having.

"We have had a good collection to-day — 8*l.* more than last year; the church much crowded. Remember me to Roberts and let me hear from you as to B——, and the result of your communication with him; especially let me know the day of poor Hook's funeral if you can ascertain it, and believe me, as ever, most truly yours,

"R. H. BARHAM."

"It was on the 29th of last month that I shook poor Hook's hand for the last time."

To Mrs. Hughes.

"MARGATE, *September* 2, 1841.

"MY DEAR FRIEND, — You do me no more than justice in supposing that the loss of my poor friend would indeed cast a gloom over me; in fact it came upon me like a thunder-clap, and I even yet can scarcely believe it real. On Monday, the 29th of July, I went down to Fulham, and spent the whole morning with him, having heard that he was out of sorts, and wishing to see him before I came down here, where I had promised to preach a sermon for the benefit of "The Sea-bathing Infirmary." *That day month* was the day of his funeral! I dreamt of no such thing then, for though I could not persuade him to taste even the fowl which we had for luncheon, yet his spirits were so high, and his countenance wore so completely its usual expression, that I thought him merely laboring under one of those attacks of bilious indigestion, through so many of which I had seen him fight his way, and which I trusted the run to the sea-side, in which he commonly indulged at this time of the year, would entirely remove.

"I was, I confess, a little startled when he told me that he had not tasted solid food for three days, but had lived upon effervescent draughts, of gentian or columba, taken alternately with rum and milk, and Guinness's porter. There was something in this mixture of medicine, food, and tonic, with the stimulants which I *knew* he took besides, though he said nothing about *them*, that gave me some apprehension as to whether the regimen he was pursuing was a right one, and I pressed him strongly to have further advice than that of the apothecary (an old friend who had attended him for many years), and not to risk a life so valuable to his family, as well as to his friends, on a point of punctilious delicacy. He promised me that if he was not better in a day or two, he would certainly do so.

"He went on to speak of some matters of business connected with the novel he was employed on, part of which he read to me; and much, my dear friend, as you, in common with the rest of the world, have enjoyed his writings, I do assure you the effect of his humor and wit was more than doubled, when the effusions of his own genius were given from his own mouth. Never was he in better cue, and his expressive eye reveled in its own fun. I shall never forget it!

"We got afterwards on miscellaneous subjects, and then he was still the Theodore Hook I had always known, only altered from him of our college days by the increased fund of anecdote which experience and the scenes he had since gone through had given him. There was the same good-nature which was one of the most distinguishing characteristics of his mind; indeed it has so happened that, intimate as has been our friendship for the last twenty years, since his return from the Mauritius renewed the connection of our earlier days, I have been but rarely a witness to that bitter and cutting sarcasm of which he had perfect command, and could employ without scruple when provoked. The reason of this, perhaps, may be that, frequently as we met, it was either in a quiet stroll or dinner by ourselves, or in the society of a few intimate friends, all of whom loved and regarded each other too well to give occasion for the slightest ebullition of temper. The only instances I can call to mind in which he has given way to any severity of expression have ever been in mixed company, and generally (with one single exception, perhaps, I might say universally), when undue liberties, taken by those whose acquaintance with him was not sufficient to justify the familiarity, drew from him a rebuff which seldom make a second one necessary. His friends *could* not provoke him.

"He read to me a letter from his son in India, a young man not yet of age, written with much of the peculiar humor of his father, combined with a degree of good feeling and affection amply justifying that extreme attachment which the latter had always felt for him. Never, I am persuaded, was a parent fonder of his children, and the way in which he now spoke to me of this one (for whom Majoribanks had about a year ago procured a commission in India), the traits he mentioned of his character, and the delight with which he dwelt upon them, were, from reasons to which I need scarcely allude, calculated to make no slight impression upon his auditor.

"After more than three hours spent in a *tête-à-tête*, I got up to leave him, and then, for the first time, remarked that the dressing-gown he wore seemed to sit on him more loosely than usual; I said, as I shook his hand, for the last time, —

"'Why, my dear Hook, this business seems to have pulled you more than I had perceived.'

"'Pulled me!' said he, 'you may well say that; look here,' and, opening his gown, it was not without a degree of painful surprise, that I saw how much he had fallen away, and that he seemed literally almost slipping through his clothes, a circumstance the more remarkable from the usual portliness of his figure.

"I was so struck with his change of appearance that I could not refrain from again pressing him to accompany me for a few days down here, but he declined it as being impossible, from the necessity of his immediately winding up 'Peregrine Bunce' and 'Fathers and Daughters' (the novel he was publishing in monthly parts in 'Colburn's Magazine'), but he added, that in a fortnight or three weeks he should so far have 'broken the necks of them both' as to admit of his running down to Eastbourne, where he said 'he could be quiet.' Alas! he little thought, or I, *how* quiet, or what his rest would be before the expiration of that term! I left him, but without any foreboding that it was for the last time.

"The first intimation I had of his danger was on Tuesday the 24th ult. in a letter from my son, who went down to Fulham to call on him on the Monday; that letter stated that, to his equal surprise and grief, the answer he received had been that Mr. Hook was given over by Dr. Ferguson who had been called in to him; that mortification had taken place, was rapidly going on, and that a few hours at farthest must close the scene. In point of fact, he expired about half-past four that same afternoon, as I heard from Bentley by the following post.

" It was well for my engagement with the latter that I had a few days before sent him up the legend I had promised for the month, for, feeling apart, the confusion of intellect I was in would have rendered it impossible for me even to have looked at a proof.

"Mathews, Frank Bacon, poor Power, Tom Hill, and James Smith — and now Hook! — he who flung his life and spirit into the rest! I question if half a dozen such associates were ever removed, or such a party broken up in so short a time. I doubt if I shall have the courage now to enter the Garrick Club again. Its glory has indeed departed!

"With the exact state of poor Hook's circumstances I am not fully acquainted. I believe he has left no tradesmen's bills unpaid, and if in debt at all, it must be to such persons as never will look to that part of their loss. But I much fear he can have left no great provision for Mrs. Hook or his children, of whom he has four besides the young man in India. I hope somebody will be found to do justice to his memory. Mr. Croker would be the man of all others, if he would undertake the task; and though I believe it has been neglected of late, yet I know my poor friend kept a diary, which I have seen, of the freaks and adventures of his earlier years. Much of this, I dare say, has been anticipated in 'Gilbert Gurney,' and much, perhaps from respect to living persons, could not, as yet at least, be given to the public; but the history of the Berners Street hoax, and some other transactions I could name, will one day, no doubt, raise a hearty laugh among those who come after us."

Sir Walter Scott.

"*November* 26, 1826. — Dined at Doctor Hughes's. Sir Walter Scott had been there the day before; and the Doctor told me the following anecdote, which he had just heard from the 'Great Unknown.' A Scottish clergyman, whose name was not mentioned, had some years since been cited before the Ecclesiastical Assembly at Edinburgh, to answer to a charge brought against him of great irreverence in religious matters, and Sir Walter was employed by him to arrange his defense. The principal fact alleged against him was his having asserted, in a letter which was produced, that 'he considered Pontius Pilate to be a very ill-used man, as he had done more for Christianity than all the *other nine apostles* put together.' The fact was proved, and suspension followed."

"*November* 20, 1828. — Carried a letter addressed by Sir Walter Scott to Mrs. Hughes, on the subject of a benefit for Mr. Terry the actor, lately afflicted with a paralytic stroke, to Stephen Price at Drury Lane Theatre. Price promised me to let him have a benefit at the proper season, if he wished it; Sir Walter undertaking to write a prologue or an epilogue. Mrs. H., in a conversation respecting the 'Bride of Lammermoor,' told me that she had been informed by Sir Walter, when she was last at Abbottsford, that the main incidents of that story were true; that the Lucy of the tale was a Miss Dalrymple; Bucklaw, who marries her, was Dunbar of Dunbar; and her lover, Hamilton of Bungany, who, however, survived her many years. The expression used by Lucy, 'So ye have taken up your bonnie bridegroom,' is historically correct; as is the whole circumstance of her stabbing her new-made husband, and her subsequent insanity. The catastrophe of Ravenswood's being overwhelmed in the sand is founded on an occurrence which took place before the eyes of Sir Walter's son, Major Scott, who saw three Irish horsedealers disappear in the manner described. A similar accident is said to have happened to the son of the celebrated Mrs. Trimmer.

"Meg Dodds, described in 'St. Ronan's Well,' is a Mrs. Wilson, who keeps the inn at Fushie Bridge, the first stage from Edinburgh on the road to Abbotsford. She adores Sir Walter, and when Dr. and Mrs. Hughes were detained for want of horses, finding out accidentally that they were friends of his, she without any scruple ordered those which were bespoken for a gentleman, then on his way to dine with Lord

Melville, to be put to their carriage. Mrs. Wilson is a strict Presbyterian, and once complained to Sir Walter that 'though he had done just right by being so much with Arnieston (Mr. Dundas of Arnieston), yet that the latter had greviously offended her. He had pit up,' she said, 'in the kirk the Lord's Prayer and the Ten Commandments, and when a remonstrance was sent to him against such *idolatry*, he just answered, that if they did not let him alone he would e'en pit up a "Belief" into the bargain!'"

"*September*, 1829. — Mrs. Hughes told me that the person whose character was drawn by Sir Walter Scott as Jonathan Oldbuck was a Mr. Russell, and that the laird whom he mentions as playing cards with Andrew Gemmell (the prototype of Edie Ochiltree) through the window was Mr. Scott of Yarrow.

"Snivelling Stone, about two miles and a half from the cromlech known as Wayland Smith's Cave, in Berkshire, is a large stone, which it is said that Wayland, having ordered his attendant dwarf to go on an errand, and observing the boy to go reluctantly, kicked after him. It just caught his heel, and from the tears which ensued, it derived its traditionary appellation. It is singular that when Mrs. Hughes, who had this story from a servant, a native of that part of the country, first told it to Sir Walter Scott, he declared that he had never heard of Wayland's having had any attendant, but had got all the materials for his story, so far as that worthy is concerned, from Camden. His creation of Dicky Sludge, a character so near the traditionary one of which he had never heard, is a curious coincidence.

"So also is his description of Sir Henry Lee and the dog in "Woodstock." There is a painting in the possession of Mr. Townsend of Trevallyn, in Wales, representing, according to a tradition long preserved in his family, Sir Henry Lee of Ditchley, with a large dog, the perfect resemblance of Bevis. Mr. Townsend, however, thinks he flourished about a century earlier than the Woodstock hero, and was the same with the Sir H. Lee whose verses to Queen Elizabeth, on his retiring from the tilt yard in consequence of old age, are preserved in Walpole's "Antiquities." The strange thing is that Sir Walter knew nothing of this picture till after "Woodstock" was published.

"Told her the story of old Steady Baker, the Mayor of Folkestone, whom I well remember. A boy was brought before him for stealing gooseberries. Baker turned over 'Burn's Justice,' but not being able to find the article he wanted in the book, which is alphabetically arranged, he lifted up his spectacles, and addressed the culprit thus: 'My lad, it's very lucky for you that instead of stealing gooseberries, you are not brought here for stealing a goose; there is a statute against stealing geese, but I can't find anything about gooseberries in all "Burn"; so let the prisoner be discharged, for I suppose it is no offense.'"

"*October*, 1831. — Sir Walter Scott came to town on his way to Malta, and visited Dr. Hughes. Is much sunk in spirits, and told the doctor, on taking leave, that 'he saw a broken man!' — in spirit, of course, as his circumstancesare now reviving. He still, however, retains gleams of his former humor, and told with almost his usual glee the story of a placed minister, near Dundee, who, in preaching on Jonah, said: 'Ken ye, brethren, what fish it was that swallowed him? Aiblins ye may think it was a shark — nae, nae, my brethren, it ways nae shark; or aiblins ye may think it was a saumon — nae, nae, my brethren, it was nae saumon; or aiblins ye may think it was a dolphin — nae, nae, my brethren, it was nae dolphin' —

"Here an old woman, thinking to help her pastor out of a dead lift, cried out, 'Aiblins, sir, it was a dunter!' (the vulgar name of a species of whale common to the Scotch coast).

"'Aiblins, madam, ye 're an auld witch for taking the word o' God out of my mouth!' was the reply of the disappointed rhetorician.

"Mr. Lonsdale, late chaplain to the Archbishop, dined there, and, in a conversation which ensued, mentioned his having, in a late tour, fallen in with the late Dominie Sampson. This gentleman was a Mr. Thompson, the son of the placed minister of Melrose, and himself in orders, though without a manse. He had lived for many years as chaplain in Sir Walter's family, and was tutor to his children, who used to take advantage of his absence of mind to open the window while he was lecturing, get quietly out of it and go to play, a circumstance he would rarely perceive. Sir Walter had many opportunities of procuring him a benefice, but never dared avail himself of them, satisfied that his absence of mind would only bring him into scrapes if placed in a responsible situation. Mr. T. was once very nearly summoned before the Synod for reading the 'Visitation of the Sick' service from our Liturgy to a poor man confined to his bed by illness."

"*July* 3, 1833. — Visit to Mrs. Hughes at Kingston, Lisle. From letters of Sir Walter Scott, it appears that Lord Webb Somerset, brother to the Duke of Beaufort, was the author of the note to 'Rokeby' containing the legend of Littlecote Hall, and that Miss Hayman furnished him with the ballad, 'The spirit of the blasted tree' in 'Marmion.'

"Dandie Dinmont was one Jamie Davison, who lived in Liddesdale, and died in September, 1823. When the minister, who had paid him several visits during his illness, called for the last time on the morning of his death, the good man inquired as to the state of his mind: —

"'Eh minister, ye 're vara gude and Ise muckle obleeged to ye; eh, sir, it 's a great mercy that I sulde be able to look out of window the morn and get a sight o' the hounds; it 's just a mercy they sulde rin this way. 'T wad ha' bin too much for a puir sinner like to ha' expeckit a sight o' the tod! sae thank the Lord for a' things!'

"The circumstances attending Tony Foster's death as described in 'Kenilworth,' are taken from a real incident recorded in the third volume of the Duc de St. Simon's memoirs. There an account is given of the death of an avaricious Master of Requests at Lyons, named Pecoil, who had contrived a recess within his cellar closed by a heavy iron door, within which he was in the habit of depositing his hoards. By some means the lock at last got hampered, and on one of his visits he was unable to let himself out again. He was eventually discovered lying on his treasures dead, and having previously begun to gnaw one of his arms.

"Mrs. Hughes repeated several anecdotes which she had heard from the mouth of Sir Walter himself; among them one of Lady Johnson, sister to the late Earl of Buchan and Lord Erskine, and widow of Sir J. Johnson. When on her deathbed, a few hours prior to her dissolution, she had her notice attracted by the violence of a storm which was raging with great fury out of doors. Motioning with her hand to have the curtains thrown open, she looked earnestly at the window through which the lightning was flashing very vividly, and exclaimed to her attendants: 'Gude faith, but it 's an unco awfu' night for me to gang bleezing through the lift!'

"Another story told by Sir Walter was of a drunken old laird who fell off his pony into the water while crossing a ford in Ettrick.

"'Eh, Jock,' he cried to his man, 'there 's some puir body fa'en into the water; I heard a splash; who is it, man?'

"'Troth, laird, I canna tell; forbye it 's no yersell,' said John, dragging him to the bank. The laird's wig meantime had fallen off into the stream, and John in putting it on again had placed it inside out. This, and its being thoroughly soaked, annoyed the old gentleman, who refused to wear it: —

"'Deil ha' my saul, it 's nae my ain wig; what for do ye no get me my ain wig, ye ne'er-do-weel?'

"'Eh, then, laird, ye 'll no get ony ither wig the night, sae e'en pit it on again. There 's nae sic a wale of wigs in the burnie I jalouse.'

"Another of his stories was of a party of Highland gentlemen who continued drinking three whole days and nights successively, without intermission: —

"'Hech, sirs,' cried one at last, 'but McKinnon looks gash!'

"'What for should he no,' returned his neighbor, 'has na the chiel been dead these twa hoors?'

"'Dead!' repeated his friend, 'an ye did na' tell us before!'

"'Hoot, man,' was the answer, 'what for should I ha' spoiled gude company for sic a puir bit bodie as yon?'"

Sir Walter Scott declared to Mrs. Hughes that, many years before the event took place, he had heard of a prophecy in the Seaforth family, uttered, or said to have been uttered by a second-sighted clansman more than a century before, to the effect that "when the Chisholm and the Fraser should be baith deaf, and the M'Pherson (? M'Kenzie) born with a buck tooth, the male line of the Fraser should become extinct, and that a white-hooded lassie should come from ayont the sea and inherit a'." All these contingencies happened in the late Lord Seaforth's time, who, on reverting to the prophecy, showed two fine lads, his sons, to Sir Walter, and observed, "After all 's said and done, I think these boys will ding the prophet after all." He was wrong, however. The two boys died immediately before their father, and the present Lady Hood, a widow, came from India after his decease and inherited the property.

The prophecy is said to have included yet another family misfortune, and to have foretold that the white-hooded lassie (the widow's cap is clearly alluded to in the epithet) should cause the death of her own sister. This also came to pass. By the upset of a pony carriage which Mrs. Stuart M'Kenzie (as Lady Hood had become by marriage) was driving, her sister was instantaneously killed on the spot, and she herself so fearfully injured about the face as to be compelled to wear, for the remainder of her life, a head-dress of a fashion which enabled her to conceal the greater part of her countenance under bands of black velvet.

"Sir Walter Scott," Mr. Barham goes on to say, "gave Mrs. Hughes an account of his visit to Warrender House, the seat of Sir George Warrender, at Burntfields, near Edinburgh. He stated that on an architect being called in to make some repairs there on a large scale, he could not make the ground plan agree with the interior measurement of the edifice. After much discussion he found an old doorway, which the servants assured him was a false one and 'led nowhere.' Recurring in his plan, however, he suspected that the deficient quantity must be in its vicinity, and accordingly determined to have it opened. It was strongly fastened, but was at length removed, when behind it he found three small rooms, the farthest one fitted up as a bed-room, with two silver candlesticks on the toilet table, the candles burnt down in the sockets. Half-burnt embers were on the hearth ; and an old-fashioned but very handsome dressing-gown was hanging over the back of a chair at the foot of which was a pair of slippers. The bed appeared to have been left disarranged as when quitted by its last occupant. Not any of the family then living were aware of the existence of these rooms, nor was there any tradition as to the name or character of their inmates. It was also said by Sir George, at the same time, that he had been assured by members of the family that at Glamis Castle there was a secret room, the mode of approaching which was never known to more than the possessor and the heir apparent of the property."

Charles Diggle.

Of Diggle Mr. Barham used to tell many absurd stories : how, for instance, he used to steal the shoe-strings of Isaac Hill, the second master, and avowed his intention of continuing the robbery till he got enough to form a line that would reach from one end of the school to the other (seventy feet), but was unluckily removed from school before he had half accomplished his task. The most amusing, however much to be condemned, of his practical jokes was one in which his friend Barham also had a share. The two boys having, in the course of one of their walks, discovered a Quakers' meeting-house, forthwith procured a penny tart of a neighboring pastry-cook ; furnished with this, Diggle marched boldly into the building, and holding up the delicacy in the midst of the grave assembly, said with perfect solemnity, —

"Whoever speaks first shall have this pie."

"Friend, go thy way," commenced a drab-colored gentleman, rising ; "go thy way and "—

"The pie 's yours, sir!" exclaimed Master Diggle politely, and placing it before the astounded speaker hastily effected his escape.

Barham's College Life.

College life, more especially at that day, was likely to present numerous and sore temptations to one who was overflowing with good-nature and high spirits, and whose early loss had not only placed a perilous abundance of funds at his disposal, but had left him, as it happened, utterly unchecked by parental counsel and authority, for his mother, a confirmed invalid, had for some time been incapable of exercising any control over his conduct. Of his guardians, on the other hand, but one busied himself at all in his affairs; and of him, the attorney before alluded to, the youth had come to conceive a strong dislike, a feeling not unmixed with suspicion, which proved but too well founded, of the man's honesty. It was scarcely to be expected that such an ordeal should be passed through without scathe. Brasenose, too, was an expensive college: it was commonly reported that the Principal "hated a college of paupers," and the young men were ready enough in this respect to follow the cue which they believed had been given. Mr. Barham, like many others, spent there a great deal of money to very little purpose. Among other extravagances gaming was the fashion there as elsewhere. Whether, indeed, college "hells" were in existence at that time, as they certainly were a generation later, I am not able to say, but a good deal of high play went on, and although this was certainly a vice to which my father had no natural inclination, he was on one occasion induced to join a party at "unlimited loo," or something of the sort, and with the happiest result — he lost heavily; a great deal more, that is to say, than he was in a condition to pay. Direct communication on such a subject with the lawyer at Canterbury was on many accounts extremely distasteful. A lecture from him would have proved particularly galling; there was nothing for it, therefore, but to apply to Lord Rokeby, and this Mr. Barham did, earnestly begging him to authorize the advance of a sum, from the property in trust, sufficient to discharge the obligation. Lord Rokeby very decidedly, and it need hardly be said very properly, declined to accede to the request. As a guardian, he said, he could not for a moment entertain the question, but he very good-naturedly added, that as a friend he would give the money. The present showed tact as well as kindness, and clearly rendered any second application of the sort impossible. And it is a fact that, from that day to his last, Mr. Barham held entirely aloof, not only from gambling in the ordinary sense of the word, but from speculation of every kind and degree. A railway investment he looked upon as a certain step towards utter ruin; and when one of the most accomplished of projectors, a gentleman who had succeeded in getting some very pretty sport, especially among the clergy, called on him with the prospectus of a certain Cornish mining company, and tried hard to persuade him to join with many of his brethren in the adventure, his habitual distrust was not to be overcome: "Tell me candidly," asked he, "all exaggeration apart, what dividend do you really calculate will be paid?"

"Not one farthing short of twenty per cent.!"

"You are in earnest?"

"Absolutely in earnest, on my honor."

"Thank you — that is rather too good a thing for me to meddle with. I wish you all possible success, and — a very good morning!" and he buttoned up his pocket, bowed out his friend, and could never be persuaded to resume the negotiation. Those who persisted in the scheme — two of his intimate friends among the number — were ruined, or nearly ruined, by its collapse.

His reply to Mr. Hodson, his tutor, afterwards Principal of Brasenose, will convey some notion of the hours he was wont to keep. This gentleman, who, doubtless discerning, spite of an apparent levity, much that was amiable and high-minded in his pupil, treated him with marked indulgence, sent for him on one occasion to demand an explanation of his continued absence from morning chapel.

"The fact is, sir," urged his pupil, "you are too *late* for me."

"Too late?" repeated the tutor, in astonishment.

"Yes, sir—too late. I cannot sit up till seven o'clock in the morning: I am a man of regular habits; and unless I get to bed by four or five at latest, I am really fit for nothing next day."

An impertinence better rebuked by the look of dignified displeasure which it called up, than by any amount of punishment that could have been inflicted. All affectation was cast aside on the instant—an apology sincerely offered, and silently accepted.

Anecdote of Harley the Comedian.

The Whig Club patronized the drama, which was then represented at Canterbury by a travelling company under the management of a certain Mrs. Baker. The principal light comedian was a youth as yet "to fortune and to fame unknown," but destined ere long to win the smiles of both—no other than the late popular favorite, Mr. Harley. He often used to tell how he was extricated from one of his early professional difficulties by the aid, good-naturedly offered, of my father. Harley had been cast for the part of Goldfinch in "The Road to Ruin," but the resources of the establishment were limited, and the wardrobe afforded no dress better suited to the character than an old tarnished lace frock of Macheath's, with a pair of jack-boots to match—the whole much too large for the figure of the young actor. There was no time—to say nothing of money—to provide a more appropriate costume, and in his embarrassment he consulted Mr. Barham, who was a constant visitor both before and behind the curtain. The latter settled the matter at once by presenting him with a complete suit of his own. It consisted of a green single-breasted coat with gilt buttons, a crimson waistcoat, edges and pockets trimmed with fur, buff buckskin breeches, top-boots, and silver spurs! Harley was delighted, so it is to be hoped was the audience; assuredly a more complete buck of the period was never before presented to their notice.

WITCHCRAFT.

Among my father's memoranda I find an account, abridged from Scott's curious work, of a case of witchcraft which occurred at the village of Westwell in the reign of Elizabeth, and which was professionally treated with marked success by the minister of the parish : —

" I will begin with a true story of a witch practicing her diabolical witchcraft and ventriloquie anno 1574, at Westwell, in Kent, within six miles of where I dwell, taken and noted down by two ministers of God's Word, four substantial yeomen, and three women of good fame and reputation, whose names are after-written. — October 13. Mildred, the base daughter of Alice Norrington, and now servant to Will. Spooner, of Westwell Co. Kent, being of the age of seventeen years, was possessed with Satan in the day and night aforesaid. About two o'clock in the afternoon of the same day there came to the said Spooner's house Roger Newman, minister of Westwell, John Brainford, minister of Kinington, with others whose names are unwritten, who made their prayer to God to assist them in that needful case, and then commanded Satan in the name of the Holy Trinity to speak with such a voice as they might understand, and to declare from whence he came."

At first the devil proved refractory, but the exorcisers insisting, he confessed that he had been sent to the girl by "old Alice," who, among other things, had moved him to kill three persons, Edward Agar, a gentleman of forty pounds by the year, his child, and Wolton's wife ; and that finally he was commissioned by the said "old Alice" to kill the possessed. The devil being exorcised and driven out, an account was drawn up, signed, and testified as aforesaid. Eventually the girl was arrested as an impostor, confessed her crime, and received "condigne punishment."

According to Scott the trick was managed by means of ventriloquism. The Holy Maid of Kent is also said by him to have practiced the same art.

A second extract from the same volume (p. 61 of the edition of 1654) runs as follows : —

"I remember another story written in 'Malleus Maleficarum,' repeated by Bodmin, that one soldier called Punker daily throughout witchcraft killed with his bowe and arrows three of the enemies as they stood peeping over the walls of a castle besieged, so as in the end he killed them all quite, saving one. The triall of the archer's sinister dealing and a proof thereof expressed is for that he never lightly failed when he shot, and for that he killed them by three a day, and had shot three arrows into a rod. *This was he that shot at a peny on his sonnes head and made ready another arrow to have slaine the Duke that commanded it.*"[1]

Query, origin of William Tell?

Barham among Smugglers.

The villages which formed his new cure (Warehorn) were about two miles apart and situated, the former in, the latter on the verge of, Rommey Marsh; and, as may be supposed, they abounded, even more than the spot he had just quitted in desperadoes engaged in what, by a technical euphemism, was termed "The Free Trade."

But, notwithstanding the reckless character of these men, the rector met with nothing of outrage or incivility at their hands. Many a time indeed, on returning homewards late at night, has he been challenged by a half seen horseman who looked in the heavy gloom like some misty condensation a little more substantial than ordinary fog, but on making known his name and office, he was invariably allowed to pass on with a "Good-night, it's only parson!" while a long and shadowy line of mounted smugglers, each with his led horse laden with tubs, filed silently by. Nay, they even extended their familiarity so far as to make the church itself a depôt for contraband goods; and on one occasion a large seizure of tobacco had been made in the Snargate belfry—calumny contended for the discovery of a keg of hollands under the vestry-table. When it is added, that the nightly wages, paid whether a cargo was run or not, were at the rate of seven and sixpence to an unarmed man,

[1] Scott's *Discovery of Witchcraft*, book vii.

and fifteen shillings to one who carried his cutlass and pistols, little surprise can be felt if nearly the whole population pursued more or less so profitable an avocation.

The district, moreover, appears up to a late period to have been utterly neglected in point of religious instruction and superintendence. It seems to have been one of the last strongholds of the Trullibers. Will it be credited that in the nineteenth century one of the reverend gentlemen in question has been known on a Sabbath-day to cart a load of bricks, in *propriâ personâ*, to the church-yard, for the purpose of repairing the chancel? Such was the fact.

Indeed, it was this gentleman's ordinary custom, living as he did at some distance from his cure, to drive over on a Sunday at any hour which might happen to be most convenient, and, having put up his horse and gig, to enter the public-house parlor and there sit down to discuss the state of the markets over a glass of toddy and a pipe with the landlord, who was parish clerk as well, together with any neighbors who might happen to drop in. Meanwhile a lad was dispatched to ring the bell, and by the time the rest of the congregation had assembled, the rector and his company were usually ready to repair to the church, where, after a fashion, divine service was performed. But one blunder Mr. ——— unfortunately committed — he outlived his age. Old friends died off, new parishioners intruded, a stricter discipline was on all sides growing up; and one day before the cheering — would that we could say not inebriating — glass was emptied, or the fragrant "screw" half consumed, the bell suddenly and unexpectedly stopped! What could it mean? off started clerk and clergyman, indignant at the interruption, to ascertain its cause, and discovered to their consternation a stranger in the reading desk. It was the Rural Dean! What steps were subsequently taken I do not remember to have heard, but they were such as to relieve Mr. —— of the necessity of hurrying over his Sunday morning's refreshment for the future.

It is recorded of the same individual that even during divine service it was not unfrequent for him to mingle secular matters with divine, in a manner no less ludicrous than indecorous — leaning, for example, over his churchwarden's pew as he passed from the reading desk to the pulpit, and observing, as the result of long and recently concluded deliberation, "Well, Smithers, I 'll have that pig."

A Case of Monomania.

I may here introduce a somewhat singular occurrence which took place at the residence of another clergyman in this neighborhood; one, however, it is to be observed, in every respect the opposite of the gentleman just mentioned. He had lost a beloved daughter, under circumstances peculiarly affecting. She was playing in the garden in high spirits and apparent health, when suddenly approaching her father she looked up in his face, and saying, "Father, take care of my fowls!" without another word laid her head upon his knees and died. The blow was stunning, and Mr. —— never entirely recovered from its effects. For some months his reason was despaired of, and though afterwards restored to cope in full vigor with ordinary subjects, it sank into monomania on the mention of one — his daughter!

A belief took full possession of his mind that he was constantly subject to the visits of his lost child; he intimated, moreover, that the spirit spoke of poison having been administered, and urgently pressed upon him the avenging of the murder. In the earlier stages of the disease, his friends entertained hopes of reasoning or rallying him out of so distressing a delusion. Mr. Barham, among the rest, being present at his table, took an opportunity of addressing to him some skeptical remarks on the theory of apparitions.

"I sincerely hope, sir," replied his host, "you may never have occasion to change your opinion; but, unless I greatly err, your unbelief will meet with a manifest check in the course of this very night."

The words had scarcely passed his lips, when the party was startled by a loud noise, as of a falling body, proceeding from the hall. Mr. —— looked round with an air of calm triumph, while his guest, not altogether convinced that the interruption was necessarily to be attributed to spiritual agency, opened the door to ascertain its cause. He returned with his own hat which had been dislodged, probably by the wind which happened to be unusually high, from the wall.

"You see, gentlemen, I am no false prophet," said the host quietly.

"Well," urged Mr. Barham, half annoyed at the aptitude of the accident, "if that be the handiwork of your familiar, I should take it as a favor if you would represent to him or her, as the case may be, that, as the hat happens to be my best" — "Oh!" interrupted the seer, "if you are still disposed to treat the matter with levity, we will drop it at once." Dropped accordingly it was, leaving the unfortunate gentleman more confirmed than ever in his visionary creed.

A Poetical Invitation.

Of the many amusing trifles which he was in the habit of addressing to his friends, one of the best, perhaps, is an invitation to Dr. Wilmot of Ashford, conveyed under the form of a parody on "O Nanny, wilt thou gang with me?"

"O Doctor! wilt thou dine with me,
And drive on Tuesday morning down?
Can ribs of beef have charms for thee —
The fat, the lean, the luscious brown?
No longer dressed in silken sheen,
Nor decked with rings and brooches rare,
Say, wilt thou come in velveteen,
Or corduroys that never tear?

"O Doctor! when thou com'st away,
Wilt thou not bid John ride behind,
On pony, clad in livery gay,
To mark the birds our pointers find?
Let him a flask of darkest green
Replete with cherry brandy bear,
That we may still, our toils between,
That fascinating fluid share!

"O Doctor! canst thou aim so true,
As we through briars and brambles go,
To reach the partridge brown of hue,
And lay the mounting pheasant low?

Or should, by chance, it so befall
  Thy path be crossed by timid hare,
Say, wilt thou for the game-bag call,
  And place the fur-clad victim there ?

"And when at last the dark'ning sky
  Proclaims the hour of dinner near,
Wilt thou repress each struggling sigh,
  And quit thy sport for homely cheer?
The cloth withdrawn, removed the tray —
  Say, wilt thou, snug in elbow-chair,
The bottle's progress scorn to stay,
  But fill, the fairest of the fair ?"

The Fate of a Hare.

Some similar lines were dispatched to the great man of the neighborhood, "Squire" Hodges, who hunted the Marsh country with a scratch pack of beagles, and had happened to lose his hare in the Rector's cabbage-garden : —

BENEVOLENCE.

"The lark sings loud, 't is early morn,
  These woodland scenes among,
The deep-toned pack and echoing horn
  Their jovial notes prolong.

"And see poor puss, with shortened breath,
  Splashed sides, and weary feet,
In terror views approaching death,
  And crouches at my feet!

"Her strength is gone, her spirits fail,
  Nor farther can she fly ;
The hounds snuff up the tainted gale,
  And nearer sounds the cry.

"Poor helpless wretch! methinks I view
  Thee sink beneath their power!
Methinks I see the ruffian crew
  Thy tender limbs devour!

"Yet oh! in vain thy foes shall come:
  So cheer thee, trembling elf!
These guardian arms shall bear thee home —
  'I 'll eat thee up myself!"

Rustic Simplicity.

A genuine and touching instance of simplicity is noted down by my father as having been told to him by Mr. Baber of the British Museum.

"A short time after Mr. Baber, who succeeded Mr. Beloe at the British Museum, had entered upon his office as one of the keepers, he attended a party from the west of England over the building, and explained, in his official capacity, many of the curiosities which it contains. In one of the rooms he pointed out to their observation a collection of beautiful antique vases, all of which, he informed them, had been dug up at Herculaneum. One of the party echoed his words with the greatest astonishment.

"'Yes, sir, dug up, sir?'

"'What, out of the ground?'

"'Undoubtedly.'

"'What, just as they now are?'

"'Perhaps some little pains may have been taken in cleaning them, but in all other respects they were found just as you see them.' The Somersetshire sage turning to one of his companions with a most incredulous shake of the head assured him in an audible whisper, —

"'He may say what he likes, but he shall never persuade me that they ever dug up ready-made pots out of the ground?'"

Anecdote of Lord Eldon.

Diary: June 1, 1822. — Anecdote of Lord Chancellor Eldon narrated to me by Dr. Blomberg.

"The Chancellor is very fond of shooting, and usually retires into the country for six weeks towards the end of the season, where he is in the habit of riding a little Welsh pony, for which he gave fifty shillings. One morning last year his lordship intending to enjoy a few hours' sport after a rainy night, ordered 'Bob,' the pony, to be saddled. Lady Eldon told him he could not have it, but company being in the room gave no reason. In a few minutes, however, the servant opened the door and announced that 'Bob' was ready.

" 'Why, bless me!' cried her ladyship, 'you can't ride him, Lord Eldon, he has got no shoes on.'

" 'Oh, yes! my lady,' said the servant, 'he was shod last week.'

" 'Shameful!' exclaimed her ladyship, 'how dared you, sir, or anybody, have that pony shod without orders?' 'John,' continued she, addressing her husband, 'you know you only rode him out shooting four times last year, so I had his shoes taken off, and have kept them ever since in my bureau. They are as good as new, and these people have shod him again; we shall be ruined at this rate!' "

"Repeated a story which I had from Dubois, that a friend of his walking one day in Hyde Park with Lord Eldon, was stopped by the latter, who pointed to a house and said:—

" 'In that house the present Lady Eldon formerly dwelt, and from that house, in consequence of my addresses being thought presumptuous, I was banished. During my exile I was informed that her father was going to give a masked ball, and I resolved to make my way in disguise. I mingled with the company, and when I came to my present lady, I said, "Don't be alarmed, my love, it is I—John Scott!" She, however, could not command herself, and screamed. I was detected and kicked out of the house.' "

"George the Third scolded Lord North for never going to the concert of ancient music: 'Your brother, the bishop,' said the King. 'never misses them, my lord.' 'Sir,' answered the premier, 'if I were as deaf as my brother, the bishop, I would never miss them either!' Told me by Dr. Blomberg, who was present."

THE BLOMBERG GHOST STORY.

The name of Dr. Blomberg is well known in connection with the celebrated ghost story so frequently narrated by George IV. As several versions of this strange occurrence are in existence, it may be worth while to give the one which Mr. Barham heard at the doctor's own table, either on the occasion when the foregoing anecdotes were told, or a few days later.

"During the American War, two officers of rank were seated in their tent, and delayed taking their supper till a brother officer, then absent upon a foraging party, should return. Their patience was well-nigh exhausted, and they were about to commence their meal, concluding something had occurred to detain the party, when suddenly his well-known footstep was heard approaching. Contrary to their expectation, however, he paused at the entrance of the tent, and without coming in called on one of them by name, requesting him with much earnestness, as soon as he should return to England, to proceed to a house in a particular street in Westminster, in a room of which (describing it) he would find certain papers of great consequence to a young lad with whom the speaker was nearly connected. The speaker then apparently turned away, and his footsteps were distinctly heard retiring till their sound was lost in distance. Struck with the singularity of his behavior, they both rose, and proceeded in search of him. A neighboring sentinel on being questioned denied that he had either seen or heard any one, although, as they believed, their friend must have passed close by his post. In a few minutes their bewilderment was changed into a more painful feeling by the approach of the visiting officer of the night, who informed them that the party which went out in the morning had been surprised, and that the dead body of poor Major Blomberg (their friend) had been brought into the camp about ten minutes before. The two friends retired in silence, and sought the corpse of the person who, as both were fully persuaded, had just addressed them. They found him pierced by three bullets, one of which had passed through his temples and must have occasioned instant death. He was quite cold, and appeared to have been dead some hours. It may easily be conceived that a memorandum was immediately made of the request they had both so distinctly heard, and of the circumstances attending it, and that on the return of the regiment to Europe, no time was lost in searching for the papers. The house was found without difficulty, and in an upper room, agreeably with the information they had received in such an extraordinary manner, an old box was discovered, which had remained there many years, containing the title-deeds of some property now in the possession of the Rev. Dr. Blomberg, who was the 'lad' mentioned by name by the voice at the tent door.

"This story," adds Mr. Barham, "was repeated to me by Mr. Atwood, the King's organist, at Dr. Blomberg's own table in his temporary absence. Mr. Atwood declared that he had heard the story related by George IV. (whose foster-brother Dr. Blomberg was) more than once, and on one occasion when the doctor himself was present. He further stated that the King had mentioned the names of all the parties concerned, but that, with the exception of Major Blomberg's, they had escaped his memory."

Since the foregoing pages were prepared for the press a very different version of the story has reached me, furnished by a member of the family to the head of which the Yorkshire property has descended. The account given by my informant contains the substance of a narrative of the circumstances under which the alleged supernatural communication was made, drawn up by the officer to whom it was more particularly addressed. It runs as follows: —

Captain (? Major) Edward Blomberg was left a widower, with one little boy, two years old, who was heir to a fair estate in Yorkshire then in the possession of Baron Blomberg. The captain's regiment being stationed in the island of Martinique, he was, in the course of duty, sent off with dispatches to a place at a considerable distance from headquarters. One night, shortly after his departure, an officer who, in consequence of the crowded condition of the barracks, was sharing his chamber with a comrade, was aroused, just as he was dropping off to sleep, by the opening of the door. Captain Blomberg entered, walked slowly to his friend's bed, and drew back the mosquito curtains.

"Why, Blomberg," exclaimed the latter in astonishment, "what on earth has brought you back?"

The intruder answered: "This night I died at ——, and I

have come hither to beg you to take charge of my little orphan boy." He then gave the address of the child's grandmother and aunt, who were residing in London, and requested that his son might be sent to them immediately; adding directions as to the searching for certain papers necessary to establish the boy's title to the property of which he was heir. This done, without waiting for a reply, the figure departed. Perplexed, not to say alarmed, and thinking it just possible that his imagination might have played him false, the officer called to the occupant of the other bed: —

"Did you," he asked, "see any one come into the room?"

"Yes," was the answer; "it was Blomberg, was it not? What did he want?"

"Did n't you hear what he said?"

"No," returned the other; "I could hear that he was talking to you, but what he said I was unable to make out."

The first speaker then related the extraordinary communication he had just received. Both officers were much affected by the strangeness of the affair, and were not a little ridiculed on the following morning when they narrated the occurence at breakfast in the mess-room. In the evening, however, a message was forwarded to the general in command to the effect that Captain Blomberg's death had taken place on the preceding night, just at the time of his appearance in the bedroom. It came out that he had died of fever, evidently brought on by depression of spirits occasioned by the loss of his wife. No time was lost in seeking out the child, who was found and dispatched to England, where he appears to have been somewhat coldly received by the grandmother. His story, however, happened to reach the ears of Lady Caroline Finch, the Queen's governess, who repeated it to her Majesty.

The Queen, struck by the interest attaching to the boy, declared that little Blomberg should never want a home; and immediately sending for him ordered that he should be brought up in the royal nursery. She afterwards provided for his education, and saw to the settlement of his property. In addition to this, when the lad reached the age of nine years, the Queen employed Gainsborough to paint his portrait, and subsequently presented the picture to the original. This lad, brought up at the palace, became in due time chaplain to George IV. and residentiary of St. Paul's. He married Miss Floyer, a Dorsetshire lady, but, continuing childless, adopted her niece; and narrative and portrait, papers and estate — to say nothing of the ghost's plates and spoons — are, I am told, at the present time in the possession of this lady's representative.

Dr. Blomberg and his Fiddles.

Dr. Blomberg was an amiable man, that he was a sound divine may be taken for granted, and assuredly he was a very excellent musician. Fiddling was his strong point and his unfailing amusement; there were people who believed that he kept a greased bow for silent play on Sundays. Three fiddles he possessed — three fiddles that he loved, I had almost said, like children. And no wonder; they were mellow, marvelous instruments — one a genuine Straduarius of incalculable value. It is curious how players become attached to their fiddles! I speak in ignorance, but I never heard of any one conceiving a strong affection for a trombone, or a big drum, or a key bugle, but there appears to be something exceptionally fascinating about a fiddle — something which commends that simple parent of sweet sounds to its master's heart in a degree not attained by organs more powerful or more elaborate. There are some fiddles too, I believe, which love their owners — at least they speak as if they do. But this by the way. One morning Dr. Blomberg came to my father in dire distress. The tears, without figure of speech, were in his eyes as he told his pitiful story. He had been robbed — robbed of his fiddles — robbed of all three — all three were gone! A former servant who had been detected in some petty dishonesty and discharged was, it was pretty clear, "the gentleman concerned in the abstraction." But what was to be done? How get at the offender — or rather at the fiddles, one of which, the solace of the Doctor's life, his incomparable Straduarius, was, as had been intimated by the culprit's wife, lying in pledge at a pawnbroker's shop in the neighborhood of Smithfield? It was impossible for Dr. Blomberg himself, a dignified clergyman in shorts and shovel hat, to penetrate the recesses of Cock Lane and Barbican. Would Mr. Barham help him at his need? This, it is needless to say, my father very readily promised to do, and as he happened to number among his acquaintances not only the chief magistrate at Bow Street, Sir Richard Birnie, but both Townshend and Ruthven, the celebrated "runners," he obtained from one or other of these experts some practical hints, acting upon which he paid a visit that very evening to the Smithfield establishment.

After an animated discussion with the proprietor, and an offer, hastily declined, to refer the matter to the arbitration of Sir Richard, the missing violin was produced, and, in consideration of the repayment of five pounds which had been advanced upon it, handed over to the applicant. Wrapping his prize up in a silk pocket-handkerchief, my father hurried off, late as it was, to the Doctor's house in Amen Corner, and restored the recovered Cremona to his arms. The old gentleman's delight was touching to witness. He jumped up, seized his bow and ran it over the strings; the tone was unimpaired; he tapped and sounded the lungs of his favorite — they were sound as ever. His gratitude was overwhelming; and my father always maintained that had the living of Tottenham been vacant at that moment, and at the Doctor's option, he would to a certainty have at once bestowed upon his benefactor the best piece of preferment in the gift of the Dean and Chapter. Eventually the other two fiddles were restored by his exertions.

Murder of Mrs. Donatty.

Mr. Barham's acquaintance with Sir Richard Birnie has been mentioned. It was of old standing and of sufficient weight to procure an entrance into the police office and a seat on the bench, during the examination of the Cato Street conspirators on the night of the 29th of February, 1820; and I have often heard him (my father) speak of the thrill of horror which ran through the court on the production of the bag which the butcher, Ings, had destined for the reception of Lord

Castlereagh's head. Happily the villains were betrayed. But about the time of which I am writing, viz.: 1822, a murder was actually committed which producèd a sensation in the town unequaled in intensity by any similar event since the massacre of the Marrs and Williamsons in Ratcliffe Highway, and which in point of dramatic interest would vie with any of later days. The spot was a house in a narrow street, at the northern end of Gray's Inn, running parallel with Bedford Row, and called Robert Street. The victim was one Mrs. Donatty, the widow of a sheriff's officer, who, in the exercise of his vocation, had amassed a considerable sum of money, a large proportion of which had been obtained by the sale of pictures painted by Morland, whose custodian he had happened frequently to be. One evening this poor woman was found lying dead in the passage of her home with her throat cut from ear to ear and a handkerchief stuffed by way of a gag into her mouth. After the removal of the body, Sir Richard Birnie and Ruthven, accompanied by Mr. Barham, went to examine the premises, and nothing in the history, genuine or fictitious, of modern detectives, can surpass the description which the latter used to give of the sagacity exhibited by the trained intelligence of the police officer — one of the most acute as well as resolute that Bow Street could boast.[1] He corrected without any affectation or failure of respect, the hasty and occasionally erroneous guesses of the magistrate; gave his reasons simply for believing that the assassin had been admitted in the usual way at the front door, and had effected his purpose as the woman was preceding him to the sitting-room — inferring that he was either an habitual visitor or that he had been expected on this particular occasion; commented on the height of the man who had inflicted the wound from its position,— a calculation curiously confirmed by a subsequent discovery; and then remarking that an inner door had been forced —

"Aye, with this chisel," interrupted the magistrate, picking up a heavy tool.

[1] He headed the officers in the attack upon the loft in Cato Street, without waiting for the arrival of the Coldstream Guards.

"Pardon me, Sir Richard, not with that; it is too large to produce the marks you see about the lock. It was done with a narrower instrument, one with which he also broke open this small box." "Why, it is merely an old tea-caddy!" objected the other. "Yes, Sir Richard, an old tea-caddy, but it has been forcibly opened, as you may see."

The party then proceeded to a small yard at the back of the house, a grimy, damp, well-like looking place, shut in by high walls, in one angle of which stood a half-rotten water-butt. After a careful examination of this spot the officer observed: —

"The man was disturbed before he had time to ransack the house, probably by a knock at the front door, which prevented his leaving by the way he entered, so he had to make his escape over that wall, and so got into Great Ormond Street. Here you see, sir," pointing out a small space on the stand of the water-butt, from which the dark green mould had lately been detached, "here he placed his left foot; there his left hand — he is a tall man, as I supposed; here came his right foot — you can see the brick scraped by the toe of his boot; there his right hand grasped the top of the wall. With a spring he raised himself up, knocking out the mortar, as you observe, in the scramble; and he then dropped easily down on the other side."

Certain slightly suspicious circumstances led to the arrest of a young man, the nephew of the deceased, indeed, the only relative she had. He was of a dissolute character, and, though as a boy a great favorite of the old lady's, had of late been known more than once to have exchanged angry words with her. In person he was *tall.* This was pretty much all that could be alleged against him at the time. On the other hand, his horror and grief at the bloody deed appeared genuine, and the magistrate, notwithstanding the opinion of the police, saw no sufficient cause for detaining him. The next day he disappeared, but many years afterwards the man, then being on his death-bed in America, confessed that he was indeed the murderer; that the murder had been effected as Ruthven had surmised; that he had broken open the tea-caddy, which he knew to contain his aunt's will, by the provisions of which, as she had informed him he was left penniless in consequence of his repeated misconduct; that he had secured the document and destroyed it, in the expectation of coming in as heir for the whole of the property, not being at the time aware that as an illegitimate child, which he was, he was debarred by law from inheriting a farthing. He added that he was disturbed by a knock at the door, and compelled to secure his retreat by the route so cleverly tracked by the Bow Street officer. Mr. Townshend's remarks, made in the hearing of my father, on the simplicity of Sir Richard Birnie in letting the fellow slip through his fingers after the police had fairly secured him, were in that worthy's usually forcible and figurative style.

MESMERISM.

It was in the spring either of this year, 1822, or of the year following, that Mr. Barham became a witness of one of those extraordinary exhibitions of the influence of the imagination or faith upon the bodily organs which forms, we are told by the orthodox physicians, the basis of the ephemeral systems, whether of the school of Mesmer or others, that are continually springing up around us. With instances indeed of the injurious effects which mental impressions are capable of producing upon the body, medical works abound. Dr. Hughes Bennett, in his "Lectures on Clinical Medicine," No. iv. p. 174, gives one especially marvelous case of what he terms "the predominance of ideas:"—

"A butcher," he says, "was brought into a druggist's shop (at Edinburgh) from the market-place opposite, laboring under a terrible accident. The man, on trying to hook up a heavy piece of meat above his head, slipped, and the sharp hook penetrated his arm, so that he himself was suspended. On being examined, he was pale, almost pulseless, and expressed himself as suffering acute agony. The arm could not be moved without causing excessive pain, and in cutting off the sleeve he frequently cried out; yet when the arm was exposed it was found to be quite uninjured, the hook having only traversed the sleeve of his coat."

The same author allows that, in like manner, so far from its being improbable that real cures are occasionally effected through the medium of the imagination, "all that we know of the effects of confident promises on the one hand, and belief on the other, render it very likely that such have occurred."

The case that fell under Mr. Barham's observation was that of an old friend, Major Hart. I can remember him (for he was fond of children, — fond, that is to say, of teasing them, — and children were of course fond of him), a slight, short man with a pale face, white hair, and glittering eyes, and the possessor of a certain bright shilling which was the object of my thoughts by day and my dreams by night. As an officer in the Rifle Brigade, he had seen a good deal of service; had been frequently and severely wounded; and was now sinking under a complication of disorders, of which partial paralysis was one. He had become utterly prostrate. The country doctors — he was living, I believe, at Maidstone — shook their heads, and admitted they could do no more. Then it was that some one whispered — "Try mesmerism!" Hart caught at the suggestion at once. There was in London, at this time, a professor of animal magnetism, whose fame had reached even unto Maidstone. His success was wonderful. Every human ill, old age scarcely excepted, was to be cured by some new and occult process, of which he was the fortunate discoverer. If men persisted in dying of disease, it was simply through their own willfulness, obstinacy, and incredulity. To this man the Major was determined to apply, and although he had been for several weeks considered incapable of quiting his bedroom, he insisted upon being placed in a carriage and conveyed to my father's house in town. With the assistance of a servant, the coachman, and Mr. Barham, he was removed from the vehicle to the apartment prepared for him. After resting a couple of days, during which he scarcely spoke, he was, in like manner, lifted into a hackney coach and driven off to the residence of the celebrated practitioner. The same care was necessary and was observed in carrying the patient into the consulting room, so completely unable was he to take a step, or even to stand, without the support of others. Placed gasping into a chair he was submitted to the keen, and for some time silent, examination of the doctor. At length the latter turned to my father and spoke to this effect: —

"You must be quite aware, sir, that exaggerated notions of my invention, as of everything displaying great and incomprehensible power, have got abroad. I am not, however, the charlatan that people would make me out. Sufferers are constantly brought here to whom I can hold out no hope of relief, and with whom I would rather have nothing to do. I am nevertheless perhaps obliged to operate, and little or no good follows. Now, sir, the case of your friend, on the contrary, I undertake with the utmost satisfaction. It is in every particular, both as regards his temperament and the character of his disorder, precisely the case adapted to the influence I shall bring to bear upon it. I have never met a subject whom I have approached with more perfect confidence. I stake my reputation upon a cure."

"*Credat Judæus!*" thought my father, and the gentleman continued: —

"A great effect will doubtless be produced this very morning, but it will be the work of some time, during which I require to be left alone with my patient. Call again in an hour and you shall judge for yourself."

My father was inclined to object to the dismissal. "Better go, Barham," said the Major in a tone distinct and clear, very different from that he had hitherto employed, and Barham went. He took the opportunity of transacting some business in the neighborhood, by which he was detained a few minutes beyond the time specified. Finding he was late, he took a coach and drove back, with the intention of carrying away his friend in it.

"Is Major Hart ready?" he inquired of the servant who opened the door.

"The Major, sir, was tired of waiting, so he has walked on; he said you would be sure to overtake him before he got home, he should n't hurry."

"Hurry!" exclaimed my father, "why he can't move — I am speaking of the gentleman you helped to carry in."

"Yes, sir; that is the gentleman — he has walked on."

At this moment out came the doctor himself, "It is quite true," he said; "Major Hart has left the house, and insisted upon walking."

"Impossible!"

"It is nevertheless so. His sensibility is even greater than I expected to find it; his cure will be proportionably rapid; meanwhile you had better perhaps overtake him as soon as you can, and persuade him to ride the remainder of the distance."

Half pleased, half alarmed, and wholly bewildered, Mr. Barham hurried away, and ere long caught sight of his friend looking contentedly into the window of a print shop. The change worked in him was certainly to all seeming nothing short of miraculous. He could walk, use his limbs freely, was free from pain, and in the highest possible spirits, overflowing with gratitude to his benefactor and respect for science. He admitted he was a little tired, so got into a coach and returned to Queen Street. Towards evening his new strength gradually died away. By next morning it was clean gone; and on the third day he was again all but speechless. A second visit to the doctor was paid, and a repetition of the treatment attempted, but faith had in the interval expired, and no further effect could be produced. He said he would go back to Kent and die comfortably at home. Happily he was enabled to reach his home alive; and the next news we heard of him was that one sunny afternoon, as he sat by the window in his easy chair with his Bible before him, he closed the book, lay back and fell asleep, passing out of life so imperceptibly that his niece, who was sitting opposite, was for some time unaware that he was dead.

Edward Cannon.

His appointment in the Chapel Royal led to an acquaintance, which quickly ripened into a warm friendship, with the

Rev. Edward Cannon, also one of the priests of the household, and who for many years previously had been on intimate terms with the family of Mrs. Barham. This singular being, introduced to the world under the name of Godfrey Moss, in Theodore Hook's celebrated novel "Maxwell," claims some notice, the more so as he has scarcely met with justice at the hands of his facetious friend.

For a general idea of his mannerism, I can but refer to the striking portrait referred to, one of the most perfect ever committed to paper. As he is there depicted, so precisely did he live and move in daily life — not an eccentricity is exaggerated, not an absurdity heightened! It is, however, to be regretted that the great master restricted himself to the delineating the less worthy features of the outward and visible man, and touched but lightly those high and noble traits of character which had gone far to relieve the mass of cynicism and selfishness but too correctly drawn.

Mr. Cannon, was, in fact, both a spoiled and a disappointed man. Brought up under the immediate care of Lord Thurlow, his brilliant wit, his manifold accomplishments, and, as may be hardly credited by those who knew him only in his decline, his fascinating manners, procured him a host of distinguished admirers and proved an introduction to the table of royalty itself. A welcome guest at Carlton House, Stow, and other mansions of the nobility, patronized by the Lord Chancellor, courted and caressed by men — to say nothing of women — of the highest rank and influence, he might possibly have become too extravagant or too impatient in his expectations; while more reasonable views would scarcely have been met by a chaplaincy to the Prince of Wales, and a lectureship at St. George's, Hanover Square — the only preferment he ever obtained. This neglect, as he esteemed it, was especially calculated to work evil on a disposition naturally independent to a fault, and associated, as it was, with a humor tinctured overmuch with bitterness. His caprices indulged and fostered, and his hope delayed, he fell gradually into utter disregard of all the amenities and conventional laws of society.

The extreme liberties he began to take, and the burst of sarcasm, which he took the less heed to restrain as he advanced in years, deprived him betimes of all his powerful patrons, and at the last alienated most of his more attached friends.

At one of the annual dinners of the members of the Chapel Royal, a gentleman had been plaguing Mr. Barham with a somewhat dry disquisition on the noble art of fencing. Wishing to relieve himself of his tormentor, the latter observed that his crippled hand had precluded him from indulging in that amusement ; but pointing to Cannon who sat opposite, he added, "That gentleman will better appreciate you ; he was an enthusiastic admirer of fencing in his youth."

After a few minutes the disciple of Angelo contrived to slip round the table, and commenced a similar attack upon Cannon. For some time he endured it with patience, till at length, on his friend's remarking that Sir George D—— was a great fencer, Cannon, who disliked the man, replied, "I don't know whether Sir George D—— is a great fencer, but Sir George D—— is a great fool."

A little startled, the other rejoined, "Well, possibly he is ; but then a man may be both."

"So I see, sir !" said Cannon, turning away.

As regards the circumstances which led immediately to his dismissal from the palace, his conduct was certainly not chargeable with blame, but was the natural working of an unbending spirit which scorned to flatter even princes.

Possessing, in addition to the attractions of his conversation, the charm of a voice so unusually sweet as to have gained him the name of Silver-tongue Cannon, he was admitted to the more select parties of the Prince of Wales, where his great musical taste and talent not unfrequently procured him the honor of accompanying his royal master on the pianoforte. On one occasion, at the termination of the piece, the Prince inquired, "Well, Cannon, how did I sing that?"

Cannon continued to run over the keys, but without making any reply.

"I asked you, Mr. Cannon, how I sang that last song, and

I wish for an honest answer," repeated the Prince. Thus pointedly appealed to, Cannon, of course, could no longer remain silent.

"I think, sir," said he, in his quiet and peculiar tone, "I have heard your Royal Highness succeed better."

"Sale and Atwood," observed the latter sharply, "tell me I sing that as well as any man in England."

"They, sir, may be better judges than I pretend to be," replied Cannon.

George the Fourth was too well bred as well as too wise a man to manifest open displeasure at the candor of his guest, but in the course of the evening, being solicited by the latter for a pinch of snuff, a favor which had been hesitatingly accorded a hundred times before, he closed the box, placed it in Mr. Cannon's hand, and turned abruptly away.[1] A gentleman in waiting quickly made his appearance, for the purpose of demanding back the article in question, and of intimating at the same time that it would be more satisfactory if its possessor forthwith withdrew from the apartment.

Cannon at first refused to restore what he chose to consider no other than a present.

"The *creetur* gave it me with his own hand," he urged, "if he wants it back let him come and say so himself."

It was represented, however, that the Prince regarded its detention in a serious light, and was deeply offended at the want of respect which had led to it. The box was returned without further hesitation, and Mr. Cannon retired for the last time from the precincts of Carlton House.

He was, however, not a man to permit a single affront to obliterate from his memory all traces of former kindness, and accordingly, when the trial of Queen Caroline had excited so much popular clamor against the Sovereign, Cannon was the first, on the termination of that affair, to get up and present an

[1] Cannon had previously succeeded in affronting Mrs. Fitzherbert. On being asked by the lady what he thought of a new upright pianoforte which she had just purchased, he replied, scarcely deigning to examine it, — "I think, Madam, it would make a very good cupboard to keep your bread and cheese in."

address from the inhabitants of the Isle of Wight to his royal master. Delighted at this seasonable exhibition of public approval, and not untouched, it may be, by the conduct of his former favorite, the King was all courtesy and condescension.

"You are not looking well, Cannon," he observed, at length.

"I am not so well, sir, as I have been," replied Cannon, with a meaning smile.

"Well, well! I must send Halford to prescribe for you," said the King. Nor did this prove to be an idle compliment; in due time the physician of the household called, having it in command to tender to the invalid his professional assistance, and at the same time to intimate that he might expect to be received again at the royal parties. This honor Mr. Cannon bluntly and resolutely declined. On being pressed to give some explanation of his refusal, he merely answered,—

"I have been early taught when I want to say 'no' and can say 'no,' to say 'no' — but never give a reason" — a maxim which he had learned from his early protector, Lord Thurlow, and a neglect of which, the latter used to boast, had enabled him to carry an important point with his late Majesty George III.

Thus it was: he had applied to that monarch on behalf of his brother for the Bishopric of Durham, and having somewhat unexpectedly met with a refusal, he bowed and was about to retire without pressing his suit, when the monarch, wishing to soften his decision as far as possible, added, "Anything else I shall be happy to bestow upon your relative, but this unfortunately is a dignity never held but by a man of high rank and family."

"Then, Sire," returned Lord Thurlow, drawing himself up, "I must persist in my request — I ask it for the brother of the Lord High Chancellor of England!"

The Chancellor was firm, and the King was compelled to yield.

"He gave me his reasons," said the former, "and I beat him."

With respect to Mr. Cannon, although he thought fit to decline giving any explanation at the time, he was not so reserved on all occasions.

"The *creetur*," he said, "has turned me out of his house once — he shall not have the opportunity of doing so again."

Of the many anecdotes of the Chancellor narrated by Cannon, I find but few preserved; the following, however, are given on his authority: —

"The great Lord Thurlow passed the latter part of his life at Brighton, and died there — it is said, while swearing at his servant. The present King (George IV.) having come down to the Pavilion, invited him to dinner, but knowing his man, thought proper to offer a sort of half apology for some of the company, among whom were Sir John Lade, and several characters of sporting notoriety. The sturdy old Chancellor leaning upon his cane, and looking his Royal Highness full in the face, replied, "Sir! I make exceptions to no man. Sir John Lade, for instance, whom your Royal Highness has thought proper to mention by name, is an excellent character in his proper place, but that, with all due deference, I humbly conceive to be your Royal Highness's coach-box, and not your table."

Again: —

"A Mr. Sneyd, a tall, thin man, nicknamed by George IV. 'The Devil's Darning Needle,' was much about Lord Thurlow during his last years, and had a sort of roving commission from him to pick up any stray genius he could lay hold of and bring him to the old nobleman's table. Coming in the stage-coach one day to Brighton Mr. Sneyd scraped an acquaintance with a fellow-traveller who turned out to be the celebrated J. P. Curran, and he eagerly invited his new friend to dine with Lord Thurlow, but some accident prevented his own attendance on the appointed day. Thurlow, who had heard much of Curran, when the cloth was removed, led the conversation to the state of the Irish bar, which Curran, who was at that time red-hot against the Union, abused in the lump with great vehemence.

"'Timidity, my lord, and venality,' said he, 'are the bane

of the Irish courts, and pervade them from the lowest to the highest.'

"'Indeed!' said Thurlow, 'pray what is the character of Lord ———?' (naming a particular friend of his own then on the Irish bench).

"'Oh,' replied Curran, 'never was man less fitted for his position; if he has any honesty in him, which is very problematical, he is infinitely too great a poltroon to let it appear.'

"'Humph!' quoth the Chancellor — 'a bad account of him indeed, Mr. Curran. And pray what do you think then of Lord ———?' (naming another old crony also in the same rank).

"'As to him,' said the barrister, 'he is ten thousand times worse than the other. The venality of that man is such that no person, however just and clear his case may be, can hope for a verdict where he presides, unless he has contrived to bribe his judge into justice. In fact these two form an admirable sample of Irish jurisprudence at it exists now — all venality and cowardice!'

"'In other words,' said the Chancellor, 'all the Irish lawyers are rascals?'

"'Pretty much so indeed, my lord.'

"Here the conversation stopped. The next day Lord Thurlow attacked Mr. Sneyd for sending such a flippant fellow to his table, adding that he saw nothing whatever in him.

"'Ah, my lord,' suggested Sneyd, 'that might be because there was no one present to draw the trigger.'

"'Sir,' replied the old nobleman, with one of his inveterate frowns, 'ask him to dine here again to-morrow, and be sure you are present and draw it yourself.'"

Whatever version of Cannon's reply to Sir Henry Halford reached the King, and however much at first he may have been disposed to resent the rejection of his advances, the offender was nevertheless again forgiven and without being forgotten. One circumstance certainly deserves to be mentioned as tending, in its degree, to invalidate those charges of selfishness and want of feeling which have been so lavishly directed against the best abused of all earthly monarchs.

Many years afterwards, when Cannon, who, though of inexpensive tastes, was utterly regardless of money and almost ignorant of its value, and who generally carried all he received loose in his waistcoat pocket, giving it away to any one who seemed to need it, was himself severely suffering from the effects of ill-health and improvident liberality, the King, who accidentally heard of his melancholy condition, instantly made inquiries with a view of presenting him with some piece of preferment that might have served as a permanent provision; but ascertaining that his habits had become such as to render any advancement in the clerical profession inexpedient, he, entirely unsolicited, sent his old favorite a check for a hundred pounds.

This assistance proved most opportune and served to supply immediate necessities. Cannon was staying at the time at a small hotel on the banks of the Thames, near Twickenham, from which he was unable, or rather unwilling to depart, till his bill which had swollen to a somewhat formidable size was discharged. Mr. Barham, therefore, and another friend hastened down to release him from a position which most people would have deemed embarrassing in the extreme. They found him, however, perfectly happy in his retirement; clothed from head to foot in mine host's habiliments, and, altogether, appearing so much better in health and spirits than could have been anticipated, that Mr. Barham was led to address some compliment to the landlady on the good looks of her guest.

"Well, sir, to be sure," replied that worthy personage, "we have done our best to keep him tidy and comfortable, and if you had only seen him last Sunday, when he was *washed and shaved*, you really might have said he *was* looking well."

He had formed, it appeared, a close intimacy with a monkey belonging to the establishment, and spent the principal portion of his time in its society, exchanging it occasionally for that of adventurous bipeds whom the steamboats, then "few and far between," landed at the Eyot, according as he found them more or less intelligent than his quadrupedal companion.

Like his friend, Cannon was one of those who gave full assent to the poet's doctrine,

> "The best of all ways
> To lengthen our days
> Is to steal a few hours from night," etc.

And so resolutely did he carry it out in practice when the opportunity offered, as at times to cause no little inconvenience to his entertainers. After a dinner, for example, given by Mr. Stephen Price of Drury Lane Theatre, all the guests, with the exception of Cannon and Theodore Hook, having long since retired, the host, who was suffering from an incipient attack of gout, was compelled to allude pretty plainly to the lateness of the hour. No notice, however, was taken of the hint, and, unable to endure any longer the pain of sitting up, Mr. Price made some excuse and slipped quietly off to bed. On the following morning he inquired of his servant—

"Pray, at what time did those gentlemen go last night?"

"Go, sir!" replied John; "they are not gone, sir: they have just rung for coffee!"

It was not to be supposed that these eccentricities could altogether escape episcopal observation, and although they met with considerable indulgence, a rebuke was sometimes unavoidable. Cannon, however, resented the slightest attempt at interference with a warmth and jealousy, ill-advised, to say the least of it. His hostility indeed to his diocesan, Dr. Blomfield, was not altogether to be attributed to private feeling; and certainly it could not have been warranted by any treatment experienced at his hands. Many, however, of the bitter satires that appeared in the periodicals, directed against certain proceedings of this eminent individual, were from Cannon's pen. More than one of the more powerful and more personal of these Mr. Barham was fortunate enough to save from publication. He borrowed the copy, and that once in his possession, he knew that Cannon was too indolent a man either to write another, or to persevere in demanding the restoration of the original. Those, however, who have read the "Dives and Lazarus," and "Lines written on the exclusion of ill-dressed persons from seats in the Chapel Royal," though they can scarcely fail to admit that nothing produced by Byron or Churchill excelled them in pungency will, nevertheless, consider their suppression justifiable even by an act of friendly felony.

That much of this caustic spirit sprang from blighted prospects, and was nurtured by the frequent supplies of his favorite "ginnums and water," there can be little doubt; his natural disposition was most amiable, and the kindness of his heart, and his complete freedom from selfishness in matters of importance, exhibited themselves in numberless instances, and never more conspicuously than in a case of self-denial which graced his declining days. He was summoned to the bedside of an old and valued friend; the lady (for a lady it was — like his "double," "Godfrey Moss," he had been a lady-killer in his time) announced to him that believing her health to be rapidly giving way she had made her will, by which, at her demise, the whole of a considerable fortune was to be placed at his disposal. Cannon looked at her doubtfully: —

"I don't believe it!" he said, at length.

The lady assured him that she was incapable of trifling on such a subject, and at such a moment; and added, that the document itself was lying in an escritoire in the room.

"I won't believe it," persisted the other, "unless I see it."

Smiling at such incredulity, the lady placed the will in his hands. Cannon took it, and read it.

"Well," said he, "if I had not seen it in your own handwriting, I would not have believed you could have been such an unnatural brute;" and he deliberately thrust the paper between the bars of the grate.

"What," he continued, "have you no one more nearly connected with you than I am, to leave your money to? No one who has better reason to expect to be your heir, and who has a right to be provided for first and best? Pooh! you don't know how to make a will. I must send Dance, a very respectable man in his way, red tape and parchment and all that — he shall make your will ; you may leave me a legacy, there 's no harm in that. I am a poor man, and want it ; but I am not a-going to be d—— to please you."

A new will was accordingly drawn up on Cannon's suggestion, bequeathing to him merely a sum of four thousand pounds. It will scarcely be credited that advantage was afterwards taken of a technical informality (in ignorance, it is to be hoped, of previous circumstances) to resist his claim even to this. It appeared that two copies of the will were executed ; one of which was retained in the custody of the testatrix, while the other was handed over to the care of a trustee. After a time, however, the lady sent for the duplicate, which was returned to her ; and on her death the two documents were found in a drawer folded up together. From one every name except Cannon's had been snipped out with a pair of scissors ; the other remained intact. Upon this it was contended that by mutilating one copy the testatrix had canceled both ; and a precedent was alleged to be found in the case of a gentleman who, taking with him to India one copy of his will, which he subsequently destroyed, left another in the charge of his solicitor at home. This on being produced was pronounced void in virtue of the canceling of its fellow. It was urged in answer, that the precedent did not apply, inasmuch as in the latter case the gentleman had revoked and destroyed the only instrument which was within his power, whereas in the former, both papers being in the hands of the testatrix, there was nothing to prevent her destroying both if she wished to make the revocation complete ; from her omitting to do so it was to be inferred that she repented of the change she had begun to make, and so reclaimed the uninjured copy of the will, to which she determined to adhere. After the delay of more than a year a decision was given in Cannon's favor, and the remainder of his life relieved from further apprehension on the score of pecuniary distress. He withdrew, shortly afterwards, to Ryde, in the Isle of Wight, taking his accustomed seat on the pier, with a pertinacity that gained for him among the boatmen the sobriquet of the "Pier Gun." Want of exercise, and the slow poison he became a slave to, at length did their work. Like Swift — to whom, in the general structure of his mind, in the power of his reasoning, and in the peculiar bent of his humor, he bore no little resemblance — his last hours were such as might well have aroused

> "The bitter pangs of humbled genius;"

they were those of one,

> "Marked above the rest,
> For qualities most dear, plunged from that height,
> And sunk, deep sunk, in second childhood's night."

He died forgotten, and almost alone; and it was left for a comparative stranger to raise the simple tablet that pleads for the memory of Edward Cannon.

Theatrical Anecdotes.

"*Diary: July* 26, 1826. — Dined with Lord Wiliam Lennox. Mr. Fawcett of Covent Garden told a story of an old woman and her daughter in a provincial town in Yorkshire.

"'Mither,' says the girl, 'there do go Mr. Irby agen.'

"'Ees, bairn, he be g'ween to ploy-house, I do suppose.'

"'Mither, what do Mr. Irby do at ploy-house? Him be never on steage?'

"'Nay, girl, him be prompter.'

"'What be prompter, mither?'

"'Why prompter, bairn, be mon wid book, and when all be fast on steage, he *lowses* 'em.'

"He also gave us an anecdote of Cooper of C. G. T., when on a provincial tour. The prompter of the company was a drunken, one-eyed fellow, who, having been born at Kidderminster, was generally known at the theatre by the name of 'Kiddy.' From frequent attacks of rheumatic gout, he had become crippled in both his hands, and as the porter pot was never absent, was compelled to support it by applying the knuckles of both his clenched fists in order to get it to his mouth. One evening, during the performance of a new play, all the *dramatis personæ* on the stage came to a stand-still. 'Kiddy' was loudly called on for the cue, but having been immersed for some minutes past, as usual, in contemplating the interior of his flagon, he had lost the place, and embarrassed at the same time with the mug, he cried out to the 'call-boy,' in a tone of voice which was heard, and caused no slight amusement in the stage boxes, —

"'Little boy, little boy, come here and hold de pot, while I sees where these thieves be.'"

Anecdote of Indian Officer.

"Cannon, who was present, and in most entertaining mood, told, among other things, his story of a general officer who, having passed many years of his life in India, was taken by a friend, on his return, to dine with some common relation. All parties being anxious to conciliate the nabob, who was rich, old, and a bachelor, every attention was shown him during dinner-time. The General, however, either from paucity of ideas, or from his regards being riveted upon the good things before him, was invincibly taciturn.

"'Pray, General,' said a female cousin on his left, 'how do you like India?'

"'Hot, ma'am,' said the commander, scarcely raising his eyes from his basin of mulligatawney, 'Hot, very hot!'

"Another pause ensued, which was broken by her brother on his right:—

"'General, we have heard much in England lately of the increase of suttees in India: may I ask if the burning of a Hindoo widow ever came under your personal notice?'

"'Widow! — burning! — Oh, aye, it was very hot, sir, devilish hot, never so hot in my life!'

"An excellent curry had now engaged his attention, when the general was again addressed by a tall, thin, antiquarian-looking personage, from the lower end of the table,—

"'Pray, General, during the many years you spent in Asia, did duty or inclination ever carry you into the neighborhood of the celebrated caves of Elephanta?'

"'Elephanta! Oh, ah, Elephanta—the caves—of course. Why, sir, it was very hot, devilish hot; hot all the time I was there; never was so hot in all my life; sir, it was as hot as H——!'

"This climax, delivered with the only spark of energy which the worthy officer had as yet exhibited, completely precluded any further attempt to engage him in conversation, and the observant veteran was permitted to relapse into silence; several of the party, however, declaring the next morning that they had derived much pleasure from their relation the General's interesting description of the state of our Oriental empire.

CANNON'S SNUFF-TAKING.

"Repeated as much as I could recollect of the handbill respecting Cannon. The latter having gone off into the Isle of Wight with Vaughan, last Lent, without making any arrangement for the performance of his duty at St. George's, Hanover Square, a placard was, a few mornings after his arrival, affixed nearly opposite his window at the Bugle Horn Hotel, near the bottom of Ryde pier, to the following effect:—

"'STOLEN OR STRAYED!

"'A stout black horse of the punch breed. Face tan, with a brown mark under the nostrils, coat rough, with brown spots, aged, but has the teeth of a young one. Fore-feet blacker than the hind. Is a little hard in the mouth, but gentle, having been ridden by a lady; goes a little lame on one leg, from having been ill-driven in a buggy, and *shies at a Churchbell;* supposed to have been carried off in Passion-week, by some itinerant musicians, who have been traced into Hampshire. Whoever will give information, etc.'"

The brown mark under the nostrils, and the blackness of the fore-feet mentioned in the description, are allusions to the enormous quantity of snuff which Cannon was in the habit, partly of taking, and partly of scattering right and left over shirt, waistcoat, table, chair, carpet — everything that he approached. Once, at the Chapel Royal he set the Bishop of London sneezing through the whole of the Communion Service, and afterwards when the Bishop remonstrated with him on having produced an old, colored, cotton handkerchief during the prayers, he merely asked in reply, — 'Pray, does your lordship take snuff?'

"Not if I can help it, Mr. Cannon."

"Ah, then, I do, my lord, a good deal."

His friend, John Wilson Croker, gave him, in lieu of the fourpenny box which he commonly used, a very handsome substitute having a gold cannon on the lid, and as a motto — "*Non sine pulvere.*"

The Dignum Brothers.

"*August* 15, 1826. — Dined with the Girdlers' Company at their Hall, after preaching to them at St. Michael Bassishaw, Mr. Taylor in the chair. Among the professional singers on the occasion was poor old Dignum. Anecdote told of him which I first heard from Nield, the lay vicar of St. Paul's. Dignum, it seems, was complaining one morning to old Knyvett, the King's composer, that his health was much impaired, and what was very extraordinary, that so strong a degree of sympathy existed between him and his brother, that one was no sooner taken ill than the other felt symptoms of the same indisposition, whatever it might be. 'We are both of us very unwell now,' added Dignum, 'and as our complaint is supposed to be an affection of the lungs, we are ordered to take asses milk, but unfortunately we have not been able to get any, though we have tried all over London; can you tell us what we had better do?'

"'Do?' answered Knyvett, 'Why the deuce don't you suck one another!'

A STRANGE FISH.

"*December* 3, 1826. — Dined for the first time with Dr. Sumner, Bishop of Llandaff, who told me as a fact that Dr. R——, a fellow of Eton, had some time since ordered one of his ponds to be cleaned out. A great number of carp, tench, eels, etc., were taken in the course of the operation. The Doctor was at dinner with some friends who had been viewing the work, when a servant came in to inform him that in draining off the water the men had found a chalybeate, 'Have they indeed?' cried he with much interest, 'I am very glad to hear it. Tell them to put it along with the other fish for the present.'

A KEW COMER.

"*May* 18, 1827. — Harry Sandford (of the Treasury), Cannon, Tom Hill, Sir Andrew Barnard, and myself, went up to Twickenham by the steamboat. On the way we talked all sorts of nonsense, and laughed at everything, and everybody. A queer-looking old gentleman served especially to amuse Sandford, who took a delight in quizzing him.

"'What is this bridge we're coming to?' asked the old gentlemen of the skipper.

"'Kew, sir,' returned the man.

"'How dare you insult a respectable individual,' cried Sandford, 'by insinuating that he is a *Kew comer?*'

"One of the company asserting that he had seen a pike caught, which weighed thirty-six pounds, and was four feet in length, —

"'Had it been a sole,' said Harry, 'it would have surprised me less, as Shakespeare tells us

"'All the *souls* that are, were *four feet* (forfeit) once.'

"On Hill's remarking on the number of publicans who had put up the Duke of Wellington's head over their doors, Sandford said, 'Yes, let his grace's death come when, and how it may, you will never be able to say of him as King Henry does of Cardinal Beaufort,

"'He dies and makes no sign!'"

OLD FRIENDS SHOULD NOT BE PARTED.

"*September* 1, 1827. — Lord William Lennox and Mr. George Hill (of the Blues) met Dick and myself at Parrock House, where we slept last night. Went out shooting this morning, killing eleven brace and a half of partridges; dined at two, and returned at four by the steamboat. On the voyage we had our profiles taken by an artist on board for a shilling a head, which he executed in ten seconds by the help of a pair of scissors only. An old woman on board told some of her friends who were very merry that, while she was at Margate in the course of the summer, the friend at whose house she had been staying had gone into the market for the purpose of purchasing a goose. There were but two in the whole place, offered for sale by a girl of fourteen, who refused to part with one without the other, assigning no other reason for her obstinacy than that it was her mother's order. Not wishing for two geese, the lady at first declined the purchase, but at last finding no other was to be had, and recollecting that a neighbor might be prevailed upon to take one off her hands, she concluded the bargain. Having paid for and secured the pair, she asked the girl at parting if she knew her mother's reason for the directions she had given. 'Oh, yes! mistress,' answered the young poultry-merchant readily, 'mother said that they had lived together *eleven years*, and it would be a sin and a shame to part them now!'"

LUTTREL'S EPIGRAM.

"*September* 20, 1827. — Walpole, Lord William, and Cannon dined here. Cannon repeated Luttrel's epigram on the illness of the King when Regent: —

"'The Regent, sir, is taken ill,
And all depends on Halford's skill.
"Pray what," inquired the sage physician,
"Has brought him to this sad condition?"
When Bloomfield ventured to pronounce,
"A little too much Cherry Bounce."
The Regent hearing what was said,
Raised from the couch his aching head,
And cried "No, Halford, 't is not so!
Cure us, O Doctor, — *Curaçoa!*"'"

THE DUCHESS OF ST. ALBANS.

"*October* 28, 1827. — Dined at Dr. Hughes's. He read, from a letter of Southey, the Laureate, a humorous account of his first introduction to the Duchess of St. Albans, *ci-devant* Miss Mellon, alias Mrs. Coutts: 'I begin to think with Sir William Curtis that wonders will never have done ceasing. Here have I been hooked into an acquaintance with a duchess, and partaken of a potatoe-pie of her grace's own making! I could tell you much of her bonnet, which our vicar has already compared to a banyan-tree. I could say much of her lip, which would seem to bespeak her a Nazarite from her mother's womb,' etc. This led the conversation to her Grace's habits and manners, when it was mentioned that, while an actress, Miss Mellon was the terror of the green-room from her violence, and that on one occasion, having taken offense at something said about her by Horace Twiss, she went up to Mrs. Henry Siddons, while sitting on a sofa, and addressed her, to her no small consternation, 'Madam, you may tell that rascal of a Twiss that the first time I meet him in a room I will shave his head with a poker!'"

THOMAS HILL.

Mr. Hill is the Mr. Hull of "Gilbert Gurney," — and he furnished the subject of Mr. Poole's admirable comedy, "Paul Pry." "Pooh pooh! everybody must happen to know *that.*" It may not, however, be so generally known that to his spirit of inquiry was owing the discovery of the celebrated American sea-serpent. Such was the fact! Hill was in the constant habit of visiting Mr. Stephen Price, the manager of Drury Lane, at his room in the theatre, and the latter soon found, to his surprise, that much that fell from him in conversation relating to engagements, the receipts of "the house," together with portions that he might have communicated of his American correspondence, appeared next day in the columns of the "Morning Chronicle."

"When I discovered this, sir," said Price, "I gave my friend a lie a day!" and accordingly the public were soon treated with the most extraordinary specimens of Transatlantic intelligence; among the rest, with the first falling in with the body of a sea monster, somewhere about the Bermudas, and the subsequent appearance of his tail, some hundred miles to the northeast.

"Well, my dear boy," used to exclaim the credulous visitor on entering the manager's sanctum, "any news; any fresh letters from America?"

"Why, sir," would reply Price, with the utmost gravity, "I have been just reading an extract, sent under cover, from Captain Lobcock's log; they 've seen, sir, that d—d long sea-sarpant again; they came upon his head, off Cape Clear, sir!"

And so the hoax continued, till the proprietors of the journal which was made the vehicle for these interesting accounts, finding they were not received with the most implicit faith, unkindly put a stop to any further insertions on the subject.

A Paradox.

"*Diary: November* 18, 1827. — Coming home in the evening from the Chapel Royal, where I had been doing duty, I overtook in the Strand two lads, having much the appearance of linen-drapers' shopmen, and endeavoring to smoke certain abominations under the semblance of cigars; both of them very tipsy. The obliquity of their motions, which resembled that sort of progress called by sailors 'tack and half tack,' rendered it difficult to pass them, and while thus kept, half voluntarily, half compulsorily, following in their wake, I heard the following conundrum put by the shorter one to his friend.

"'I say, Tom, do you know where that place is in the world where two friends, let them be ever so intimate — as good friends as you and me, Tom — can't be half an hour together without quarreling? Now there is a *paradox* for you!'

"'A what? a Paradise?'

"'No, you fool, a *paradox*.'

"'A paradox is it? Very well, and what's that?'

"'What, don't you know what a *paradox* is? Why, a paradox is a — what a fool you must be not to know what's a paradox; it's a sort of — oh, it's no good talking to a chap that don't know what a paradox is!'

"Here the speaker relapsed into an indignant silence, which he maintained till I was obliged to pass them, and I remain to this hour as ignorant of the meaning, or rather solution (for meaning it may have none), of the conundrum, as his antiparadoxical ally."

A Dubious Acquaintance.

On his first arrival in London, Mr. Barham had become acquainted with a young man named Graham, who may be remembered as moving some years ago in respectable literary circles; he was possessed of considerable intellectual attainments, a prepossessing appearance, and very pleasing manners. The history of his career, detailed in the following extract, is not without interest, presenting, as it does, the melancholy spectacle of one endowed with great abilities, all blighted and rendered barren through want of principle.

"*December* 2, 1827. — Dined with Price, the manager of Drury Lane Theatre. The company were Const the magistrate, Tom Hill, Jerdan, Broderip, Braham the singer, and myself. Braham sang beautifully. . . . . Had some conversation with Price respecting W. Graham, late editor of 'The Literary Museum,' whom I knew well when he filled that situation. He was a tall, slight, gentlemanly young man; rather, but not offensively, dandified, and with abilities and information which might have made him anything he chose to be. He was, I found, on comparing notes with Price, an American by birth, and at the age of seventeen had committed a forgery on a person of high respectability at Philadelphia. He was detected, but pardoned by the gentleman whom he had attempted to defraud, on account of his youth, and out of regard to his family, but on the express condition that he should leave the country. Graham went, at first, no farther than New York, where Mr. Price was then practicing at the American Bar. The latter received a letter from the gentleman alluded to, requesting him to call on the young man, and either compel him to quit America forthwith, or send him back in custody to Philadelphia. This commission Price executed to the letter, allowing him four days for departure ; and Graham, sailing for England, landed at Plymouth. Here he was for a short time in the company of Mr. Foote, the manager of the Plymouth Theatre, and father to the (subsequently) celebrated Miss Foote, of Covent Garden Theatre, to whose Juliet, I have heard him say, he played Romeo ; he also performed the part of Frederic in 'The School of Reform,' she playing the heroine. With Miss Foote he was, according to his own account, much 'smitten' at the time, and to this early attachment was owing several of his rhyming effusions later in life ; one I recollect ran the round of the newspapers, and was attributed to others, but I have heard Graham claim it. The only verse I can call to mind runs : —

'Had I the land that's in the Strand, —
Gentles, I beg your pardon, —
I'd give each Foot, and more to boot,
For one of Covent Garden.'

"An opportunity occurring for a literary engagement in London, Graham came to town, when he distinguished himself as a contributor to the magazines, and other periodicals. It was about this time I first knew him. A gentleman with whom he had become acquainted in the course of business had, I understood, taken a great fancy to him, had sent him for a while to Cambridge, and at his death bequeathed him an annuity of 300*l.* This, however, was soon disposed of, and the sum raised was, according to some accounts, lost in speculation, while others said it was spent in debauchery. Of this I know nothing; the only reason I ever had for suspecting he was of a dissipated turn, was an account he himself once gave me, when we met accidentally — that a young woman had that evening called at his lodgings in a hackney-coach, and (I think on his declining to see her) had cut her throat on the spot. She was not dead at the time he mentioned this, and the result I never learned. The nature of this circumstance, and the want of feeling exhibited in the recital, were of course sufficient to check any favorable opinion I might have formed of him, and to replace our acquaintance on the most distant footing.

"When Mr. Price first came to London, with the view of taking a lease of Drury Lane Theatre, he was walking one evening with a friend in the lobby of that house, when he met Graham, but without recognizing him; the latter, however, watched his opportunity, and drawing him aside, inquired if he did not recollect him.

"'Why, sir,' said Price, 'I have certainly seen you before, but where, and under what circumstances, I cannot at present call to mind. The impression I feel, however, respecting you is a painful one; and it strikes me that either in my professional capacity, or otherwise, I have seen you involved in some disgrace.'

"Graham did not hesitate to prompt a memory which further reflection might render less treacherous, but avowed himself at once, adding that he was now prospering and filling a respectable situation in the world, and begging Price not to betray that they had ever met before. This Price promised. Some short time after, the latter was called to dine with Mr. R——, to whom he had been recently introduced; Graham was also asked for the same day, and had unhesitatingly accepted the invitation, but happening afterwards to hear that he would meet his countryman Mr. Price, he at once recollected 'a previous engagement at Chelsea,' and that in so marked a manner that his friend perceived it was a disinclination to meet the person he had just named which occasioned his retracting. He of course said no more to Graham ; but having a very slight acquaintance at the time with Mr. Price, actually went to a common friend to ask 'if he were quite sure of Mr. Price's respectability, as Graham evidently would not meet him ?'

"The real state of the case he did not learn for a long time after, when Graham, having run through all he possessed or could borrow, drew several forged bills on Mr. C. Knight, Mr. Whitaker, and others, and absconded with the money. He succeeded in returning to America, and there became sub-editor of a periodical paper, when a quarrel arising between him and a young man at a dinner party, Graham struck him ; a challenge was the consequence, and the assailant, being shot through the body at the first fire, died almost immediately. This happened in the autumn of 1827."

John Wilson.

"*May* 14, 1828.—Acted as one of the stewards of the Literary Fund dinner with Lord F. L. Gower, Mr. Buckingham the traveller, Bishop of Winchester (Sumner), Hobhouse, Colonel Fitzclarence, and others. Duke of Somerset in the chair. Fitzgerald the *poet* spouted as usual, and broke down. Cannon observed 'Poeta nascitur son *Fitz*—I beg his pardon, I am afraid I am wrong in a letter!' Supped afterwards with Blackwood of Edinburgh, who dined with us, at his rooms at the Somerset Coffee House. Jerdan, Crofton Croker, Rev. M. Stebbing present, with whom was passed an extremely pleasant evening, till 'Ebony' fell asleep. Amusing story told of John Wilson, the Professor of Morality, editor of 'Blackwood's Magazine,' and my old college acquaintance. He had taken Mrs. Wilson, her sister, and her sister's husband, in the summer of 1824, to the inn at Bowness for the purpose of viewing the Lake district. On the morning after their arrival the gentlemen walked out, leaving the ladies at their breakfast. Suddenly the latter were most unceremoniously broken in upon by Lord M——, a young nobleman recently expelled from Christ Church, and three of his companions, one of whom was in orders. In spite of the interference of the landlady, they acted very rudely, insisting on saluting the ladies, and in the scuffle overturned the table. Having been with much difficulty induced to quit the room, they next proceeded to stroll by the margin of the magnificent piece of water in the immediate vicinity. On his return, Mr. Wilson was made acquainted by the landlady with what had occurred in his absence, and became, as may be supposed, violently angry. In vain did his brother-in-law and the ladies endeavor to pacify him, and as they locked the door to prevent his going in search of the intruders, he sprang through the window, and made off to the shore of the lake, where he found the party amusing themselves with throwing stones into the water. Instantly addressing them, he insisted on knowing which was Lord M——. The gentlemen at first were silent, but on his declaring, if he were not informed, he should treat the person nearest as the object of his inquiry, his lordship avowed himself, and was immediately knocked down! The other three closed on the Professor; but he, being a very athletic man, as well as possessed of considerable skill in the art of boxing, soon gave the whole four a very severe drubbing, and compelled them to apologize for their improper conduct. The next morning the clergyman, mounting a very respectable pair of black eyes, called on him, having learnt his name in the interval, and renewing his excuses, hinted that for the sake of all parties it would be better that the affair should be buried in silence. Mr. Wilson replied that he was not in the least ashamed of what *he* had done, and that if his Professor's grown had been on his back at the time he should have had no hesitation in laying it aside on such an occasion; but that his object of inflicting a due chastisement having been accomplished, any publicity which might arise would be owing only to their own indiscretion, as he should think no more of the matter. And thus the affair terminated."

A Ghost Story.

With his vivid imagination, and appreciation of the marvellous, it is not to be altogether wondered at if Mr. Barham himself appeared a little disposed to give credence to the existence of things undreamed of in our philosophy.

People who heard him narrate some tale of mystery with a dramatic power and flow of impressive language that riveted the attention of a youthful audience, whom he always loved to amuse, and with whom he loved to be amused, might easily allow the undercurrent of humor to escape their notice. And really he seemed at times to endeavor to persuade himself into credulity, much in the way that some people strive to convict themselves of a bodily ailment. He sought, as it were, to lull reason to sleep for a while, and leave an uninterrupted field for the wildest vagaries of fancy. Unlike poor Lady Cork, whose enjoyment of "her murders" sensibly declined, he never lost his relish for a "good ghost story;" nothing delighted him more than to listen to — unless it were to tell — one of those "true histories," properly fitted with the full complement of names, dates, and locale, attested by "living witnesses of unblemished reputation," and hedged in on all sides by circumstantial evidence of the most incontrovertible nature; one, in short, of those logical *culs de sac* which afford no exit but by unceremoniously kicking down the opposing barrier. It was Sir Walter Scott, I believe, who was thus driven to extricate himself from a dilemma of this sort, when, being asked "how he accounted" for some strange tale he had related on no less authority than that of his own grandmother, he was forced to reply, after some deliberation, — "Aiblins my grandmither was an awfu' leear!"

That the lovers of well-authenticated ghost stories owe a good deal of their delectation to the ingenuity of the "awfu' leears" is, I fear, not to be gainsaid. The diary seems to supply an instance with which this chapter may conclude: —

"It is a singular thing that, of all the numerous writers who have told this celebrated ghost story (that of Sir George

Villiers [1]), not one that I have ever seen has alluded to a story precisely similar in all its details which is recorded by the Duc de St. Simon, in the first volume of his memoirs, as having happened to Louis XIV. A man brings the same message of secret advice, together with a secret known only to the King himself, which he declares he has received three different times from a phantom representing the late Queen, in the forest of St. Germain, and which had been confided to the speaker for the purpose of securing attention to his message. The King receives the man more than once, rebukes his ministers for thinking him mad, and treats the whole business very gravely, ordering the messenger to be provided for comfortably in his own sphere of life for the rest of his days. This happened in 1691, and St. Simon conjectures it to have been a trick of Maintenon's to induce Louis to own their marriage. It is difficult to believe that one of these stories is not a mere variation of the other."

THOMAS HUME.

One of the earliest and closest intimacies which Mr. Barham contracted, after his settlement in London, was with Dr. Thomas Hume, who, like Cannon, had been for many previous years a constant guest of Dr. Bond, the husband of Mrs. Barham's sister, at Hanwell. Hume must have been naturally a man of strange temper, and time and circumstances had combined to deepen his peculiarities. Tall, upright, stern, with a cold, colorless, impassive face over which a smile rarely flitted,

[1] The particulars of the Villiers story are briefly these: A certain M . Twose, an old school-fellow of Sir George Villiers, father of the first Duke of Buckingham, being asleep in his lodging in Drury Lane, was disturbed by the apparition of the knight, who enjoined him to visit the Duke and admonish him as to his conduct and policy, and assure him, if he attended to the warning, of life and prosperity, but to predict his death before St. Bartholomew's Day if he neglected it. The man not obeying, the visit was repeated thrice, and on the last occasion the ghost told him certain secrets to be used as credentials. Mr. Twose, having with difficulty obtained access to the Duke, delivered the message. The Duke, on receiving it, consulted with his mother, who was much affected, but paid himself no further heed to the admonition, and was soon after assassinated at Portsmouth by Felton, as he was about to set out for the relief of Rochelle, then besieged by the French.

he was assuredly not one either to invite or to accept any hasty demonstration of friendship. There was, indeed, something cynical about him which had the effect of keeping people in general at a distance; and at a distance people in general were best pleased to keep. The absence of all outward show of geniality, and the seeming want of sympathy which he displayed, rendered it impossible for mere acquaintances to feel at ease in his company. And yet, notwithstanding his repellant manner, he was blessed with a heart warm, true, and largely generous — qualities which endeared its possessor to a chosen few, among whom may be numbered Thomas Moore and my father. Moreover, he was a perfect gentleman — an Irish gentleman, and endowed with a courteous gravity of demeanor which lent an uncommon force to anything of a sarcastic turn to which he might be provoked into giving utterance.

One instance, in particular, of his dry humor my father used to relate. They had walked together to the office of one of the morning newspapers, and there the doctor silently placed upon the counter an announcement of the death of some friend, together with five shillings, the usual charge for the insertion of such advertisements. The clerk glanced at the paper, tossed it on one side, and said gruffly, "Seven and six!"

"I have frequently," replied Hume, "had occasion to publish these simple notices, and I have never before been charged more than five shillings."

"Simple!" repeated the clerk without looking up; "he 's universally beloved and deeply regretted! Seven and six."

Hume produced the additional half-crown and laid it deliberately by the others, observing as he did so, with the same solemnity of tone he had used throughout, — "Congratulate yourself, sir, that this is an expense which your executors will never be put to."

Dr. Hume was, as I observed, an Irishman; he was in the army, had done some service, and had attained, I believe, the rank of physician to the forces. He was married twice: in his first choice he was not fortunate; and to this early disappointment of his hopes something of the sternness of his disposition is in fairness to be attributed. His first wife was the daughter of a clergyman, rector of a parish which now may almost be reckoned in the suburbs of London, whose tragic end shocked the town some sixty years ago, and has since been introduced in at least one work of fiction. The particulars, as my father heard them on good authority, are certainly remarkable. The gentleman, whom I need designate no further than by the initial G——, was a tolerably well-known, and accomplished member of society, an elegant scholar, distinguished for much of that facility in the composition of Latin verse which has rendered Father Prout famous, and one who called great folks — even royal dukes — his friends. More than one of these illustrious personages occasionally did him the honor of visiting his rectory. As may be supposed, he was not long in finding out that the entertaining royalty is a sort of hospitality far too splendid for the fortune of a simple clergyman. Perhaps, like so many men under the like circumstances, and yet without reason, he vaguely hoped that something would be done for him. But whether or not he had been beguiled by others, or by himself, in this respect, one thing was clear — the something was too long a-doing! Ruin was inevitable, and was at hand! Resolving to anticipate the wreck, he got together all that was available of his remaining property and departed suddenly and secretly for London. It so happened that one of his friends, residing at Hanwell, had invited him to join a party at dinner on the following day. The guests, with the exception of Mr. G——, arrived in due time. At first there was the usual disposition shown, on the part of the host, to await his coming; then a little whispering among the gentlemen took place; and by degrees a gloom, felt but not comprehended by all, stole over the company, who sat down to table without the rector and quitted it at an unusually early hour. It was not till the next morning that the hostess (a near relative of my own) was informed of the cause of her friend's absence. A rumor of its nature had reached the village the day before, and had been communicated to her husband in the drawing-room; the report was now confirmed, and there was no further use in maintaining silence on the subject. Mr. G——, it appeared, had reached London safely and had been driven to one of the large coaching inns in the city; I believe it was "The Spread Eagle," in Gracechurch Street. Here he supped and retired, as it was supposed, to rest, having given orders to be called in the morning in time to enable him to start off by the first stage bound for Dover. Noises, it came out afterwards, were heard in the course of the night proceeding from his room, but as they probably had not reached the ears of any of the servants of the house, no notice was taken of the occurrence. At the appointed hour "boots" rapped at the traveller's door. No answer was returned; the summons was repeated, but in vain. The man became alarmed, called his master, under whose directions the door was forced, and a strange and shocking sight was disclosed. Suspended from the bedstead, strangled and long dead, hung the occupant of the apartment. Bed and bedding were tumbled in confusion on the floor; every article of clothing, the curtains, even the sheets, were torn to shreds and scattered in all directions; the furniture was overthrown and broken, and the work of destruction was completed by the self-murder of its perpetrator. For some little time no clew to the mystery could be gained, but ere long a discovery was effected by means the most unlooked for. A hackney coachman was taken into custody for drunkenness. On being examined by the police there was found in his possession a pocket-book containing bank notes for a very large amount. Inquiry elicited the fact that he had lately obtained change for others; and, finding evasion impossible, the man confessed that he had a few days before driven a gentleman to the inn in question, and that, on examining the carriage after depositing his fare, a pocket-book lying among the straw at the bottom caught his eye, and he could not resist the temptation to appropriate its contents. Meanwhile the wretched owner evidently had not become aware of his loss till he had reached his bed-room. Then there must have flashed upon him the hopelessness and horror of his position — a penniless fugitive, with disgrace and ruin confronting him turn which way he would! One may well imagine the despair and agony which accompanied the frantic search for his treasure, and finally the mania which drove him to his death.

CHARLES MATHEWS THE ELDER.

In 1829 Mr. Barham appears to have met for the first time, at the table of their common friend, Theodore Hook, Charles Mathews the elder. Their acquaintance was of some years' duration, but never reached intimacy; it was accompanied, nevertheless, certainly on the part of Mr. Barham, by feelings of no ordinary regard. It may, indeed, be questioned whether the golden opinions won by this accomplished actor in his professional career upon the stage were more than commensurate with the esteem which he inspired in private life.

"*Diary: May* 5, 1829. — Dined at Hook's. Horace Twiss, Lord W. Lennox, Jerdan, Cannon, Mathews, Yates, Professor Millington, Allan Cunningham, Price, Denham, brother to Colonel Denham the traveller, Milan Powell, F. Broderip, Doctors Arnott and Whimper, with myself, formed the party. Sir A. Barnard being engaged with the king, Lockhart with his wife, and Charles Kemble laid up with a bilious attack. Mathews told an excellent story of an Irish surgeon named Maseres, who kept a running horse, and who applied to him on one occasion for his opinion respecting a disputed race.

"'Now, sur,' commenced the gentleman, 'Mr. Mathews, as you say you understand horse-racing, and so you do, I 'll just thank ye to give me a little bit of an opinion, the least taste in life of one. Now, you 'll mind me, sur, my horse had won the first *hate*, well, sur, and then, he 'd won the second *hate*, well" —

"'Why, sir,' said Mathews, 'if he won both the heats, he won the race.'

"'Not at all, my dear fellow, not at all. You see he won the first *hate*, and then, somehow, my horse fell down, and then the horse (that 's not himself, but the other), came up" —

"'And passed him, I suppose,' said Mathews.

"'Not at all, sur, not at all; you quite mistake the gist of the matter. Now, you see, my horse had lost the first *hate*"—

"'Won it, you mean — at least, won it, you said.'

"'Won it! of course, I said won it; that is, the other horse won it, and the other horse, that is, *my* horse, won the second *hate*, when another, not himself, comes up and tumbles down — but stop! I'll demonstrate the circumstances ocularly. There — you'll keep your eye on that decanter; now, mighty well; now, you'll remember that's *my* horse, that is, I mane it's not my horse, it's the other, and this cork — you observe this cork — this cork's my horse, and my horse, that is this cork, had won the first *hate*'—

"'Lost it, you said, sir, just now,' groaned Mathews, rapidly approaching a state of complete bewilderment.

"'Lost it, sur, by no manes; won it, sur, I maintain — 'pon my soul, your friend[1] there that's grinning so is a mighty bad specimen of an American — no, sur, *won* it, I said; and now I want your opinion about the *hate*, that is, not the *hate*, but the race, you know, not, that is, the first *hate*, but the second *hate*, that would be the race when it was won.'

"'Why, really, my dear sir,' replied the referee, 'I don't precisely see the point upon which'—

"'God bless me, sur! do ye pretind to understand horse-racing, and can't give a plain opinion on a simple matter of *hates?* Now, sur, I'll explain it once more. The stopper, you are aware, is my horse, but the other horse — that is, the other *man's* horse,' etc., etc.

"And so poor Maseres went on for more than an hour, and no one could tell at last which horse it was that fell; whether he had won the first *hate*, or lost it; whether his horse was the decanter or the cork; or what the point was, upon which Mr. Maseres wanted an opinion."

[1] Mr. Stephen Price.

The Portsmouth Ghost Story.

"A story with much more of the supernatural about it was related to me by Mrs. Hughes the other day, which is, I think. one of the best authenticated ghost stories in existence. It was narrated to her by Mrs. Hastings, wife of Captain Hastings, R. N., and ran to the following effect: —

"Captain and Mrs. Hastings were driving into Portsmouth one afternoon, when a Mr. Hamilton, who had recently been appointed to a situation in the dockyard there, made a third in their chaise, being on his way to take possession of his post. As the vehicle passed the end of one of the narrow lanes which abound in the town, the latter gentleman, who had for some little time been more grave and silent than usual, broke through the reserve which had drawn a remark from the lady, and gave the following reason for his taciturnity: —

"'It was,' said he, 'the recollection of the lane we have just passed, and of a very singular circumstance which occurred to me at a house in it some eighteen years ago, which occupied my thoughts at the moment, and which, as we are old friends, and I know you will not laugh at me, I will repeat to you.

"'At the period alluded to, I had arrived in the town for the purpose of joining a ship in which I was about to proceed abroad on a mercantile speculation. On inquiry, I found that the vessel had not come round from the Downs, but was expected every hour. The most unpleasant part of the business was, that two or three king's ships had just been paid off in the harbor, a county election was going on, and the town was filled with people waiting to occupy berths in an outward bound fleet which a contrary wind had for some days prevented from sailing. This combination of events, of course, made Portsmouth very full and very disagreeable. To me it was particularly annoying as I was a stranger in the place, and every respectable hotel in the place was quite full. After wandering half over the town without success, I at length happened to inquire at a tolerably decent looking public-house, situate in the lane alluded to, where a very civil, though a very cross looking landlady at length made me happy by the intelligence that she would take me in, if I did not mind sleeping in a double-bedded room. I certainly did object to a fellow-lodger, and so I told her, but, as I coupled the objection with an offer to pay handsomely for both beds, though I should occupy only one of them, our bargain was settled, and I took possession of my apartment.

"'When I retired for the night I naturally examined both beds, one of which had on a very decent counterpane, the other being covered with a patchwork quilt, coarse, but clean enough. The former I selected for my own use, placed my portmanteau by its side, and having, as I thought, carefully locked the door to keep out intruders, undressed, jumped beneath the clothes, and fell fast asleep.

"'I had slept, I suppose, an hour or more, when I was awakened by a noise in the lane below; but being convinced that it was merely occasioned by the breaking up of a jolly party, I was turning round to recompose myself, when I perceived, by the light of the moon which shone brightly into the room, that the bed opposite was occupied by a man, having the appearance of a sailor. He was only partially undressed, having his trowsers on, and what appeared, as well as I could make it out, to be a Belcher handkerchief, tied around his head by way of a nightcap. His position was half sitting, half reclining on the outside of the bed, and he seemed to be fast asleep.

"'I was, of course, very angry that the landlady should have broken her covenant with me and let another person into the room, and at first felt half disposed to desire the intruder to withdraw; but as the man was quiet, and I had no particular wish to spend the rest of the night in an altercation, I thought it wiser to let things alone till the morning, when I determined to give my worthy hostess a good jobation for her want of faith. After watching him for some time, and seeing that my chum maintained the same posture, though he could not be aware that I was awake, I reclosed my eyes and once more fell asleep.

"'It was broad daylight when I awoke in the morning, and

the sun was shining full in through the window. My slumbering friend apparently had never moved, for there he was still, half sitting, half lying on the quilt, and I had a fair opportunity of observing his features, which, though of a dark complexion, were not ill-favored, and were set off by a pair of bushy black whiskers that would have done honor to a rabbi. What surprised me most, however, was that I could now plainly perceive that what I had taken in the moonlight for a red handkerchief on his forehead was in reality a white one, but quite saturated in parts with a crimson fluid, which trickled down his left cheek and seemed to have run upon the pillow.

"'At the moment the question occurred to me — how could the stranger have procured admission into the room? as I saw but one door, and that I felt pretty confident I had myself locked on the inside, while I was quite positive my gentleman had not been in the chamber when I retired to bed.

"'I got out and walked to the door, which was in the centre of one side of the room, nearly half-way between the two beds; and as I approached it, one of the curtains interposed for a moment so as to conceal my unknown companion from my view. I found the door, as I had supposed it to have been, fastened, with the key in the lock, just as I had left it, and, not a little surprised at the circumstance, I now walked across to the farther bed to get an explanation from my comrade, when to my astonishment he was nowhere to be seen! Scarcely an instant before I had observed him stretched in the same position which he had all along maintained, and it was difficult to conceive how he had managed to make his exit so instantaneously, as it were, without my having perceived or heard him. I, in consequence, commenced a pretty close examination of the wainscot near the head of the bed, having first satisfied myself that he was concealed neither under it nor by the curtain. No door nor aperture of any kind was to be discovered, and, as the rawness of the morning air began by this time to give me a tolerably strong hint that it was time to dress, I put on the rest of my clothes, not, however, without occasionally pausing to muse on the sailor's extraordinary conduct.

"'I was the first person up in the house; a slipshod, ambiguous being, however, in whom were united all the various qualities and functions of "boots," chambermaid, waiter, and potboy, soon made its appearance, and yawning most terrifically began to place a few cinders, etc., in a grate not much cleaner than its own face and hands, preparatory to the kindling of a fire. From this combination I endeavored to extract some information respecting my nocturnal visitor, but in vain; it "knowed nothing of no sailors," and I was compelled to postpone my inquiries till the appearance of the mistress, who descended in due time.

"'After greeting her with all the civility I could muster—no great amount by the way as my anger was in abeyance only, not extinct—I proceeded to inquire for my bill, telling her that I certainly should not take breakfast, nor do anything more "for the good of the house," after her breach of promise respecting the privacy of my sleeping-room. The good lady met me at once with a "Marry come up!" a faint flush came over her cheek, her little gray eyes twinkled, and her whole countenance gained in animation what it lost in placidity.

"'What did I mean? I had bespoke the whole room, and I had had the whole room, and, though she said it, there was not a more comfortable room in all Portsmouth; she might have let the spare bed five times over, and had refused because of my fancy; did I think to "*bilk*" her? and called myself a gentleman she supposed!

"'I easily stopped the torrent of an eloquence that would have soon gone near to overwhelm me, by depositing a guinea (about a fourth more than her whole demand) upon the bar, and was glad to relinquish the offensive for the defensive. It was therefore with a most quaker-like mildness of expostulation that I rejoined, that certainly I had not to complain of any actual inconvenience from the vicinity of my fellow-lodger, but that, having agreed to pay double for the indulgence of my whim, if such she was pleased to call it, I of course expected the conditions to be observed on the other side; but I was now convinced that it had been violated without her privity, and that some of her people had doubtless introduced the man into the room, in ignorance probably of our understanding.

"'"What man?" retorted she briskly, but in a much more mollified tone than before the golden peacemaker had met her sight — "There was nobody in your room, unless you let him in yourself; had you not the key, and did not I hear you lock the door after you?"

"'That I admitted to be true; "nevertheless," added I, taking up my portmanteau and half turning to depart, as if I were firing a last stern-chaser at an enemy whom I did not care longer to engage, "there certainly was a man — a sailor — in my room last night; though I know no more how he got in or out than I do where he got his broken head, or his unconscionable whiskers."

"'My foot was on the threshold as I ended, that I might escape the discharge of a reply which I foreboded would not be couched in the politest of terms. But it did not come, and as I threw back a parting glance at my fair foe, I could not help being struck with the very different expression of her features from that which I had anticipated. Her attitude and whole appearance were as if the miracle of Pygmalion had been reversed, and a living lady had been suddenly changed into a statue; her eyes were fixed, her cheek pale, her mouth half open, while the fingers, which had been on the point of closing on the guinea, seemed arrested in the very act.

"'I hesitated, and at length a single word, uttered distinctly but lowly, and as if breathlessly spoken, fell upon my ear; it was "WHISKERS!"

"'"Aye, *whiskers*," I replied; "I never saw so splendid a pair in my life."

"'"And a broken— For Heaven's sake come back one moment," said the lady, whom I now perceived to be laboring under no common degree of agitation.

"'Of course I complied, marveling not a little that a word, which though, according to Mr. Shandy, it once excited a powerful commotion in the court of Navarre, is usually very harmless in our latitudes, should produce so astounding an effect on the sensorium of a Portsmouth landlady.

"'"Let me entreat you, sir," said my hostess, "to tell me, without disguise, who and what you saw in your bed-room last night."

"'"No one, madam," was my answer, "but the sailor of whose intrusion I before complained, and who, I presume, took refuge there from some drunken fray, to sleep off the effects of his liquor, as, though evidently a good deal knocked about, he did not appear to be very sensible of his condition."

"'An earnest request to describe his person followed, which I did to the best of my recollection, dwelling particularly on the wounded temple and the remarkable whiskers, which formed, as it were, a perfect fringe to his face.

"'"Then, Lord have mercy upon me!" said the woman, in accents of mingled terror and distress, "it's all true, and the house is ruined forever!"

"'So singular a declaration only whetted my already excited curiosity, and the landlady, who now seemed anxious to make a friend of me, soon satisfied my inquiries in a few words which left an impression no time will ever efface.

"'After entreating and obtaining a promise of secrecy, she informed me that, on the third evening previous to my arrival, a party of sailors from one of the vessels which were paying off in the harbor were drinking in her house, when a quarrel ensued between them and some marines belonging to another ship. The dispute at length rose to a great height, and blows were interchanged. The landlady in vain endeavored to interfere, till at length a heavy blow, struck with the edge of a pewter pot, lighting upon the temple of a stout young fellow of five-and-twenty, who was one of the most active on the side of the sailors, brought him to the ground senseless and covered with blood. He never spoke again, but, although his friends immediately conveyed him up-stairs and placed him on the bed, endeavoring to stanch the blood and doing all in their power to save him, he breathed his last in a few minutes.

"'In order to hush up a circumstance which could hardly

fail, if known, to bring all parties concerned "into trouble," the old woman admitted that she had consented to the body's being buried in the garden, where it was interred the same night by two of his comrades. The man having been just discharged, it was calculated that no inquiry after him was likely to take place.

"'" But then, sir," cried the landlady, wringing her hands, "it's all of no use. Foul deeds will rise, and I shall never dare to put anybody into your room again, for there it was he was carried; they took off his jacket and waistcoat, and tied his wound up with a handkerchief, but they never could stop the bleeding till all was over; and, as sure as you are standing there a living man, he is come back to trouble us, for if he had been sitting to you for his picture, you could not have painted him more accurately than you have done."

"'Startling as this hypothesis of the old woman's was, I could substitute no better, and as the prosecution of the inquiry must have necessarily operated to delay my voyage, and, perhaps involve me in difficulties, without answering, as far as I could see, any good end, I walked quietly, though certainly not quite at my ease, down to the Point; and my ship arriving in the course of the afternoon, I went immediately on board, set sail the following morning for the Mediterranean, and though I have been many years in England since, have never again set foot in Portsmouth from that hour to this.'

"Thus ended Mr. Hamilton's narrative.

"The next day the whole party set out to reconnoitre the present appearance of the house, but some difficulty was experienced at first in identifying it, the sign having been taken down, and the building converted into a greengrocer's shop about five years before. A dissenting chapel had been built on the site of the garden, but nothing was said by their informant of any skeleton having been found while digging for the foundation, nor did Mr. Hamilton think it advisable to push any inquiries on the subject. The old landlady, he found, had been dead several years, and the public-house had passed into other hands before the withdrawal of the license and its subsequent conversion to the present purposes."

Funeral of Sir T. Lawrence.

"*Diary: January* 21, 1830.— Attended the public funeral of Sir Thomas Lawrence. An immense throng, but all conducted with great order and splendor. The coffin was carried into the vaults, and brought under the brass plate in the centre of the dome, after the part of the service usually performed in the choir had been gone through. The mourners formed a large outer circle, in the centre of which, close round the plate, was an inner one composed of the members of the cathedral. Among the mourners were Sir G. Murray, Peel, Lord Aberdeen (who seemed almost frozen while bearing the pall from the west door), C. Kemble, Horace Twiss, Derham, Gwilt, T. Campbell, John Wilson Croker, conspicuous in a black velvet cap, and old Nash, the architect, still more so in a Welsh wig. My poor little Emma being very ill, I had some doubt as to going, but Dr. Bowring and Mr. Rothwell with the Crombies coming, I was obliged to conduct them, and we got in with no little difficulty through the crowd, already assembled at twelve, though the funeral was not appointed to take place till two o'clock. Dr. Hughes, a very old friend of the deceased, was so affected that it was with the greatest difficulty he got through the lesson. After the ceremony the body was conveyed to a brick grave under the south aisle, where it lies, thus:—

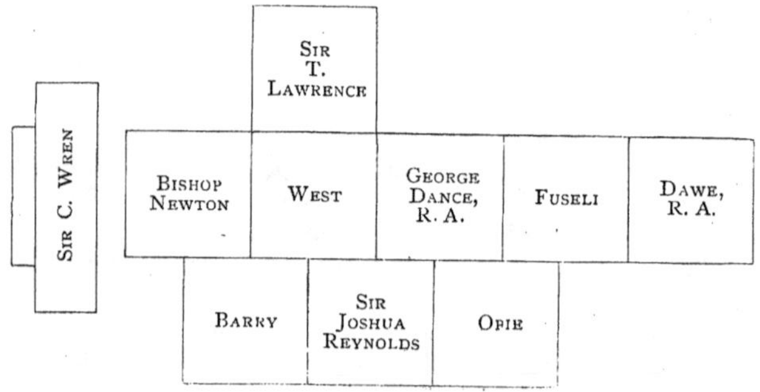

"Mrs. Hughes mentioned to me a singular story respecting the deceased, which she had from his intimate friend, Miss C——. This lady told her, while in the gallery during the ceremony, that the evening before his decease she had seen him. He seemed, she said, a little out of spirits, and asked her somewhat abruptly if she had ever heard a death-watch? She replied that she had; on which he requested her to describe the noise it made, which she did. On hearing her description he replied, "Aye, that is it exactly!" and relapsed into a thoughtful silence which he scarcely broke during the rest of her visit.

JOHN FROST.

"All the papers of this date [*January*, 1830] were full of the quarrel between the Medico-Botanico Society and its Director, as he was called, and founder, Mr. John Frost, a gentleman remarkable equally for his modest assurance and the high estimate he had formed of his own pretensions, on what many persons thought singularly insufficient grounds. The Royal Society, as a body, were unquestionably of this opinion, as, on his name being submitted to the ballot, he was almost unanimously blackballed. His perseverance, however, in beating up for recruits for his favorite society was unparalleled. It was his custom to run about with a highly ornamented album to every distinguished person, British or foreign, to whom he could by any possibility introduce himself, inform them that they were elected honorary members of the Medico-Botanico Society, and give a flourishing account of its merits; and as one of the rules required that a member should write his own name in their book, Mr. F. procured by these names a valuable collection of autographs.

"The best of the joke was, that, having written to several foreign princes through the medium of their ambassadors, and under Lord Aberdeen's government franks, procured through the interest of Lord Stanhope, the President and head of the Society (for the high-sounding office of Director was, in fact, that of Secretary), he contrived to get no less than a dozen potentates of various grades to consent to their enrolment, and to acknowledge the compliment. Two indeed of them — the Emperor of the Brazils was one — went so far as to inclose the insignia of one of their minor orders, addressed to 'the Director,' as they had never heard of any higher officer, and these Jacky Frost, as he was commonly called, lost no time in mounting upon his coat, much to the annoyance of Lord Stanhope and the rest of the body.

"It was determined, in consequence, to get rid of Mr. Frost, by doing away with the office of Director altogether; the orders, however, and the album he could not be induced to part with. His honors after all were dearly purchased, as the Royal Humane Society, thinking, perhaps, that it was sadly *infra dig.* for a chevalier with two crosses on his breast to be holding the bellows to the nose of every chimney-sweeper picked out of the Serpentine, dismissed him from the employment he held under them, whereby he lost 200*l.* a year and a good house in Bridge Street.

"Among the cool stratagems which he occasionally made use of to procure signatures to his book, was one which he played off on the Duke of Wellington, which, had it not been vouched for by Mr. Wood, F. R. S., I should hardly have credited. Having failed in repeated attempts to get with his quarto into Apsley House, he heard by good luck that his Grace, then Commander-in-chief, was about to hold a levee of general officers. Away posted Jacky to a masquerade warehouse, and hired a Lieutenant-general's uniform, under cover of which he succeeded in establishing himself fairly in the Duke's anteroom, among thirteen or fourteen first-rate Directors of strategetics.

"Everybody stared at a general whom nobody knew, and at length an aide-de-camp, addressing him, politely requested to know his name.

"'What general shall I have the honor of announcing to his Grace?'

"'My name is Frost, sir.'

"'Frost, General Frost! I beg your pardon, but I really do not recollect to have heard that name before!'

"'Oh, sir, I am no general, I have merely put on this costume as I understood I could not obtain access to his Grace without it; I am the Director of the Medico-Botanico Society, and have come to inform his Grace that he has been elected a member, and to get his signature.'

"'Then, sir, I must tell you that you have taken a most improper method and opportunity of so doing, and I insist upon your withdrawing immediately.'

"Jacky, however, was too good a general to capitulate on the first summons, and he stoutly kept his ground, notwithstanding a council of war at once began to deliberate on the comparative eligibility of kicking him into the street, or giving him in charge to a constable. Luckily for him the aide-de-camp thought his Grace had a right to a voice in the matter, as the offense was committed in his own house. On the business, however, being mentioned to him, the hero of Waterloo, not choosing perhaps to risk the laurels he had won from Napoleon in a domestic encounter with so redoubtable a champion, said, 'Let the fellow in,' cut short Jacky's oration by writing his name hastily in the book, and gave the sign 'to show him out again.' It was doubtful, however, whether any other sanctuary than the house he was in would have sheltered him from the indignation of the *militaires* in waiting, at the sight of what they considered a degradation of the national uniform.

"Quite as amusing was this gentleman's interview with the Duke of St. Albans. The 'Director' easily got his Grace's consent to be elected a member, and the book was produced for his signature. The latter took up a pen, and commenced '*Du* —,' when he was interrupted by his visitor, —

"'No, I beg pardon, it is your Grace's title we require, written by your own hand.'

"'Well, my title is Duke of St. Albans, is it not?'

"'Yes, your Grace, undoubtedly, but your signature merely — the way in which your Grace usually signs.' — Here the Duchess interfered, and 'St. Albans' was soon written, in a large German-text, school-boy hand, the '*Du*' having been previously expunged by a side wipe of his Grace's forefinger. Mr. Frost bowed, pocketed the subscription, pronounced all to be *en règle*, congratulated his noble friend on having become a brother Medico-Botanico, and quitted Stratton Street in high glee.

"Not long afterwards it was his good fortune again to encounter his Grace, on some public occasion. Of course he paid his respects, and equally of course the Duke inquired of 'Mr. *Thingumee*,' as he called him, how that 'medical thing' that he belonged to, went on.

"'Exceedingly prosperous, indeed, my Lord Duke,' was the answer; 'we are increasing both in numbers and respectability every day; I have got twelve Sovereigns down since the commencement of the present year.'

"'Oh, if you have only got twelve *sovereigns* in all that time, I don't think you are getting on so very fast; you know I gave you *five guineas* of them myself.'"

This anecdote may easily be believed of a duke who soon after his wedding wrote to the editor of "Debrett's Peerage," then Mr. Townshend, Rouge Dragon, saying, "Sir, I have to inform you that I am married to Mrs. Coutts, and Mrs. Coutts desires you will put it into your next edition." This Townshend told me himself.

Poetical Epistle to his Son.

Some slight difference of opinion I remember to have arisen between my father and myself respecting the comparative merits of the box-seat and a place inside the coach, which was to convey me to Tunbridge. My fare paid, I was handed, under protest, into the interior of the "machine," and on my naturally availing myself of the opportunity offered by the first stoppage to mount the roof, in which position I accomplished the remainder of the journey, some mistake arose respecting my identity and the sum disbursed on my behalf. Thence ensued, to my confusion, a disclosure of the masterly movement that had been effected, and a consequent remonstrance conveyed in terms more indulgent than, I fear, I deserved:—

To R. H. D. Barham.

"St. Paul's, *July* 5, 1830.

"I find, Mister Dick,
That you 've played me a trick,
For which you deserve a reproof—
Not to say a reproach;
You got out of the coach,
And settled yourself on the roof.

"You knew you 'd a cough,
And when you set off,
I cautioned you as to your ride,
And bade you take care
Of the damp and cold air,
And above all to keep withinside.

"This they tell me that you
Did not choose to do,
But exchanged with some person, they said;
And so Easton mistook
Your name in his book,
And charged you what he should have paid.

"I found them quite willing
To refund every shilling,
And render to Cæsar his due;
They gave me back three,
Which I take to be
The overplus forked out by you.

"Now don't do this again;
Indeed, to be plain,
If you mount, when you come back to town,
Your namesake the 'Dicky,'
I shall certainly lick ye,
And perhaps half demolish your crown.

"Mamma means to inclose
Two white 'wipes' for your nose;
As your purse may be run rather hard,
I shall also attack her
To augment your exchequer
With a sovereign stuck in a card.

"But my note I must end it,
Or 't will be too late to send it

To-day, which I much wish to do;
So remember us, mind, enough
To our friends who are kind enough
To be bored with such a nuisance as you.

"Write as soon as you can,
That's a good little man,
And direct your epistle to me;
Meanwhile I remain.
Till I see you again,
Your affectionate sire, — R. H. B."

Sydney Smith.

The appointment of Mr. Sydney Smith to one of the canonries of St. Paul's proved the means of introducing Mr. Barham to the society of that distinguished individual, and circumstances led afterwards to a pretty frequent correspondence between them, chiefly indeed bearing reference to matters of business, but abounding, on the part of the latter, with instances of that decided spirit and peculiar humor inseparable from his writings and conversation. At first, I believe Mr. Barham looked upon the introduction of the great Whig wit into the chapter with some feeling of misgiving, but the thorough honesty and kind-heartedness of the new canon soon made themselves manifest to the apprehension of the candid observer. And differing, as they always did more or less, in political opinion, an appreciation of each other's worth gradually sprang up sufficient to induce a greater degree of intimacy than might, under the circumstances, have been expected.

The first appearance of Mr. Smith at the Cathedral, for the purpose of taking possession of his stall, is thus briefly noted: —

"*October* 2, 1831. — Rev. Sydney Smith read himself in as Residentiary at St. Paul's; dined with him afterwards at Dr. Hughes's. He mentioned having once half offended Sam Rogers by recommending him, when he sat for his picture, to be drawn saying his prayers with his face in his hat."

Townsend the Bow Street Officer.

"Cannon called in the evening, and told us an adventure of his with Townsend, the Bow Street officer, at Brighton. A little Jew boy had been plaguing him the day before to buy pencils, saying that he had a sick mother, thirteen brothers and sisters, and that his father was dead, etc. Cannon gave him a trifle, but desired him not to bother him again. The next day, however, the little Israelite attacked him as before, when he called to Townsend, standing on the Steyne, and told him not to be rough with the lad, but to prevent his continuing to annoy him.

"Townsend commenced a regular examination of the youth. 'Do you know Mr. Goldsmith? Do you know Houndsditch?' etc., till he made Cannon open his eyes by asking, 'When were you last at Purim?'

"The boy's answer was satisfactory, and when he was dismissed Cannon turned to the officer and inquired how *he* came to know anything about the Jewish festivals.

"'Why God *blesh* you,' says Townsend, 'Purim's one of these rascals' grand feasts; the High Priest wets his thumb, and the fellows fall a knocking as if they was all at Bartle-my fair. Why blesh your soul! there was a Queen Easter, you know, once, and if it had not ha' been for her, all these scamps would have been hanged altogether. Now you know how I respect "The Establisment," so you won't be offended at what I am going to say, which is this — you remember these "Smouches" are said to be "whited sepulchres," well enough to look at outside, but good for nothing within — well, so they continues to be to this very day — and I 'm blessed if you 'll find any lead in that chap's pencils!' — The illustration proved perfectly correct."

Another Ghost Story.

"*Diary: November* 4, 1832. — Mrs. Hughes told me the following ghost story. Her own grandfather had carried on a flirtation with Miss Richards of Compton, one of the richest heiresses in his native country, but being, for a gentleman, in comparatively narrow circumstances, did not venture to propose for her; nor was it till after he had engaged himself to another lady that he discovered the heiress might have been his but for the faint heart which prevented him from winning the fair lady. Miss Richards, however, remained a spinster for his sake, formed a strict intimacy with his sister, whom she prevailed upon to live with her, and when he had children adopted one of them — a girl — aunt to the lady from whom I had this story, and from whom she had it.

"At the death of her father, Miss Richards inherited, among other possessions, the home farm called Compton Marsh, which remained in her own occupation under the management of a bailiff. This man, named John ——, was engaged to be married to a good-looking girl, to whom he had long been attached, and who superintended the dairy.

"One morning Miss Richards, who had adopted masculine habits, was going out with her greyhounds, accompanied by her *protégée*, and called at the farm. Both the ladies were struck by the paleness and agitation evinced by the dairymaid. Thinking some lover's quarrel might have taken place, the visitors questioned her strictly respecting the cause of her evident distress, and at length, with great difficulty, prevailed upon her to disclose it.

"She said that on the night preceding she had gone to bed at her usual hour, and had fallen asleep, when she was awakened by a noise in her room. Rousing herself she sat upright and listened. The noise was not repeated, but between herself and the window, in the clear moonlight, she saw John standing within a foot of the bed, and so near to her that by stretching out her hand she could have touched him. She called out immediately, and ordered him peremptorily to leave the room. He remained motionless, looking at her with a sad countenance, and in a low but distinct tone of voice bade her not be alarmed, as the only purpose of his visit was to inform her that he should not survive that day six weeks, naming at the same time two o'clock as the hour of his decease. As he ceased speaking, she perceived the figure gradually fading, and growing fainter in the moonlight, till, without appearing to move away, it grew indistinct in its outline and finally was lost to sight.

"Much alarmed she rose and dressed herself, but found everything quite quiet in the house, and the door locked on the inside as usual. She did not return to bed, but had prudence enough to say nothing of what she had seen, either to John, or to any one else. Miss Richards commended her silence, advising her to adhere to it, on the ground that these kinds of prophecies sometimes bring their own completion along with them.

"The time slipped away, and, notwithstanding her unaffected incredulity, Miss Richards could not forbear, on the morning of the day specified, riding down to the farm, where she found the girl uncommonly cheerful, having had no return of her vision, and her lover remaining still in full health. He was gone, she told the ladies, to Wantage market, with a load of cheese which he had to dispose of, and was expected back in a couple of hours. Miss Richards went on and pursued her favorite amusement of coursing. She had killed a hare, and was returning to the house with her companion, when they saw a female, whom they at once recognized as the dairymaid, running with great swiftness up the avenue which led to the mansion.

"They both immediately put their horses to their speed, Miss Richards exclaiming, 'Good God! something has gone wrong at the farm!' The presentiment was verified. John had returned looking pale and complaining of fatigue, and soon after went to his own room, saying he should lie down for half an hour while the men were at dinner. He did so, but not returning at the time mentioned, the girl went to call him, and found him lying dead on his own bed. He had been seized with an aneurism of the heart!"

The Beefsteak Club.

"*February* 9, 1833. — Dined, for the first time, at the Beefsteak Club, held at the Bedford till the rebuilding of Arnold's theatre. The members present were Mr. Lewin (in the chair), Stephenson (vice), the Duke of Leinster, Lord Saltoun, Sir Andrew Barnard, Sir Ronald Ferguson, Sir John Cam Hobhouse, Messrs. Hallett, Peake, Linley, and Arnold. All very amusing. Jokes of Lord Alvanley mentioned. At the late *fête* at Hatfield House, *tableaux vivants* were among the chief amusements, and scenes from 'Ivanhoe' were among the selections. All the parts were filled up but that of Isaac of York. Lady Salisbury begged Lord Alvanley 'to make the set complete by doing the Jew.' 'Anything in my power your ladyship may command,' replied Alvanley, 'but though no man in England has tried oftener, I never could *do a Jew* in my life.'

"He half affronted Mr. Greville, with whom he was dining. The dining-room had been newly and splendidly furnished, whereas the dinner was but a very meagre and indifferent one. While some of the guests were flattering their host on his taste, magnificence, etc., 'For my part,' said his lordship, 'I had rather have seen less gilding and more carving.'"

Of the Mr. Samuel Arnold just mentioned, Mr. Barham observes elsewhere: "I first met him at Hawes's, several years before the institution of the 'Garrick,' where he was a member of the committee at the same time with myself. I encountered him the morning after his theatre (the English Opera-house, afterwards the Lyceum) was burnt down, by which he lost 60,000*l.*, and never saw a man meet misfortune with so much equanimity. His new theatre, which was raised by subscription completely failed, and when Osbaldiston took Covent Garden in 1835, and reduced the admission to the boxes to four shillings, Arnold reduced his price to two, but this did not succeed, while the property was materially depreciated by the measure. Arnold was one of the leading members of the Beefsteak Club where he was called 'the Bishop.'"

Denials of Authorship.

To authors' oaths, as well as those of lovers, Jove, it is to be hoped, is particularly indulgent; for, assuredly, whatever amount of affirmative perjury may be incurred by the latter, it is to the full paralleled by the ample negations put forth by the former. Southey distinctly denied the authorship of "The Doctor." But, perhaps, a greater degree of "nerve" was exhibited by Mr. Sydney Smith, who, positively disowning all connection with the "Plymley Letters" in one edition, actually published them in a collection of his acknowledged works some few months after. The mystery that hung so long around the Wizard of the North is yet more notorious; the anecdote which follows may serve to show the anxiety of the "Great Unknown" to preserve his incognito: —

"*February* 11, 1833. — Dined with Sir George Warrender at his house in Albemarle Street. Met Lord Saltoun, John Wilson Croker, Sir Andrew Barnard, Mr. Barrow of the Admiralty, John Murray, the publisher, Mr. Littleton, Sir Charles Bagot, Mr. Lee, an artist, Francis Mills, and James Smith.

"Murray told me that Sir Walter Scott, on being taxed by him as the author of 'Old Mortality,' not only denied having written it, but added, 'In order to convince you that I am not the author, I will review the book for you in the "Quarterly" — which he actually did, and Murray still has the MS. in his handwriting.

Suett's Funeral.

"*Diary: March* 24, 1834. — Dined at the 'Garrick;' Mr. Williams, the banker, in the chair, Fladgate, croupier, Charles Mathews (the father), E. Parrott, Westmacott, the sculptor, Mortimer Drummond, T. Clarke, Tom Hill, J. R. Durrant, W. Beloe, myself, and John Murray. We twelve were seated when Hook arrived. He looked at first very blank on finding himself the *thirteenth*, but being told that Charles Young the actor was expected immediately took his seat, and we had a very pleasant evening. C. Mathews gave a very amusing account of poor Dicky Suett's funeral which he had attended as a mourner. Suett lies buried in St. Paul's Church-yard, in the burial-ground belonging to St. Faith, nearly opposite the shop of Dollond the optician, and just within the rails. Suett had been brought up originally as a boy in the choir. Mathews and Captain Caulfield (whom I have often seen perform, and whose personation of Suett, Mathews said, was much more perfect than his own) were in the same coach with Jack Banister and Palmer. The latter sat wrapt up in angry and indignant silence at the tricks which the two younger *mourners* (who, by the way, had known but little of Suett, and were invited out of compliment) were playing off; but Banister, who was much affected by the loss of his old friend, nevertheless could not refrain from laughing occasionally in the midst of his grief and while the tears were actually running from his eyes. Mr. Whittle, commonly called 'Jemmy Whittle,' of the firm of Laurie and Whittle, stationers, in Fleet Street, was an old and intimate friend of Suett's. As the procession approached, he came and stood at his own door to look at it, when Caulfield called out to him from the mourning-coach in Suett's voice,

"'Aha! Jemmy — O la! I 'm going to be buried! O la! O lawk! O dear!'

"Whittle ran back into the house absolutely frightened. Similar scenes took place the whole of the way. The burial service was read, when, just as the clergyman had concluded it, an urchin seated on a tombstone close by the rails began clapping his hands. The whole company were struck by this singular conclusion to a theatrical funeral; but the boy when questioned and taken to task for the indecency said, —

"'La! there was only them two dogs outside as wanted to fight, and was afraid to begin, so I did it to set 'em on.'

"Mathews also gave a very entertaining account of his having been recommended by Mr. Lowdham, a member of the club, to stop at a particular inn in Nottingham, when upon his last theatrical tour. He found it, however, quite a third-rate inn, and could get no attendance. Half a dozen different people successively answered the bell when he rang, stared at him, said 'Yes, sir!' and went away; nor could he get any one to show him into a private room, though he had bespoken one. At last a great lubberly boy came blubbering into the room, when Mathews addressed him very angrily: —

"*M.* — When am I to have my private room?

"*Boy.* — We ha'n't got none but one, and that 's bespoke for Mathews the player.

"*M.* — Well, I am Mathews the player, as you call him.

"*Boy.* — Oh, then you may come this way!

"He was ushered at length into a room with a fire just lighted, and full of smoke; still there was nothing to be got to eat, while Mathews, who had travelled between forty and fifty miles that day, was very hungry.

"*M.* — Send me up the master of the house! Where is the master?

"*Boy.* —He 's dead, sir!

"*M.* — Then send the mistress.

"*Boy.* — Mother 's gone out!

"*M.* — Well, do let me have something to eat at all events; can you get me a mutton chop?

"*Boy.* — Not till mother comes home.

"*M.* — Well, then, some cold meat — anything. Confound it, boy, have you got nothing in the house?

"*Boy.* — Yes, sir!

"Well, what is it then?

"Here the poor boy burst into a flood of tears and blubbered out — 'An execution, sir!'

"Late in the evening Young did come, and sang with great taste and feeling Sheridan's 'When 't is Night.' Hook improvised, as usual with him, on the company, but was not altogether so happy as I have sometimes heard him."

"My Cousin Nicholas."

The completion and publication of "My Cousin Nicholas" were immediately owing to the kindly interference of Mrs. Hughes. Having read "Baldwin," and having learnt that another tale was lying unfinished in Mr. Barham's desk, she prevailed upon him to lend her the manuscript. So favorable was her opinion of its merits that without more ado she submitted it to the inspection of Mr. Blackwood, and the first intimation the author received of the circumstance was conveyed in the shape of a packet containing the proof-sheets of the opening chapters. As his zealous friend had pledged her word for the continuation of the work all retreat was cut off; there was nothing for it but diligently to take the matter in hand, and endeavor to surmount those obstacles that had caused him to lay his pen aside. Whatever the difficulties may have been, they were speeeily overcome, "My Cousin's" adventures were carried on monthly with spirit, and the catastrophe was worked up in a manner that certainly brought no discredit on the earlier portions of the novel.

Mr. Barham always asserted that he was singularly deficient in the faculty of invention. "Give me a story to tell," he would say, "and I can tell it, in my own way; but I can't invent one!" and although "My Cousin Nicholas" might, I think, be fairly cited as a witness to the injustice of the disclaimer, there is no doubt that the character of his hero's escapades was suggested by an event which occurred in the life of the author's father, and which the former once thought of producing under the title of "My Grandfather's Knocker!" The circumstances, as nearly as I can recollect them, were as follows: —

Somewhere about a century ago, rather more than less, Richard Barham, of Parmstead, became by marriage the owner of some property — principally hop-gardens — lying in close vicinity to Canterbury, and also of a large red-brick house situated within the city walls. It is, I believe, still in existence, inclosed by its high garden walls, above which the tops of a few trees look down refreshingly upon the narrow streets of Burgate. But in addition to house and land, Mrs. Barham brought her husband in due time a son and heir — Richard Harris, the father of the subject of this memoir. Having reached man's estate, Richard Harris declined longer residence in the red-brick house — which was only occasionally inhabited by his father, who spent a good deal of his time at Tapton Wood — and set up a bachelor's establishment for himself. One morning the elder gentleman, who seems to have been of a peppery turn, was roused to fury by the disappearance of a magnificent brass knocker which had hitherto formed the glory of his front door. It had clearly been wrenched off in the course of the night, by way of a "spree," as this lively diversion afterwards came to be called. Mr. Barham, *senior*, raved; Mr. Barham, *junior*, condoled; both were indignant. But nothing came of raving, condolence, or indignation! The offender could not be punished, for the offender could not be found, and so by degrees the offense dropped out of memory. It chanced, some time after, that on a certain day the old gentleman rode in from the country, and, not disposed to spend the evening alone in his own rather gloomy mansion, he betook him to the lodging of his son. Richard Harris was of course delighted to see his father, and taxed his resources to the uttermost in the endeavor to entertain him. Dinner was discussed, and after dinner a liberal allowance of port wine,[1] and then, according to the fashion of the age, preparations were made for winding up the feast with a bowl of punch. "The materials" were at hand, and available — all save the sugar, and the sugar was in large refractory lumps that defied ordinary manipulation. The housekeeper was accordingly summoned, and desired to reduce a sufficient quantity of the "best loaf" to powder. Quietly proceeding to a cupboard in the room, the woman provided herself with an implement which, if not expressly constructed for the purpose of trituration, was evidently well enough adapted to it,

[1] I am not speaking at hap-hazard here. My grandfather always drank a bottle of port wine a day. The doctors interfered at last when his bulk became enormous and limited him to a pint. "Well, said he, "if I am to have only a pint, a pint it shall be; I will not be fobbed off with one of those abominations that contain little more than a half." And so, anticipating the Imperial measure movement, he had a number of bottles made expressly for him, holding each a legitimate pint. A few of these with his cipher stamped upon the shoulder I still possess. One pint of wine, however, he found scarcely sufficient, and so he tried two, thus, in place of reducing his former allowance by half, increased it by about a third. They argued with him, but he persisted in his opinion that two pints were equal to one bottle, and that one bottle of port could not hurt any man. He died at forty-eight.

and commenced pounding away. The old gentleman raised his eyes at the noise, then sprang to his feet, then fired off expression after expression of a sort that no old gentleman ought to fire off. It must, however, be admitted that the provocation was not a slight one, for there was the solution of the mystery — there in calm complacency was his son's cook hammering away at the loaf sugar with the desecrated brass knocker of which he had, so heartlessly bereaved! Mr. Barham *senior* left the house immediately, would listen to no excuses, but executed a fresh will forthwith, leaving his property to be divided between his two daughters, and refused to hold any further communication with his truly penitent son. The alienation lasted for a year or two. Then at length the remonstrances of friends prevailed, and forgiveness was extended, I am exceedingly happy to say, to my too mercurial grandfather.

Of the minor characters presented in the novel, one at least was taken from the life. There are doubtless many Oxford men yet living who can remember "Doctor Toe," as from a peculiarity of his gait he was nicknamed, the Dean of Brasenose, and the hero of Reginald Heber's "Whippiad." Not only defeated in battle within his very stronghold —

> "Where whitened Cain the wrath of Heaven defies,
> And leaden slumbers close his brother's eyes,
> Where o'er the porch in brazen splendor glows
> The vast projection of the mystic nose,"

but — more bitter humiliation still — jilted in love, deserted by his affianced bride, who ran off with her father's footman, the unfortunate doctor formed the subject of a number of University squibs, and among them of an epigram worth repeating:

> 'Twixt Footman John and Doctor Toe
> A rivalship befell,
> Which of the two should be the beau
> To bear away the belle.
>
> "The Footman won the lady's heart,
> And who can blame her? No man —
> The whole prevailed against a part,
> 'T was *Foot-man versus Toe-man!*"

The burlesque personification of "Doctor Toe" is said to have been actually perpetrated by an ancestor of the present Lord Lyttleton. And again, the denial of his father by Nicholas — an incident subsequently introduced by Mr. Boucicault in his popular comedy of "London Assurance" — is no fiction, but owes its origin to a similar prank played by the well-known humorist, Bonnell Thornton.

William Linley.

"*Diary : May*, 1834. — William Linley, brother to the first Mrs. Sheridan, though a man of the world, and a member of the celebrated 'Beefsteak Club,' the hoaxing propensities of whose members are so proverbial, was a man of great good-nature and still greater simplicity of mind. He always occupied a particular table at the 'Garrick,' and, though a general favorite, was somewhat too fond of reciting long speeches from various authors, generally Shakespeare. It was one day in this month that he had begun to spout from the opening scene in 'Macbeth,' and would probably have gone through it if I had not cut him short at the third line —

'When the hurly-burly 's done,'

with 'What on earth are you talking about? Why, my dear Linley, it is astonishing that a man so well read in Shakespeare as yourself should adopt that nonsensical reading! What is '*hurly-burly*,' pray? There is no such word in the language; you can't find an allusion to it in Johnson.' Linley, whose veneration for Dr. Johnson was only inferior to that which he entertained for the great poet himself, said, —

"'Indeed! are you sure there is not? What can be the reason of the omission? The word, you see, is used by Shakespeare.'

"'No such thing,' was the reply; 'it appears so indeed in one or two early editions, but it is evidently mistranscribed. The second folio is the best and most authentic copy, and gives the true reading, though the old nonsense is still retained upon the stage!'

"'Indeed, and pray what do you call the true reading?'

"'Why, of course, the same that is followed by Johnson and Steevens in the edition up-stairs: —

"When the *early purl* is done;"

that is, when we have finished our "early purl," *i. e.* directly after breakfast.'

"Linley was startled, and after looking steadily at me to see if he could discover any indication of an intention to hoax him, became quite puzzled by the gravity of my countenance, and only gave vent in a hesitating tone, half-doubtful, half-indignant, to the word 'Nonsense!'

"'Nonsense? It is as I assure you. We will send for the book, and see what Steevens says in his note upon the passage.'

"The book was accordingly sent for, but I took good care to intercept it before it reached the hands of Linley, and taking it from the servant pretended to read from the volume —

'When the hurly-burly 's done.

'Some copies have it, "When the *early purl* is done;" and I am inclined to think this reading the true one, if the well-known distich be worthy of credit —

"Hops, reformation, turkeys, and beer,
Came to England all in one year."

This would seem to fix the introduction of beer, and consequently of early purl, into the country to about that period of Henry VIII.'s reign when he intermarried with Anne Boleyn, the mother of Queen Elizabeth, Shakespeare's great friend and patroness, and to whom this allusion may perhaps have been intended by the poet as a delicate compliment. Purl, it is well known, was a favorite beverage at the English court during the latter part of the sixteenth century; and from the epithet then affixed to it "early," an adjunct which it still retains, was no doubt in common use for breakfast at a time when the China trade had not yet made our ancestors familiar with the produce of the tea-plant. Theobald's objection, that, whatever may have been the propriety of its introduction at the court of Elizabeth, the mention made of it at that of Macbeth would be a gross anachronism, may be at once dismissed as futile. Does not Shakespeare, in the very next scene, talk of

"Cannons overcharged with double cracks?"

and is not allusion made by him to the use of the same beverage at the court of Denmark, at a period coeval, or nearly so, with that under consideration —

"Hamlet, this purl is thine?"'

"'But, dear me!' broke in Linley, 'that is *pearl*, not purl. I remember old Packer used to hold up a pearl, and let it drop into the cup.'

"'Sheer misconception on the part of a very indifferent actor, my dear Linley, be assured.'

"Here Beazley, who was present, observed, '"Early purl" is all very well, but my own opinion has always leaned to Warburton's conjecture that a political allusion is intended. He suggests

"When the *Earl of Burleigh's* done;"

that is, when we have "done," *i. e.*, cheated or deceived, the Earl of Burleigh, a great statesman, you know, in Elizabeth's time, and one whom, to use a cant phrase among ourselves, 'you must get up very early in the morning to take in!'"

"'But what had Macbeth or the witches to do with the Earl of Burleigh? Stuff! nonsense!' said Linley, indignantly. And though Beazley made a good fight in defense of his version, yet his opponent would not listen to it for an instant.

"'No, no,' he continued, 'the Earl of Burleigh is all rubbish, but there may be something in the other reading.'

"And as the book was closed directly the passage had been repeated, and was replaced immediately on the shelf, the unsuspicious critic went away thoroughly mystified, especially as Tom Hill, for whose acquaintance with early English literature he had a great respect, confirmed the emendation with

"'"Early purl!" Pooh! pooh! to be sure it is "early purl;" I 've got it so in two of my old copies.'"

HAYNES BAYLEY.

Nothing on earth, by the way, is so soothing as that gentleman's verses; but that he would be thought a plagiarist, I think Nicholas might do a little in that way, to the tune of "Oh, no! we never mention him," etc.

"They say that I am silent, and my silence they condemn,
For oh! although they talk to me, I never talk to them!
I heed not what they think, although I know 't is thought by some
That I am dumb or deaf, but oh! I 'm neither deaf nor dumb!

"They say I 'm looking sick and pale; and well indeed they may;
They tell me, too, that I am sad; I 'm anything but gay!
They smile — but oh! the more they smile, the more, alas! I sigh;
And when they strive to make me laugh, I turn me round and cry!

"They bid me sing the song I sung, as I have sung before,
The song I sung no more I sing — my singing days are o'er!
They bid me play the fiddle, too — my fiddle it is mute!
Nor can I, as I used to do, blow tunes upon the flute!

"The feeling fain would soothe my woe, the heartless say I sham;
The ribald mock my grief, and call me — Sentimental Sam!
They cannot guess what 't is I want — There 's few indeed that can:
I want —
I want —
I want to be a butterfly, and flutter round a fan!"

"GETTING A LITTLE FISHING."

During the months of June and July, 1834, Mr. Barham spent his summer holidays at Strand-on-Green, where he had engaged a snug little cottage. Hanwell was his usual retreat, his duties rarely allowing him to select one beyond the reach of the great bell of Paul's; but this year he pitched upon Strand-on-Green, with some design, I believe, of "getting a little fishing." And for the first week or two attempts were occasionally made upon the wary gudgeons of Kew, but the expedition generally ended in some grave piscatorial disaster — the line became inextricably tangled in a worse than Gordian knot, or the hooks got foul, and had to be extracted by a surgical operation from calf or coat-tail, or the worms broke loose and buried themselves in inaccessible corners of the waistcoat pocket; and then rods and winches would be packed up, and the pleasure of the day began in earnest. At times, but not without expression of utter distrust of my competency as a waterman, he would permit me to scull him about the river, and one afternoon, on our finding ourselves opposite the house of Theodore Hook at Fulham, he determined to land and make a call on his friend. Hook was not at home; so, having no card with him, Mr. Barham asked for pen and paper, and while standing in the hall scribbled off, in as short a time as the reader would take to copy them, the following: —

LINES LEFT AT HOOK'S HOUSE IN JUNE, 1834.

" As Dick and I
Were a sailing by
At Fulham Bridge, I cocked my eye,
And says I, 'Add-zooks!
There 's Theodore Hook's,
Whose Sayings and Doings make such pretty books.

" 'I wonder,' says I,
Still keeping my eye
On the house, 'if he 's in — I should like to try;'
With his oar on his knee,
Says Dick, says he,
'Father, suppose you land and see!'

" 'What! land and *sea*,'
Says I to he;
'Together! why, Dick, why how can that be?'
And my comical son,
Who is fond of fun,
I thought would have split his sides at the pun.

" So we rows to shore,
And knocks at the door —
When William, a man I 'd seen often before,
Makes answer and says,
'Master 's gone in a chaise
Called a homnibus, drawn by a couple of bays.'

"So I says then,
'Just lend me a pen;'
'I wull, sir,' says William — politest of men,[1]
So having no card, these poetical brayings
Are the record I leave of my doings and sayings.'"

Anecdotes of Talleyrand.

"*Diary: August* 26, 1834. — Party at Williams's. Macready, Jerdan, etc. Abbot had just disappeared, an execution having been put into the Victoria Theatre by Randle Jackson. Talleyrand spoken of as 'having a cold gray eye and perfect impassibility of feature.' He being asked if Sebastiani was not a relative of Napoleon, answered, 'Yes, while he was emperor; not now!' Meeting the Duke of Wellington on his return from his installation as Chancellor of Oxford, he (Talleyrand) told him that he was now covered with glory; adding that no doubt they would end by making him a bishop; '*Vous finissez où j'ai commencé!*'"

Bon Mot of Power's.

"Macready told a story of George B—— the actor, who, it seems, is not popular in the profession, being considered a sort of time-server: 'There goes Georgius,' said some one. 'Not Georgium Sidus,' replied Keeley; 'Yes,' added Power, 'Georgium *Any*-sidus.'"

Sydney Smithisms.

"*Diary: November* 16, 1834. — Dined with Sydney Smith. He said that his brother Robert had, in George III.'s time, translated the motto, *Libertas sub rege pio*, 'The pious King has got liberty under;' also, that he had originally proposed to Jeffrey, Horner, and Brougham, as a motto for the 'Edinburgh Review,' *Musam meditamur avenâ*, 'We cultivate literature on a little oatmeal.'

[1] This proved eventually not to be a well-placed epithet; William, who had lived many years with Hook, grew rich and saucy. The latter used to say of him, that for the first three years he was as good a servant as ever came into a house; for the next two a kind and considerate friend: and afterwards an abominably bad master.

"'If ever a religious war should arise again,' he said, 'I should certainly take arms against the Dissenters. Fancy me with a bayonet at the heart of an Anabaptist, with, "Your church-rate or your life!"'

"He said nothing should ever induce him to go up in a balloon, unless indeed it would benefit the Established Church. I recommended him to go at once, as there would at least be a chance of it."

Story of Yates.

"*Diary: January* 1, 1835. — The following story was told me as a fact by George Raymond. Yates (the well-known actor and manager of the Adelphi Theatre) met a friend from Bristol in the street, whom he well recollected as having been particularly civil to his wife and himself when at that town, in which the gentleman was a merchant. Yates, who at that time lived at the Adelphi Theatre, invited his friend to dinner, and made a party, among whom were Hook and Mathews, to meet him. On reaching home he told his wife what he had done, describing the gentleman, and calling to her mind how often they had been at his house near the cathedral.

"'I remember him very well,' said Mrs. Yates, 'but I don't just now recollect his name — what is it?'

"'Why, that is the very question I was going to ask you,' returned Yates. 'I know the man as well as I know my own father, but for the life of me I can't remember his name, and I made no attempt to ascertain it, as I made sure you would recollect it!'

"What was to be done? all that night and the next morning they tried in vain to recover it, but the name had completely escaped them. In this dilemma Yates bethought him of giving instructions to their servant which he considered would solve the difficulty, and calling him in told him to be very careful in asking every gentleman, as he arrived, his name, and to be sure to announce it very distinctly. Six o'clock came, and with it the company in succession, Hook, Mathews, and the rest — all but the anonymous guest, whom

Yates began to think, and almost to hope, would not come at all. Just, however, before the dinner was put on the table, a knock was heard, and the lad being at that moment in the kitchen, in the act of carrying up a haunch of mutton which the cook had put into his hands, a maid-servant went to the door, admitted the stranger, showed him up-stairs, and opening the drawing-room door allowed him to walk in without any announcement at all. At dinner-time everybody took wine with the unknown, addressing him as 'Sir,' — 'A glass of wine, sir?' 'Shall I have the honor, sir?' etc., but nothing transpired to let out the name, though several roundabout attempts were made to get at it. The evening passed away, and the gentleman was highly delighted with the company, but about half-past ten o'clock he looked at his watch and rose abruptly, saying, —

"'Faith, I must be off, or I shall get shut out, for I am going to sleep at a friend's, in the Tower, who starts for Bristol with me in the morning. They close the gates at eleven precisely, and I sha'n't get in if I am a minute after, so good-by at once. Be sure you come and see me whenever you visit Bristol."

"'Depend on me, my dear friend; God bless you, if you must go!'

"'Adieu,' said the other, and Yates was congratulating himself on having got out of so awkward a scrape, when his friend popped his head back into the room, and cried hastily, —

"'Oh, by the bye, my dear Yates, I forgot to tell you that I bought a pretty French clock as I came here to-day, at Hawley's, but as it needs a week's regulating, I took the liberty of giving your name, and ordering them to send it here, and said that you would forward it. It is paid for.'

"The door closed, and before Yates could get it open again, the gentleman was in the hall.

"'Stop!' screamed Yates over the balusters, 'you had better write the address yourself, for fear of a mistake.

"'No, no, I can't stop, I shall be too late; the old house, near the cathedral; good-by!'

"The street door slammed behind him, and Yates went back to the company in an agony.

"Douglas repeated a story very similar of King the actor, who, meeting an old friend, whose name he could not recollect, took him home to dinner. By way of making the discovery, he addressed him in the evening, having previously made several ineffectual efforts: —

"'My dear sir, my friend here and myself have had a dispute as to how you spell your name; indeed, we have laid a bottle of wine about it.'

"'Oh, with two P's,' was the answer, which left them just as wise as before.'"

The Canister.

"We are by no means out of spirit here; though Sir Robert has given in for the present, his character and that of his Ministry is so raised by his manly and able fight, in the opinion of all classes, save and except the mere Marats and Robespierres, who are happily contemptible in point of numbers, that it is quite clear — indeed, many of his opponents admit it — that no stable administration can be formed without him. Even my poor friend V. — that 'delicately tinted Radical,' as 'The Age' not unhappily calls him — admits this, sore as he is at having been just turned out of his seat, when he was settling himself quietly down and half making up his mind to turn Conservative. After all, he is a gentleman, and a good-natured one, as you will admit when I tell you he did not knock me down for the following piece of impertinence. They were roasting him at the Garrick Club, just before he was unseated, and charging him with belonging to 'The Tail,' which he indignantly denied. 'I will appeal,' said he, 'to the biggest Tory in the room; Barham, what say you? Do I deserve, after the manner I have twice voted, to be called a part of the "Tail?"' 'Certainly not,' was the reply: 'you are the canister!' He did not seem so flattered by my taking his part as he ought to have been, but I escaped a broken head."

A Dinner at Charles Kemble's.

"*Diary : December* 12, 1835. — Dined at Charles Kemble's : a quiet dinner. In the evening Mr. Trelawney (Byron's Trelawney) came in : very like a goodish-looking bandit ; radical to the extreme ; talked of having 'no objection to calling a man a king, with a moderate salary, when the House of Peers should be purged,' etc. ; said that women might induce him to commit murder, or, 'what was *worse*, petty larceny ! '

"Story of Edward Walpole, who, being told one day at the 'Garrick' that the confectioners had a way of discharging the ink from old parchment by a chemical process, and then making the parchment into isinglass for their jellies, said, 'Then I find a man may now eat his deeds as well as his words.' This has been very unfairly, like a great many other bons mots, attributed to James Smith.

Thomas Moore.

"*April* 18, 1836. — Dined with Owen Rees in Paternoster Row. Present, Mr. Longman, senior, Messrs. C. Longman, T. Longman, W. Longman, Tom Moore, Dr. M'Culloch, Mr. Green, the host, and myself. Dr. Hume, Sydney Smith, and Mr. Tate asked, but could not come.

"Moore gave an account of the King's (George IV.) visit to Ireland. One man, whom the King took notice of and shook hands with, cried, 'There, then, the divil a drop of wather ye shall ever have to wash that shake o' the hand off of me!' and by the color of the said hand a year after it would seem that he had religiously kept his word. Moore told this story to Scott, together with another referring to the same occasion. He spoke of Jeffrey as an excellent judge, and remarked on the difference between his conversation and that of Scott. Scott all anecdote, without any intermediate matter — all fact; Jeffrey with a profusion of ideas all worked up into the highest flight of fancy, but no fact. Moore preferred Scott's conversation to Jeffrey's : the latter he got tired of.

"Anecdote of the little Eton boy invited to dinner at Windsor Castle, and being asked by Queen Adelaide what he would like, replied, 'One of those two-penny tarts, if you please, ma'am.' Lord Lansdowne's description of Sydney Smith as 'a mixture of Punch and Cato.' Moore lamented that though his son had just distinguished himself by gaining an exhibition at the Charter House, when his historical essays had been particularly applauded, the prize would be of no use to him, barring the honor, as he is determined to enter the army. His father consoled himself by reflecting that he had given up his original wish, which was for the navy.

"J. Longman's story of the rival convents, each possessing the same (alleged) relics of St. Francis, the one having furnished its reliquary with the beard of an old goat belonging to the establishment, the other asserting its superiority *non pour la grandeur, mais pour la fraîcheur.*

"Moore talked of O'Connell, and said that he had recently met him in a bookseller's shop ordering materials, in the shape of books, for his new 'Quarterly Review,' and that he had inadvertently offered to lend him a small volume respecting Ireland, but added that he must manage to slip out of his promise somehow.

"Dan, he said, manœuvred evidently that they might walk away together, but he (Moore) fought shy of the companionship and outstayed him. He spoke of O'Brien, the author of the 'Round Towers,' and said that that person's hostility to him was occasioned by his declining a proposal for a sort of partnership in publication. O'Brien wrote to him when he undertook the 'History of Ireland,' saying that he had a complete key to the origin and meaning of the 'Round Towers,' and proposed to communicate his secret. If Moore used O'Brien's MS., the compensation was to be a hundred pounds; if he took the materials and worked them up in his own way, a hundred and fifty was to be the sum. This was refused, and O'Brien was deeply offended. He died of an epileptic fit at Hanwell in 1835, and lies buried in the extreme northwest corner of the church-yard, close to the rector's garden. I happened accidentally to be present at his funeral. Mr. Mahony, the Father Prout of "Fraser," was a mourner, and, as I have heard, paid the expenses.'

"Conversation respecting Hook's proposed 'History of Hanover' — all of opinion that it would not answer. Moore said that he had met Hook twice only, once at Croker's, in Paris; that he was very silent both times, and called Croker 'Sir.'"

It was, I believe, on this occasion that one of the Messrs. Longman present mentioned to my father the following quaint answer returned by Sydney Smith to an invitation to dinner: —

"DEAR LONGMAN, — I can't accept your invitation, for my house is full of country cousins. I wish they were once removed. Yours, SYDNEY SMITH."

"I dined in company with Tom Moore the other day, who talked to me a good deal about him, and said that Lord Lansdowne, in allusion to his severity as a man of business and levity at the dinner-table, described him as being 'an odd mixture of Punch and Cato.' He could hardly have hit him off better. I know you are not over fond of Moore: *I* hate his politics, but he is a very amusing companion.

"I must tell you one of his stories, because as Sir Walter Scott is the hero of it, I know it will not be unacceptable to you. When George IV. went to Ireland, one of the 'pisintry,' delighted with his affability to the crowd on landing, said to the toll-keeper as the King passed through, —

"'Och, now! and his Majesty, God bless him, never paid the turnpike! an' how 's that?'

"'Oh! kings never does: we lets 'em go free,' was the answer.

"'Then there 's the dirty money for ye,' says Pat. 'It shall never be said that the King came here, and found nobody to pay the turnpike for him.'

"Moore, on his visit to Abbotsford, told this story to Sir Walter, when they were comparing notes as to the two royal visits.

"'Now, Mr. Moore,' replied Scott, 'there ye have just the advantage of us. There was no want of enthusiasm here: the Scotch folk would have done anything in the world for his Majesty, but — pay the turnpike.'"

Barham's Love of Children and Cats.

In his intercourse with his children, but more particularly with his youngest son, Ned, my father was always playful and affectionate. He loved to have them about him, and would continue to read and write, keeping them up of an evening far beyond the canonical hours, wholly unmindful of the chattering that raged around. Our delight was at its height when he could be coaxed into laying aside pen and book, and induced to draw round to the fire and "tell us a story." He had a manner of doing this, half thrilling, half comic, leaving the audience in a pleasing state of excitement, mingled with uncertainty as to the exact amount of credit to be given to the narrative, that proved strangely fascinating to us young folks, to say nothing of our elders. The pleasure second only in degree was to receive a letter from him. This would not unfrequently be written in verse, but always with a liveliness and easy humor which, while specially adapted to the taste and capacity of the child, may be read perhaps with some degree of amusement by those of larger growth. At all events, a trait of character is exhibited in these unstudied effusions, without some notice of which the present slight sketch would be yet more incomplete.

TO MASTER EDWARD BARHAM (*ætat.* 8).

"*August* 17, 1836.

"My dear little Ned,
As I fear you have read
All the books that you have, from great A down to Z,
And your aunt, too, has said
That you 're very well bred,
And don't scream and yell fit to waken the dead,
I think that instead
Of that vile gingerbread
With which little boys, I know, like to be fed

(Though, lying like lead
On the stomach, the head
Gets affected, of which most mammas have a dread),
I shall rather be led
Before you to spread
These two little volumes, one blue and one red.
As three shillings have fled
From my pocket, dear Ned,
Don't dog's-ear nor dirt them, nor read them in bed!
"Your affectionate Father, R. H. B."

Next to his wife and children, I verily believe my father loved his cats. One or two would commonly be seen sitting on his table — sometimes on his shoulder — as he wrote; and these animals, constantly taught and tended by his youngest daughter, attained a degree of docility and intelligence that in good King James's day might have brought their mistress into disagreeable communication with His Majesty's Witchfinder-General. The progenitor of the race was brought home by Mr. Barham, not without serious detriment to his broadcloth, one wet night soon after his arrival in London. He had rescued the poor little creature, bleeding and muddy, from a band of juvenile street Arabs, who were engaged in studying practically "the art of ingeniously tormenting." The progeny survived, and was ever held in high esteem. One of my father's last injunctions was "Take care of 'Chance' (an interloper) for my sake: Jerry (the representative of the true breed) will be taken care of for his own." On the back of an old letter there is scribbled a sort of remonstrance addressed to the latter: —

TO JERRY.

"Jerry, my cat,
What the deuce are you at?
What makes you so restless? You 're sleek and you 're fat,
And you 've everything cozy about you, — now that
Soft rug you are lying on beats any mat;
Your coat 's smooth as silk,
You 've plenty of milk,
You 've the fish-bones for dinner, and always o' nights
For supper you know you 've a penn'orth o' lights!
Jerry, my cat,
What the deuce are you at?

What is it, my Jerry, that fidgets you so?
What is it you're wanting?
(Jerry) Moll roe! Moll roe!

"Oh, don't talk to me of such nonsense as that!
You 've been always a very respectable cat;
As the Scotch would say, 'Whiles'
You 've been out on the tiles;
But you 've sown your wild oats, and you very well know
You 're no longer a kitten.
(Jerry) Moll roe! Moll roe!

"Well, Jerry, I 'm really concerned for your case;
I 've been young, and can fancy myself in your place:
Time has been I 've stood
By the edge of the wood,
And have mewed — that is, whistled, a sound just as good;
But we 're both of us older, my cat, as you know,
And I hope are grown wiser.
(Jerry) Moll roe! Moll roe!"

Mrs. Ricketts' Ghost Story.

"It was about the period when Captain Jervis, afterwards Earl St. Vincent, commanded the *Thunderer* (Foudroyant?) in which he so much distinguished himself, that on the return of that gallant commander to England, he found his sister, Mrs. Ricketts, the wife of Mr. Ricketts of Jamaica, a bencher of Gray's Inn, residing in a house between Alston and Alsford in Hampshire, about four or five miles from Abingdon, the seat of the Buckingham family. This house, then called 'New House,' was part of the property of the noble family of Legge, and of that particular branch of it of which the Lord Stawell (a peerage now extinct) had been the head. It had been principally occupied during his life by a Mr. Legge, a scion of the family, notorious for his debauched and profligate habits, and after his decease had remained for some time unoccupied, gradually acquiring, as is the case with most unoccupied mansions of a similar description, the reputation of being the resort of supernatural visitants.

"To this circumstance, perhaps, and the consequent difficulty of finding a tenant, may be attributed the easy terms on which Mr. Ricketts obtained it as a residence for his wife and family, during his own absence on a visit to his estates in the West Indies. This gentleman seems to have held the stories connected with the building in thorough contempt, a sentiment partaken of by Mrs. Ricketts herself, who was naturally a strong-minded woman, and whose good sense had acquired additional strength from the advantages of an excellent education.

"To 'New House' then the lady had repaired almost immediately after her husband's departure for Jamaica, purposing in quiet retirement to superintend there the education of her daughter (afterwards married to the Earl of Northesk).

"Mrs. Ricketts had not long been located in her new domicile, before the servants began to complain of certain unaccountable noises which were heard in the house by day as well as by night, and the origin of which they found it impossible to detect. The story of the house being haunted was revived with additional vigor, especially when its mistress became herself an ear-witness of those remarkable sounds, and an investigation, set on foot and carried on under her own immediate superintendence, assisted by several friends whom she called in upon the occasion, had proved as ineffectual as those previously instituted by the domestics. The noises continued, as did the alarm of the servants, which increased to an absolute panic, and the whole of them at length, with the exception of an old and attached attendant on Mrs. Ricketts' person, gave warning and left their situations in a body.

"A thorough change in the household, however, produced no other effect than that of proving beyond a doubt that the noises, from whatever cause they might proceed, were at least not produced by the instrumentality or collusion of the domestics. A second and a third set were tried, but with no better result; few could be prevailed upon to stay beyond the month.

"It was at this time that Mrs. Gwynne, from whose mouth Mrs. Hughes had this relation, came to reside a short time with her old and dear friend, and being a woman of strong nerve, she remained with her longer than she had originally intended, although not a day or night passed without their being disturbed. Mrs. Gwynne described the sounds as most frequently resembling the ripping and rending of boards, apparently those of the floor above, or below (as the case might be) that in which her friend and herself were sitting; but on more than one occasion she herself distinctly heard the whisperings of three voices, seemingly so close to her that, by putting out her hand, she fancied she could have touched the persons uttering them. One of the voices was clearly that of a female, who appeared to be earnestly imploring some one with tears and sobbings; a manly, resolute voice was evidently refusing her entreaty, while rough, harsh, and most discordant tones, as of some hardened ruffian, were occasionally heard interfering; these last were succeeded by two loud and piercing shrieks from the female; then followed the crashing of boards again, and all was quiet for the time.

"The visitations were so frequently repeated that, at length, even Mrs. Gwynne's constancy began to give way, and she prepared to leave her friend. Previously to her departure, however, she was aroused one night by Mrs. Ricketts' cries (who slept in the next chamber to her), and on running to her assistance, was informed that, just before, she, Mrs. Ricketts, had distinctly heard some person jump from the window-sill down on the floor at the foot of the bed, and that, as the chamber door had continued bolted, he must still be in the room. The strictest search was made, but no one was discovered.

"Various were the causes assigned in the neighborhood by the peasantry for these supernatural visitations, the history of which had now become rife all over that country side. Among other things it was said that Mr. Legge had always been a notorious evil liver, that he had held in his employ one Robin, as butler, a man with a remarkably deep-toned, hoarse, guttural voice, who was well known as a pander to all his master's vices and worst passions, and the unprincipled executor of all his oppressive dealings with his tenantry. That there was also a niece of Mr. Legge's resident with her uncle, and that dark rumors had been afloat of her having been at one time in the family way, though, as they said, 'nothing' ever came of it,' and no child was ever *known* to have been born; heavy suspicions, indeed, had been entertained on that score by the village gossips, which had gone so far that nothing but the wealth and influence of the squire had stifled inquiry. What had eventually become of the young lady no one knew, but it was supposed she had gone abroad before her uncle's death.

"Mrs. Ricketts and her friends endeavored to follow up these rumors, but the only thing they could arrive at with any degree of certainty was what they learned from an aged man, a carpenter, who declared that many years ago he had been sent for to the Hall, and had been taken by Robin up into one of the bedrooms, where, by his direction, he had cut out a portion of one of the planks, and also part of the joist below; upon which the butler had brought a box, which he said contained valuable title deeds that his master wished to have placed in security, and having put it into the cavity ordered him to nail down the plank as before. This, he said, he had done, and could easily point out the place.

"Mrs. Ricketts ordered the man to be conducted up-stairs, when he at once fixed on the door of her own sleeping apartment, saying, that, though it was a good many years ago, he was certain that was the room. On being introduced, he looked about for an instant, and then pointed out a part of the floor where there was evidently a separation in the plank, and which Mrs. Ricketts declared was the precise spot, as near as she could have described it, where the supposed intruder had alighted on his jump from the window.

"The board was immediately taken up; the joist below was found to be half sawn through, and the upper portion removed, precisely as the carpenter had described it; the cavity, however, was empty, and the box, if box there had been, must have been removed at some previous opportunity. After this investigation which ended in nothing, the noises and the whisperings, through never distinct, continued with but little diminution in frequency, and proved sufficient to render the house exceedingly uncomfortable to its inmates.

"Matters were in this state, when Captain Jervis, on his return to England, made his appearance at New House, with his friend Colonel Luttrell, to pay a visit to his sister. He had already heard of her annoyance, by letter, and of her disinclination to take the step he recommended, of removing, from the fear of offending her husband, who was somewhat of a martinet at home, and would of course treat the whole story as a fable. Captain Jervis seemed himself very much inclined to look upon it at first in the same light, or rather to consider it as a trick — for he had no doubt of his sister's veracity — and a trick which he was determined to find out.

"With this view, the Colonel and himself, sending all the rest of the family to bed, sat up, each in a separate parlor on the ground-floor, with loaded pistols by their side, and all other appurtenances most approved, when people have the prospect before them of a long night to be spent in ghost-hunting.

"The clock had stricken 'one,' when the sounds already mentioned, as of persons ripping up the floor above, were simultaneously heard by both. Each rushed from the parlor he occupied, with a light in one hand and a cocked pistol in the other, and encountered his friend in the passage. At first, a slight altercation ensued between them, each accusing the other of a foolish attempt at a hoax; but the colloquy was brought to an abrupt termination by the same sounds which each had heard separately being now renewed, and to all outward seeming, immediately above their heads. The whispering, too, at this juncture, became audible to both.

"The gentlemen rushed up-stairs, aroused their servants, and commenced a vigorous and immediate search throughout the whole premises; nothing, however, was found more than on any former occasion of the same kind, with this exception, that in one of the rooms sounds were distinctly heard of a different character from any before noticed, and resembling, as Mrs. Gwynne averred, 'the noise which would be produced by the rattling dry bones in a box.' They seemed to proceed from one of two presses which filled up a portion of the apartment; the door was immediately burst open, and the piece of furniture knocked to pieces; every search was made around, and even in the wall to which it had adjoined; but still, as heretofore, all investigation was fruitless. Captain Jervis, however, at once took upon himself the responsibility of removing his sister and her family to a farm-house in the same parish, where they remained till Mr. Ricketts' return.

"That part of the county of Hants being much the resort of smugglers, an attempt has been made to account for these events by attributing them to their agency, aided by the collusion of the servants. The latter part of the supposition could not be true, — the whole household having been so frequently changed. Even Mrs. Ricketts' favorite maid had at last, most reluctantly, abandoned her; besides which Mrs. R. had, throughout the whole business, kept a diary of the transaction, which she had regularly caused all the domestics, as they left her service, to sign, in attestation of its truth, as far as their own personal experience had qualified them so to do. Mrs. Gwynne herself, as well as a few other visitors, had done the same, and this diary coming into the hands of her daughter at her mother's decease, had been in the same way transmitted to the granddaughter, in whose possession it now is.

"It remains to be added, that with Lord St. Vincent the subject was a very sore one to the day of his death; and any allusion to it always brought on a fit of ill-humor, and a rebuke to him who ventured to make it. The house has been since, I believe, pulled down, but it does not appear that anything has occurred to throw any light on the mystery, or to strengthen or refute the suspicions which the good folks in the neighborhood entertained of the crime of Mr. Legge, and the unrest which his spirit, and those of his supposed coadjutor and victim, had experienced from the date of his delinquency.

"Mrs. Hughes expressed her doubt as to the accuracy of the name of the mansion in which all these strange occurrences took place, but of the fact she was positive. The way in which she first became acquainted with them was as follows: Mrs. Gwynne, being a visitor at her mother's house, was about to relate the story, when she was checked by the hostess, who requested her to wait till Mary Anne (Mrs. Hughes), at that time a child, was gone to bed. This so excited the girl's curiosity, that she contrived to hide herself behind the curtains of the room till the 'ghost story' was told."

According to another version which was given by an elderly lady named Hoy, to Lady Douglas, from whom I heard it, the scene of these strange events was Marwell Hall, a lonely mansion situated between Bishopstoke and Winchester. The house had been the residence of Jane Seymour, and preparations for her marriage with Henry are said to have been going on within its walls during the very day appointed for the execution of the hapless Anne Boleyn. Miss Hoy maintained that it was no other than the ghost of the unfeeling Queen Jane who used to disturb the inmates, and whose uncomfortable habits led eventually to the destruction of her former abode. For the old lady went on to say that Captain Jervis, having watched in the haunted room alone one night, during which he was heard to fire a couple of pistol shots, appeared next morning with a grave and troubled countenance; that he positively refused to answer any questions as to what had taken place, but at once sought an interview with the landlord, and in consequence of the communication made to him, but withheld from all others, the house was shortly after demolished, and a modern habitation erected in its place. It is obvious that these two versions may be partially reconciled on the very probable supposition that it is the present building which is known as the "New House," and that it has been confounded by Mrs. Hughes with the original Marwell Hall. Of course considerable difference of opinion must continue to exist respecting the identity of the ghost, unless, indeed, it should be allowed that the two, like rival tragedians engaged at the same theatre, used to perform on alternate nights.

PICKLED COCKLES.

"A certain notable housewife — he [Cannon] used to say — had observed that her stock of pickled cockles was running remarkably low, and she spoke to the cook in consequence, who alone had access to them. The cook had noticed the same serious deficiency: 'she could n't tell how, but they certainly *had* disappeared much too fast!' A degree of coolness, approaching to estrangement, ensued between these worthy individuals, which the rapid consumption of the pickled cockles by no means contributed to remove. The lady became more distant than ever, spoke pointedly and before company of 'some people's unaccountable partiality to pickled cockles,' etc. The cook's character was at stake: unwilling to give warning, with such an imputation upon her self-denial, not to say honesty, she, nevertheless, felt that all confidence between her mistress and herself was at an end.

"One day, the jar containing the evanescent condiment being placed as usual on the dresser, while she was busily engaged in basting a joint before the fire, she happened to turn suddenly round, and beheld, to her great indignation, a favorite magpie, remarkable for his conversational powers and general intelligence, perched by its side, and dipping his beak down the open neck with every symptom of gratification. The mystery was explained — the thief detected! Grasping the ladle of scalding grease which she held in her hand, the exasperated lady dashed the whole contents over the hapless pet, accompanied by the exclamation, —

"'Oh, d— me, *you've* been at the pickled cockles, have ye?'

"Poor Mag, of course, was dreadfully burnt; most of his feathers came off, leaving his little round pate, which had caught the principal part of the volley, entirely bare. The poor bird moped about, lost all his spirit, and never spoke for a whole year.

"At length, when he had pretty well recovered and was beginning to chatter again, a gentleman called at the house, who, on taking off his hat, discovered a very bald head! The magpie, who happened to be in the room, appeared evidently struck by the circumstance: his reminiscences were at once powerfully excited by the naked appearance of the gentleman's skull. Hopping upon the back of his chair, and looking him hastily over, he suddenly exclaimed in the ear of the astounded visitor, —

"'Oh, d— me, *you've* been at the pickled cockles, have ye?'"

GEAME FEATHERS.

"Mr. Wood, the conchologist, once told me a story, which I think carries friendly consolation and good offices *in extremis* to even a higher pitch.

"He was once a surgeon at Windham, in Kent, and said that, in the course of his practice, he had to pay what he considered would be his last visit to an elderly laboring man on Adisham Downs. He had left him in the last stage of illness the day before, and was not surprised on calling again to find him dead, but did experience a little astonishment at seeing the bed on which he had been lying now withdrawn from under the body, and placed in the middle of the floor. To his remarks, the answer given by her who had officiated as nurse (?) was, —

"'Dearee me, sir, you see there was partridge-feathers in the bed, and folks can't die upon *geame* feathers, nohow, and we thought as how he never *would* go, so we pulled the bed away, and then I just pinched his poor nose tight with one hand, and shut his mouth close with t' other, and, poor dear! he went off like a lamb!'"

POETICAL EPISTLE TO DR. HUME.

On the ninth November of this year (1837), the Queen came in state to dine with the Lord Mayor at the annual banquet at Guildhall. Preparations on the most magnificent scale were made to receive her; throughout the whole line of march scaffoldings were erected, windows were fitted up, balconies thrown out, the most conspicuous positions being occupied by ladies in rich and varied raiment, all glorious to behold. Seats commanding a view of the procession were sold at extravagant prices, and were with difficulty to be procured on any terms. Mr. Barham's house in St. Paul's Church-yard was of course thronged with visitors,[1] and an invitation was conveyed in the following terms to his old friend Dr. Hume: —

TO DR. HUME.

"St. P. C. Y., *November* 4, 1837.

"Doctor dear! the Queen's a coming!
All this ancient city round;
Scarce a place to squeeze one's thumb in,
High or low, can now be found;

"So my spouse — you 'll hardly thank her —
Thus in substance bids me say —
'Bring your sweet self to an anchor,
Doctor dear, with us that day!'

"If no haunch your palate tickles,
If no turtle greet your eye,
There 'll be cold roast beef and pickles,
Ox-tail soup, and pigeon pie.

"Fear not then the knaves who fleece men —
Johnny Raws, and country muffs!
There 'll be lots of new policemen
To control the rogues and roughs.

"Doctor darling! think how grand is
Such a sight! the great Lord May'r
Heading all the city dandies
There on horseback takes the air!

"Chains and maces all attend, he
Rides all glorious to be seen;
'Lad o' wax!' great Heaven forfend he
Don't get spilt before the Queen!

"Blue-coat boys with classic speeches, —
From our windows you shall view

[1] Among those present was Mr. Poole. At the dinner which followed the spectacle one of the guests, moved by enthusiasm and loyalty, to say nothing of champagne, rose to propose the health of the Queen. "We have heard to-day," he commenced, "many hurrahs" — "Yes," interrupted Poole, "and we have seen to-day many *hussars!*"

Their yellow stockings, yellow breeches,
And 'long togs' of deepest blue.

"Here the cutlers, — there the nailers, —
Here the barber-surgeons stand,—
Goldsmiths here — there merchant tailors,
And in front the Coldstream Band!

"Gas-lights, links, and flambeaux blazing,
These will shame the noon-tide ray;
'Night! — pooh! — stuff! 't is quite amazing!
Why 't is brighter far than day!'

"But a scene so brilliant mocks all
Power its beauties to declare;
Once beheld, poor Gye of Vauxhall
Hangs himself in deep despair!

"Come then, Doctor, quit your shrubbery,
Cock your castor o'er your ear;
Come and gaze, and taste the grubbery,
Ah, now join us, Doctor dear!
"R. H. B."

An Accomplished Swindler.

By the detection of an accomplished swindler Mr. Barham was the means of relieving a friend from a burden borne cheerfully for some years. He (my father) received a note one morning from the Bishop of —— begging him to call as soon as possible, the writer being about to leave town in a few hours. The Bishop was found immersed in business, and he hastily explained the cause of the summons he had sent.

"I have been in the habit," he said, "of paying quarterly a small sum to the relict of a deceased clergyman. He was a worthless fellow enough, and on his death his widow and daughter were left without a farthing and without a friend. They called upon me, and I was much struck by their ladylike and refined manners, by their grief and by their poverty, evidences of which were painfully conspicuous. I promised some periodical assistance, and I have never failed to send it punctually till now, when I find to my horror that I have permitted the lapse of nearly a week. Now I want you to call and explain to these poor people the cause of my neglect, which is illness, and express my sorrow at any inconvenience it may have caused them. At the same time you can hand them my usual contribution, and should their circumstances seem to require it, you may increase it according to your discretion."

In the course of that afternoon Mr. Barham called at a house in Salisbury Street, Strand. Was Mrs. —— at home? It appeared, after a prolonged and audible discussion carried on above, that Mrs. —— was at home; would the gentleman "leave his business?" The gentleman would with pleasure leave his business with the person whom it concerned. Well, he could walk up-stairs — "first floor, front." And up-stairs accordingly he walked. On entering the drawing-room he found it very showily, if not handsomely furnished; as much or more might be said of the two ladies who occupied it. One, the elder, was reclining in an arm-chair, and comforting herself in her bereavement with a tumbler of what smelt suspiciously like grog — hot! The younger, somewhat more *décolletée* than was quite suitable to the time of day, or indeed to any time of day, was dressed in great splendor, and was warbling her woes to a pianoforte accompaniment. The entrance of the intruder, for such he at once perceived himself to be, produced a decided effect upon both. The younger swung gracefully around upon her music stool and faced him; the elder arose, and in an angry tone demanded whom he was and what he wanted. He was a friend of the Bishop of ——, and what he wanted was to apologize for mistaking the ladies before him for Mrs. and Miss ——.

"That 's my name, and that 's my daughter," was the reply.

"Indeed!" observed Mr. Barham, "then, Madam, the mistake is the Bishop's, and not mine." Upon this the lady, who was a trifle thick of speech, and had seemingly required a good deal of stimulating to raise her spirits, began to use language which would rather have astonished his lordship if he could have heard and comprehended it. But the daughter interposed and begged politely to know the object of the visit.

"My object, Madam, was to convey to your mother a communication from the Bishop of ——, but it is one which I now feel to be so completely out of place that I must ask you to apply for it to his lordship in person, on his return from the country — *if you think fit.*"

So saying, Mr. Barham retreated as speedily as possible from the house, and no more was ever heard, so far as I am aware, of the distressing case he had left there unrelieved.

A Song of Sixpence.

"*Diary: October*, 1838. — The following is a doggerel versification of a correspondence between M—— B——, the celebrated singer and surgeon, and the committee of the Garrick Club. The question arose about the charge of 'sixpence for the table' always added to the bill when refreshments are ordered between the hours of four and nine. Mr. B—— angrily insisted on this sum being deducted, as at a quarter before eight he had ordered *supper* and not dinner. The stanzas are almost literal versions of the original letters put into rhyme.

A SONG OF SIXPENCE.

No. I.

" Mr. B—— sends his bill back — won't pay it — and begs
To inform the Committee they're regular 'legs,'
And have charged him too much for his ham and his eggs! "

No. II.

"Dear Sir, — The Committee direct me to say
That the bill's quite correct which was sent you to day;
It was not eight o'clock when you sat down to dine,
And we charge for the table from four until nine.
They have not the least wish your remonstrance to stifle,
But you're wrong — and they'll thank you to pay that 'ere trifle!
I am further desired to inform Mr. B.
That, in calling them 'legs,' he makes rather too free. J. W."

No. III.

" You may tell that banditti, the —— Committee,
Not a chop-house would charge me so much in the City.
'T was no dinner at all; I meant only to sup;
If you say that I *dined*, you 're a lying old pup!
You may tell the Committee again — and I say it,
They *are* 'legs' — and sixpence! — I 'm hanged if I pay it. W B."

No. IV.

"Sir, — Once more the Committee direct me to state,
When you sat down to dinner it had not struck eight;
When you come to consider what 'table' means here —
Cloth, napkin, wax, vinegar, mustard, oil, beer,
Pepper, pickles, and bread at discretion — it's clear
The additional sixpence can never be dear!
So you'd better fork out, sir, at once; if you won't
They must really enforce it — and blessed if they don't! J. W."

No. V.

"Take the sixpence, you thieves! I say still it's a chouse;
Your threat to 'enforce' I don't value one ——
And hang me if I ever set foot in your house! W. B."

No. VI.

"Sir, — Since writing my last I have asked the advice
Of my friends Mr. Bacon and Governor Price,
And the Governor says 'he'll be —— sir' if I'm
Not a jackass for writing what I thought sublime;
'It's just what the —— fellows wanted; you'd better
Get somebody else, sir, to write you a letter
Withdrawing your own.' So I have, and I'll thank
The Committee to mark that this comes by a frank."

No. VII.

"Mr. Winston presents his best compliments — begs
To inform Mr. B—— he is somewhat mistaken
If, having got into his scrape by his eggs,
He thinks to get out of it now by his *Bacon!*"

The Queen of the Belgians.

"What think you of a visit from, and confabulation with, the Queen of the Belgians! On Saturday, I was in the library at St. Paul's, my 'custom always in an afternoon,' with a bookbinder's 'prentice and a printer's devil, looking out fifty dilapidated folios for rebinding; I had on a coat which, from a foolish prejudice in the multitude against patched elbows, I wear nowhere else, my hands and face encrusted with the dust of years, and wanting only the shovel — I had the brush — to sit for the portrait of a respectable master chimney-sweeper, when the door opened, and in walked the Cap of Maintenance bearing the sword of, and followed by the Lord Mayor in full fig, with the prettiest and liveliest little Frenchwoman leaning upon his arm. Nobody could get at the 'Lions' but myself; I was fairly in for it, and was thus presented in the most *recherché*, if not the most expensive, court dress that I will venture to say the eyes of royalty were ever greeted withal. *Heureusement pour moi*, she spoke excellent English, however, and rattled on with a succession of questions, which I answered as best I might. They were sensible, however, showed some acquaintance with literature, and a very good knowledge of dates.

"My *gaucherie* afforded her one opportunity of displaying her acquaintance with chronology which she did not miss. The date of a MS. was the question; I unthinkingly referred to that of the *Battle of Agincourt* an allusion which a courtier would have shunned as a rock ahead, considering the figure an Orleans cut in that fight. It was not quite so bad certainly as the gentleman telling Prince Eugene that 'a certain event took place in the year the Countess of Soissons (his mother) poisoned her husband,' but it was enough to have made poor Colonel Dalton faint. She relieved me, however, in an instant by saying, 'Ah! 1415,' while George C——, who was with her, coolly asked 'when it was *printed?*' She turned to him briskly, and said at once, 'You see it is a manuscript,' which satisfied the gentleman of the bedchamber, and saved my reply."

MONCRIEF, THE DRAMATIST.

"*October* 17, 1839.—Went with W. Harrison Ainsworth to call on Mr. Moncrief, author of the forthcoming version of 'Jack Sheppard' for the Victoria Theatre. Moncrief was quite blind, but remarkably cheerful. He gave us in detail the outline of the plot as he had arranged it, all except the conclusion, which had not as yet been published in the novel, but which Ainsworth promised to send him. Moncrief, in a very extraordinary manner, went through what he had done, without having occasion to refer to any book or person, singing the songs introduced, and reciting all the material points of the dialogue. He adverted to his literary controversy with

Charles Dickens, respecting the dramatic version of 'Nicholas Nickleby,' which he declared he would never have written, had Dickens sent him a note to say it would be disagreeable to him."

The Sentimental Child.

"It reminded me of what passed between myself and Dr. Wilmot's little daughter, many years ago; I accompanied the little body, a fine, intelligent, and, as I thought, too *sentimental* child of nine years old, out into the poultry yard, to look at her 'dear little chicks,' during the awkward half-hour before dinner. We were great friends; and after introducing me to the 'gray hen who was *cluck*,' and to the 'bantams,' and to the 'everlasting layers,' I was at length ushered to the pig-sty to look at her 'own dear little pig,' whom 'she loved so much.' All due commendation was of course lavished on my side upon such a pet; and when we took leave of the little brute, whose eyes really seemed to look gratefully towards its too partial mistress, the young lady concluded her *au revoir* with 'Bless you, dear little piggy! how pretty you are; and how nice you will be when we come to eat you!' It was impossible to doubt the probability of the prophecy; but however I might revere her as a sage, the young lady sank to zero as a sentimentalist. After all this *nouvelle Heloise* was right perhaps, and only working out her great namesake's problem, —

"'What *pork* we doat on, when 't is *pigs* we love!'"

The Unlucky Present.

An old gentleman, a merchant in Bush Lane, had an only daughter, possessed of the highest attractions, moral, personal, and pecuniary; she was engaged, and devotedly attached, to a young man in her own rank of life, one in every respect well worthy of her choice. All preliminaries were arranged, and the marriage, after two or three postponements, was fixed, "positively for the last time of marrying," to take place on Thursday, April 15, 18—.

On the preceding Monday, the bridegroom elect (who was to have received £10,000 down on his wedding-day, and a further sum of £30,000 on his father-in-law's dying, as there was hope he soon would) had some little jealous squabbling with his intended at an evening party; the "tiff" arose in consequence of his paying more attention than was thought justifiable to a young lady with sparkling eyes and inimitable ringlets. The gentleman retorted, and spoke slightingly of a certain cousin, whose waistcoat was the admiration of the assembly, and which, it was hinted darkly, had been embroidered by the fair hand of the heiress in question. He added, in conclusion, that it would be time enough for him to be schooled when they were married; that (reader, pardon the unavoidable expression!) she was "*putting on the breeches*" a little too soon.

After supper, both the lovers had become more cool; iced champagne and cold chicken had done their work, and leave was taken by the bridegroom *in posse*, in terms kindly and affectionate, if not so enthusiastic as those which had previously terminated their meetings.

On the next morning, the swain thought with some remorse on the angry feeling he had exhibited, and the cutting sarcasm in which he had given it vent, and, as a part of his *amende honorable*, packed up with great care a magnificent satin dress, which he had previously bespoken for his beloved, and which had been sent home to him in the interval, and transmitted it to the lady, with a note to the following effect: —

"DEAREST * * *, — I have been unable to close my eyes all night, in consequence of thinking on our foolish misunderstanding last evening. Pray, pardon me; and, in token of your forgiveness, deign to accept the accompanying dress, and wear it for the sake of your ever affectionate * * *"

Having written the note, he gave it to his shopman to deliver with the parcel; but as a pair of his nether garments happened, at the time, to stand in need of repairing, he availed himself of the opportunity offered by his servant having to pass the tailor's shop, in his way to Bush Lane, and desired him to leave them, packed in another parcel, on his road.

The reader foresees the inevitable *contretemps*. Yes, the man made the fatal blunder! consigned the satin robes to Mr. Snip, and left the note, together with the dilapidated habiliment, at the residence of the lady. Her indignation was neither to be described nor appeased. So exasperated was she, at what she considered a determined and deliberate affront, that when her admirer called she ordered the door to be closed in his face, refused to listen to any explanation, and resolutely broke off the match. Before many weeks had elapsed, means were found to make her acquainted with the history of the objectionable present, but she, nevertheless, adhered firmly to her resolve, deeply lamenting the misadventure, but determined not to let the burden of the ridicule rest upon her.

Anecdotes.

"*Diary : July*, 1842.—The Bishop of London mentioned that at the recent grand meeting at Cambridge, at which the Duke of Cambridge attended, he (the Bishop) was appointed to preach, and had no sooner commenced with 'Let us pray,' than his Royal Highness rose up in the pew below, and exclaimed with great fervor, 'Certainly, by all means.' The Duke used invariably to read aloud all the service, including the Absolution; and when the King of Prussia visited St. Paul's, I saw him put that potentate out sadly by his over-officiousness in finding the place for him in the prayer-book. All had been properly marked, but his Royal Highness took the volume from him, began turning it over, and finally left his Majesty in much greater mystification than he found him. He appears to be a really devout man, but is absent and flighty.

"Tate told us a story of Mr. Ottley, a great connoisseur in paintings and articles of virtu, whom I once met at his house—now dead. Ottley, while at Rome, when all the treasures of art were yet contained within its limits, and long before its spoliation by the French, was much bothered by foolish people, who inquired of him whether Raphael or Titian or Corregio, etc., was the best painter, to whom he used to reply by a story: —

"There was an old woman, living at Naples, very devout, who went to her confessor on a case of conscience. Her object was to learn whether San Gennaro or the Virgin Mary was the greater Saint.

"'Why, daughter,' said the padre, 'that is a very nice question, and perhaps it might puzzle the Holy Father himself to decide upon it. However, for your comfort it may perhaps be satisfactory to know that both of them were Apostles!'

"I mentioned that, examining one of the Sunday-school boys at Addington, I asked him what a prophet was. He did not know.

"'If I were to tell you what would happen to you this day twelve-month, and it should come to pass, what would you call me then, my little man?'

"'A fortune-teller, sir,' said the boy.

"There was an end of the examination for that day."

FACETIÆ.

"*Diary: May*, 1843. — Dinner of the Sons of the Clergy at Merchant Tailors' Hall. The Archbishop, a nervous man [Dr. Howley], by a ludicrous *lapsus linguæ* gave as a toast, instead of 'Prosperity to the Merchant Tailors' Company,' 'Prosperity to the Merchant Company's Tailor!'

"Dr. Taylor read to me the following extract from a letter just addressed to him by Archbishop Whately: 'O'Connell has spoilt the dog. The story is of a traveller, who, finding himself and his dog in a wild country and destitute of provisions, cut off his dog's tail and boiled it for *his own* supper, giving the "dog *the bone*."'

"Abingdon, a gentleman of property, first an amateur and afterwards a professional actor, and manager of the Southampton Theatre, told me that once, when he was playing Hamlet there, Rosencrantz, who ought to say, —

'My lord, you once did love me,'

forgot his part and failed in giving the cue, till the prompter, seeing Hamlet could not go on for the want of it, stepped forward and said —

'My lord, you once did love *this gentleman!*'

This enabled Abingdon to reply —

'And do still by these pickers and stealers.'

Like most good-natured people who do good-natured things, the prompter got hissed by the audience for having kept the stage so long in waiting. I was terribly abused by the mob once for going to bury a corpse which my neighbor H—— had forgotten, after it had been detained by *his* carelessness more than an hour in the church-yard."

SYDNEY SMITH'S NOVEL.

"*Diary: December* 2, 1843. — Dined at Charles Dickens's. Present — Sydney Smith, my wife, Serjeant Talfourd, Albany Fonblanque, Miss Eley, Rev. —— Taggart, Mrs. Talfourd, Maclise, Mr. Forster, Sam Rogers, etc. Sydney Smith gave an account of Colburn's calling upon him with an introduction from Bulwer. The bibliopole, he said, opened with a condolence, delicately conveyed, on his recent losses in American securities, and then proposed, by way of repairing them, the production of a novel in three volumes, for which he should be most happy to treat on liberal terms.

"'Well, sir,' said Mr. Smith, after some seeming consideration, 'if I do so, I can't travel out of my own line — *ne sutor ultra crepidam*, you know — I must have an archdeacon for my hero, to fall in love with the pew-opener, with the clerk for a confidant — tyrannical interference of the church-wardens — clandestine correspondence concealed under the hassocks — appeal to the parishioners, etc., etc.'

"'With that, sir,' said Mr. Colburn, 'I would not presume to interfere; I would leave it all entirely to your own inventive genius.'

"'Well, sir,' returned the canon, with urbanity, 'I am not prepared to come to terms at present; but if ever I do undertake such a work, you shall certainly have the refusal.'"

Duke of Sussex and Mr. Offor.

For some years during the latter portion of his life my father devoted much of his leisure, not only to the prosecution of genealogical and antiquarian inquiries, to which he had always been addicted, but also to the acquiring a knowledge of the various editions of the Bible. His means were not sufficiently ample to enable him to form a collection of the rarer copies, but he made himself well acquainted with those extant, and expended a great deal of time and industry, to the severe injury of his eyesight, in preparing fac-similes of the remarkable passages and wood-cuts by which the various translations are distinguished. In this pursuit he received considerable assistance from Mr. George Offor, whose library was especially rich in specimens of early typography. Of these the choicest were very wisely kept behind a screen of brass-work, securely locked, a circumstance which Mr. Offor used to say immediately attracted the notice of the Duke of Sussex, when his Royal Highness honored him with a visit.

"Ah! I see," said the Duke, "you lock up your best books — very necessary, very proper — no collector is to be trusted; they are all thieves, every one of them!"

"I presume, sir," replied Mr. Offor, with a low bow, "I might suggest an exception?"

"You mean me? Oh! you 're quite mistaken — I could n't resist the temptation, if it came in my way, better than any one else."

Parson O'Beirne's Sermon.

"*Diary: May* 11, 1844. — Dined at Sir Thomas Wilde's. Among the company — Sir John Hobhouse, Mr. and Lady Anne Welby, Mr. Horsman, Tom Duncombe, etc. Hobhouse told a story of the Rev. — commonly called 'Parson' — O'Beirne, which he had from old Richard Brinsley Sheridan. Sheridan had been dining with O'Beirne, and, it being Saturday, the host was anxious to bring the sitting to an earlier termination than usual, as he had no sermon ready for next day. Sheridan pleaded hard for another bottle.

"'Then you must write a sermon for me,' was O'Beirne's answer, which Sheridan at once undertook to do. There was a certain Mr. ——, a neighboring squire, who was proverbial for grinding the poor, and had recently prosecuted some of the laborers in the parish for stealing turnips. Sheridan's sermon, which, true to his word, he produced in the morning, was a regular attack upon this gentleman. It was filled with all sorts of pretended quotations from St. Paul and the Fathers, sentences denouncing illiberality, tyranny, and oppression of the poor, some of them referring particularly to the especial sinfulness of prosecutions for stealing turnips. Mr. O'Beirne, who had no time to read over the composition before morning prayers, commenced his discourse and went on with it till he fairly drove the indignant squire out of the church. The latter, indeed, was so savage at the personalities, that he made a formal complaint to the bishop of the diocese.

"'And how did the matter end?' asked Hobhouse.

"'Oh, just as such a thing should end,' said Sheridan; 'O'Beirne got a better living!'"[1]

[1] The Rev. Thomas Lewis O'Beirne, afterwards Bishop of Meath, is evidently the person here referred to. A somewhat more probable version of the story is given in *Sheridaniana*. It is there stated that Mr. O'Beirne, having arrived at Sheridan's house, near Osterley, was requested to preach on the following Sunday, but, having no sermon, accepted Sheridan's offer to provide one. Next morning Mr. O'Beirne found the manuscript by his bedside, the subject of the discourse being the "Abuse of Riches." Having read it over, and corrected some theological errors (such as "it is easier for a camel," as Moses says, etc.), he delivered the sermon in his most impressive style, much to the delight of his own party, and to the satisfaction, as he unsuspectingly flattered himself, of all the rest of the congregation, among whom was Mr. Sheridan's wealthy neighbor, Mr. C——. Some months afterwards, however, Mr. O'Beirne perceived that the family of Mr. C——, with whom he had been previously intimate, treated him with marked coldness, and, on his expressing some innocent wonder at the circumstance, was at length informed, to his dismay, by General Burgoyne, that the sermon which Sheridan had written for him was throughout a personal attack upon Mr. C——, who had at that time rendered himself very unpopular in the neighborhood by some harsh conduct to the poor, and to whom every one in the church, except the unconscious preacher, applied almost every sentence of the sermon. — *Sheridaniana*.

A Nobleman who would sell Anything.

"On our way to Dover Sir W. Betham told us a story of Lord M——, a gentleman who would sell anything, even the commissions in the militia regiment he commanded, and when it was objected to him replied that he did it 'to assimilate his regiment as much as possible to the line, which was in general orders.' A pew in a parish church near his family property was supposed to belong to him, and the building having been repaired, three old ladies were anxious to possess what it is scarcely necessary to say was of little use to his lordship. One of them waited on him at the barracks, and proposed purchase.

"'Oh, bother, Ma'am, divil a pew has my Lord M—— in any such place.'

"'Ah then and indeed it's your lordship's own, and sure everybody says so.'

"'Everybody lies, sure — but what is it, ma'am, ye'll be giving for the pew?'

"After a little hesitation and fencing, the lady offered to give twenty pounds for the pew rather than suffer Mrs. Magrath to take her place in it.

"'Twenty pounds! is it twenty pounds! twenty pounds rather than be bragged by Mrs. Magrath! Sure it's forty pounds ye mane — Oh, it's a beautiful pew!'

"The old lady stood out for twenty, but his lordship was firm, and at last she agreed to give the sum demanded rather than be 'bragged' by Molly Magrath. His lordship therefore made over his right and title to the pew in something like the following words: 'Lord M—— agrees to sell to Mrs. Bridget Maloney all his right and title, if he has any, to a pew in the parish church of —— for value this day received.'

"The lady had scarcely retired when another was announced on the same errand, who succeeded in making the same purchase on rather reduced terms, as eventually did also a third. On the following Sunday the case of title was of course warmly gone into, all the three parties claiming possession. After some pains had been taken in the inquiry, the dispute was decided in favor of a fourth claimant, whose uncle had bought the pew years before of Lord M——'s father. This decision brought all the three purchasers back to the barracks in the hope of getting their money again, but 'any restitution' formed no part of Lord M——'s politics.

"'Sure he had sold them the pew if he had got one, and if he had not how could he help it!'

"'But you must give us our money back, my lord, anyhow.'

"'Aisy, aisy! how will I do that, I'd be proud to know, when it's all spent and gone — every farthing of it?'

"'But if you don't we shall tell everybody, and then what becomes of my Lord M——'s character?'

"'Oh, tell away and welcome; the character's spent and gone too, and long before, for the matter of that.' And so the matter terminated."

SCRAPS.

"*No date.* Dined at the Adolphuses: met there a Mr. or Doctor Vicesimus Knox, who talked away famously and was very funny. Told us of a story of a Mr. ——, and how he thought the word 'clause' of an Act of Parliament was the plural number, and asked him, the said Vicesimus, which *claw* of the Act he was speaking of.

"Chief Justice Bushe was dining with the late Duke of Richmond, when Lord Lieutenant of Ireland, at Sir Wheeler Cuff's. On their entertainer getting drunk and falling from his chair, the Duke good-naturedly endeavored to lift him up, when Bushe exclaimed, 'How, your Grace! you, an Orangeman and a Protestant, assist in elevating the host!' Told to me by Dr. Hume."

"Serjeant Murphy observing part of the Bench (including Sir C. Williams) leaving the court early, while two only remained to finish the causes, said, loud enough to be heard by all present, 'As a papist, I am not of course permitted to know much of Scripture, or I should say, there is on one side Exodus and on the other Judges."

"When a certain Mr. ——, of the Temple, was expelled from that Society by the Benchers for conduct unbecoming a gentleman, Thesiger, who is a very kind-hearted man, was much affected by the situation of his wife and children, who would necessarily be ruined by the decision, and burst into tears.

"'Well,' said he afterwards to Rose, who was then Judge of the Court of Review, 'I should never do for a Criminal Judge, and after the way in which I have exposed my weakness to-day, you will agree with me.'

"'Why, yes,' said Rose, 'I think you would make an indifferent Judge, but then, you know, you would make an uncommonly good Cryer.'"

"Sydney Smith, speaking of his being shampooed at Mahomet's Baths at Brighton in 1840, said they 'squeezed enough out of him to make a lean curate.'"

"Hearing Shutte's little girl give vent to a prolonged 'Oh!' at the sight of a dahlia, he (Sydney Smith) said 'it was worth a page of eulogy.'"

"In Brazil, an opinion prevails that whoever has been bitten by a boa-constrictor has nothing to fear from any other snake. What a happy illustration of a man who has undergone a blackguarding from O'Connell!"

The following was an early hoax upon a Canterbury paper, and was freely copied by the provincial press: —

"*Fact for the Naturalist.* — A terrier dog in Romney Marsh, having been desperately maltreated and bitten by a savage mastiff, ran off nine miles to the house of Mr. Strickland, a justice of the peace, where he had often before been with his master, who was a parish constable; he got into the library, jumped upon Mr. Strickland's table, seized a blank assault warrant in his jaws, and bolted with it; he then ran back to his master with the instrument in his mouth, and wagging his tail, did all in his power to induce the latter to follow him and take his assailant into custody. It cannot, however, fail to be remarked, how the omission to obtain a signature to the paper serves to confirm the fact, that the sagacity of the most intelligent brute never passes that mysterious line which invariably separates instinct from reason."

"*Judge Maule.* — A young barrister pleading before Judge Maule, described an attorney's bill as 'a diabolical one.' 'That may be,' said the Judge, 'but the devil must have his due. Gentlemen of the jury, you will find for the plaintiff.'"

Seeing Richard Price at the Garrick with half a pint of port, he accused him of studying "*Winer's* abridgment."

"When George IV. was at Lord Lothian's during his visit to Scotland, the youngest scion of the family was a little impudent, spoiled boy in petticoats, who had got a way of calling everybody 'you old fat goose.' The King inquiring as to the number of her ladyship's children, was informed of course, and also of course desired to see them all. This little urchin, therefore, whom they had intended to keep out of the way, was perforce exhibited, when his father seeing the twinkle in his eye and the curl of his lip which betokened the forthcoming expression, caught him up in his arms, while the mother sat in agony, and bore him out of the room just in time to prevent the explosion."

"Ensign White of the Forty-fourth, the regiment that was so cut up in India, told me that on the march to Scinde, they used to encourage private theatricals among the soldiers to keep them out of mischief. On one occasion, when Richard III. was the play, the Catesby of the evening (a worthy and gallant corporal) thus addressed his sovereign: —

> "''T is I, my lord, — the early village cock
> Has been crowing away this half hour,
> Your friends are up and buckle on their armor —
> And why ain't you a buckling on o' yourn?'"

A Frenchman's Criticism.

"*Wallack's account of French criticism.* — When in America, Mr. Wallack became associated with a French actor, a great admirer of Shakespeare, but who wished to become more familiarized with his beauties. Wallack being an indifferent French scholar, it was agreed that instruction should be mutual; that the Frenchman should give lessons in his own language, which Wallack should return by lending his assistance towards producing a more perfect understanding, on the part of his tutor, of the bard who 'was not for an age but for all time.'

"'Ah! *ma foi*, dat is eet, Racine is good, Corneille is good, but Mons. Shakespeare — he is de bard of all time, of nature, of what you call common sense — so everybody say.'

"Wallack proposed, by way of commencement, that his new friend, who knew enough of English to read, though not to relish his author, should go over attentively and make himself master of the text of a play, which his preceptor should afterwards read over again with him, explaining difficulties and expounding beauties. 'Macbeth' was selected, but they did not get beyond the first scene.

"'Mons. Vallake, you have told me dat Shakespeare is de poet of nature and common sense; good! now vat is dis? Here is his play open — Macbess — yes! good, very good — well, here is tree old — old vat you call veetch, vid de broom and no close on at all — yes! upon the blasted heath — good! von veetch say to de oder veetch, 'ven shall ve tree meet agen?' De other veetch she say — "in tondare!" de other she say "in lightning!" — and she say to dem herself again "in rain!" *Eh bien!* now dis is not nature! dis is not common sense! Oh, no! De tree old veetch shall nevare go out to meet again upon de blasted heath with no close on in tondare, lightning, and in rain. Ah no! It is *not* common sense! *ma foi*, dey stay at home! aha!'

"Of course there was no possibility of proceeding with such a critic, and the arrangement ceased."

Macready in America.

"*Diary: December* 5, 1844. — Dined with Charles Dickens, Stanfield, Maclise, and Albany Fonblanque at Forster's. Dickens read with remarkable effect his Christmas story, 'The Chimes,' from the proofs. Anecdote told of Macready at New Orleans looking at a paper in the reading-room, when a stranger put his arm across his (Macready's) neck, and, leaning on his shoulder, asked if he knew Colonel Johnson ?

"Macready, shrinking from the familiarity, replied coldly enough, 'No, sir, I do not.'

"'Well I guess now he 'd like to know you.'

"'Possibly, sir.'

"'Well now, Colonel Johnson, walk this way ; I calculate this is Mr. Macready, the British actor.'

"'And pray who are you, sir ?' demanded Macready.

"'Me ? Oh, I guess I 'm Major Hitchins, I am. What, you 're ryled a leetle grain, are you ? You 'll have to get over that if you mean to progress in this great country, sir.' Free and enlightened society this, at any rate !"

Barham's Surgeon.

"And now as to our state here, — it is mended, and I would fain hope mending, but very, very slowly. I am still not allowed — nor if I were could I avail myself of the permission — to answer, except in a whisper, and that only to ask for what I want, and answer medical inquiries. Luckily I have assigned to me one of the greatest chatterboxes of a surgeon, to take the poking and blistering department of my treatment upon him, that can well be imagined. If in the multitude of counselors there be wisdom, in that of apothecaries there is jaw, and with such a one as my adviser possesses, Samson might have laid waste all Mesopotamia, let alone Philistia. He has the art of saying nothing in a cascade of language comparable only to that 'almighty water privilege,' Niagara, and were I in better spirits would delight instead of boring me. Galt's 'wearifu' woman' was but a type of him.

"'Well, sir, how are we to day — better, eh ! well, sir, go on with the iodine ? does it act ?'

"'Why that is what I wanted to ask, how do you mean it to act ? as a sudorific ?'

"'Diaphoretic we say, not but sudorific will do ; it comes from *sudo*, but we seldom now say sudorific ; but, sir, the iodine, does it act ?'

"'That is what I want to know ; how do you mean it to act, on the throat or' —

"'Act ? iodine ? on the throat ? why the throat, sir, is very singularly constructed — very singularly ; it's beautiful, the mechanism of the throat ! If it gets out of order — now yours, sir, is out of order, and we have been giving you iodine — for Mr. —— agrees with me that iodine is an excellent medicine, and what I want to know is, does it begin to produce any effect ?"

"'Why that is what I want to know, and therefore I ask what effect is it intended to produce, is it to act on' —

"'What effect ? my dear sir, there are few medicines now in better repute than iodine ; we give it in many cases — dropsy, sometimes — not that yours is dropsy ; you have nothing dropsical about you ; your complaint is an affection of the throat, and we have been giving iodine in your case — you have had it now three days — twice a day. Do you take it regularly twice a day ?'

"'I take what you send me twice a day, and you tell me it is iodine, but' —

"'And does it begin to produce its effect ; does it act ?'

"'Why that's what I'm asking you — now is it intended to act as a sedative, or' —

"'A sedative ? what, is your cough more troublesome ? We give sedatives sometimes for troublesome coughs, and then in nervous complaints, but then congestion is a thing to be avoided, not that I see any symptoms of congestion in your case ; yours is an affection of the throat, and so we give you iodine, and as we are a little particular in proportioning our doses, I want to ascertain whether what you have been taking acts ?'

"Oh dear, oh dear ! never were two philosophers more deeply engaged in pursuing the same inquiry, each endeavoring to extract information out of the other. And then such lectures on the 'anatomy of the parts,' 'the beautiful mechanism, etc.' ! that I, who never yet could comprehend the mechanism of a mousetrap, and hardly that of a poacher's wire, am just in the position of a blind man listening to a discourse on colors, and yet in the end completely worked up into a something derived from *sudo.* Heaven knows I am at this moment as innocent of any knowledge of the mode of operation of 'iodine' as a 'blessed babe,' though taking 'two tablespoonfuls a day' with this tea-spoonful of learning, and only hope for your sake, as well as my own reputation for good manners, that it is in no unseemly one."

THE BULLETIN.

9 DOWRY SQUARE, HOT WELLS, *May* 29, 1845.

Hark! — the doctors come again,
Knock — and enter doctors twain —
Dr. Keeler, Dr. Blane: —
"Well, sir, how
Go matters now?
Please your tongue put out again!"
Meanwhile, t' other side the bed,
Doctor Keeler
Is a feeler
Of my wrist, and shakes his head: —
"Rather low, we're rather low!"
(Deuce is in 't, an' 't were not so!
Arrowroot, and toast-and-water,
Being all my nursing daughter,
By their order, now allows me;
If I hint at more she rows me,
Or at best will let me soak a
Crust of bread in tapioca.)
"Cool and moist though, let me see —
Seventy-two, or seventy-three,
Seventy-four, perhaps, or so;
Rather low, we're rather low!
Now, what sort of night, sir, eh?
Did you take the mixture, pray?
Iodine and anodyne,
Ipecacuanha wine,
And the draught and pills at nine?"

PATIENT (*loquitur*).

"Coughing, doctor, coughing, sneezing,
Wheezing, teasing, most unpleasing,
Till at length I, by degrees, in-
Duced 'Tired nature's sweet restorer,'
Sleep, to cast her mantle o'er her
Poor unfortunate adorer,
And became at last a snorer.
Iodine and anodyne,
Ipecacuanha wine,

Nor the draughts did I decline ;
But those horrid pills at nine !
Those I did not try to swallow,
Doctor, they 'd have beat me hollow.
    I as soon
    Could gulp the moon,
Or the great Nassau balloon,
Or a ball for horse or hound, or
Bullet for an eighteen-pounder."

DOCTOR K.

" Well, sir — well, sir — we 'll arrange it,
If you can't take pills, we 'll change it;
    Take, we 'll say,
    A powder gray,
All the same to us which way ;
    Each will do ;
    But, sir, you
Must perspire whate'er you do,
(Sudorific comes from *sudo !*)
Very odd, sir, how our wills
Interfere with taking pills!
I 've a patient, sir, a lady
Whom I 've told you of already,
    She 'll take potions,
    She 'll take lotions,
She 'll take drugs, and draughts by oceans ;
She 'll take rhubarb, senna, rue ;
She 'll take powders gray and blue,
Tinctures, mixtures, linctures, squills,
But, sir, she will *not* take pills!
Now the throat, sir, how 's the throat ? "

PATIENT.

" Why, I can 't produce a note!
I can't sound one word, I think, whole,
    But they hobble,
    And they gobble,
Just like soapsuds down a sink-hole,
Or I whisper like the breeze,
Softly sighing through the trees ! "

DOCTOR.

" Well, sir — well, sir — never mind, sir,
We 'll put all to rights, you 'll find, sir:
    Make no speeches,
    Get some leeches ;
    You 'll find twenty
    Will be plenty,

Clap them on, and let them lie
On the *pomum Adami;*
Let them well the trachea drain,
    And your larynx,
    And your pharynx —
Please put out your tongue again!
    Now the blister!
    Aye, the blister!
Let your son, or else his sister,
Warm it well, then clap it here, sir,
All across from ear to ear, sir;
    That suffices,
    When it rises,
Snip it, sir, and then your throat on
Rub a little oil of Croton:
Never mind a little pain!
Please put out your tongue again!
Now, sir, I must down your maw stick
This small sponge of lunar caustic,
    Never mind, sir,
    You'll not find, sir,
I, the sponge shall leave behind, sir,
Or my probang make you sick, sir,
I shall draw it back so quick, sir; —
This I call my prime elixir!
    How, sir! choking?
    Pooh! you 're joking —
Bless me! this is quite provoking!
What can make you, sir, so wheezy?
Stay, sir! — gently! — take it easy!
    There, sir, that will do to-day.
    Sir, I think that we may say
    We are better, doctor, eh?
Don't you think so, Doctor Blane?
Please put out your tongue again!
    Iodine and anodyne,
    Ipecacuanha wine,
And since you the pills decline,
Draught and powder gray at nine.
There, sir! there, sir! now good-day,
I 've a lady 'cross the way,
I must see without delay!" [*Exeunt Doctors.*

TO THE GARRICK CLUB.

Ye shepherds give ear to my lay,
  Who have nothing to do about sheep,
While, as Shenstone, the poet, would say, —
  I have nothing to do but to weep.

For here I sit all the day long,
  And must do so, I dare say, all June,
While so far from singing a song,
  I can't even whistle a tune.

For the probang, the blister, and leech,
  So completely my notes have o'erthrown,
When I try the sweet music of speech,
  I start at the sound of my own.

It 's useless attempting to speak,
  For my voice is beyond my control;
If high, it 's an ear-piercing squeak,
  If low, it 's a grunt or a growl!

Can Clifton those beauties assume,
  Which patients have found in her face,
When shut up all day in a room,
  One can't get a peep at the place?

Ye Garrickers, making your sport,
  As ye revel in gossip and grub,
Oh! send some endearing report
  Of how matters go on at the Club.

When I think on the rapid mail train,
  In a moment I seem to be there,
But the sight of N. E. on the vane
  Soon hurries me back to despair.

The Committee, oh, say do they send
  A blessing — or ban — after me?
Mr. Gwilt, does he duly attend
  To his salad and little *roti*?

Davy Roberts, that glorious R. A.,
  Does he still smoke his hookha in peace?
Is Millingen there every day?
  Is Mills a trustee to the lease?

Does the claret suit Thornton? and how
  Does Lord Tenterden like the cigars?
Has any one yet in a row
  Kicked impudent —— down-stairs?

For methought that a sweet little bird
  In my ear of its likelihood sung,
And I loved it the more when I heard
  Such tenderness fall from its tongue.

Oh, say is the story a hoax,
  Or one to be classed among fibs.

That Murphy 's upset with his jokes
  Colonel Sibthorpe, and broken his ribs?

Has Durant got rid of his cough?
  Are Sav'ry's rheumatics quite gone?
And how do the dinners go off,
  And how does the ballot go on?

Does Stanhope's good humor endure?
  What are White and Sir Henry about?
Is Talfourd gone up to his tour,
  Or Arden gone down to his trout?

Does the Cook keep his character still?
  Has the Fishmonger been in disgrace
For, in lieu of a turbot or brill,
  Substituting a horrible plaice?

Does Calcraft, who saved us from blazing,
  Still watch o'er our int'rests at night?
Does Ovey still drive up his chaise in?
  Is Rainy as ever polite?

Charles Kemble, his nose is it aching
  As yet from his fall, or got well?
Has Harley decided on making
  Miss —— a church-going belle?

Is Titmarsh on anything clever,
  Or bent on returning to France?
Is Planché as bustling as ever,
  Avowedly going to Dance?[1]

Say where — but ah me! wherefore ask
  When there 's none to reply or to care,
And Echo herself scorns the task
  Of answering gloomily "Where?"

But Fladgate will write, or George Raymond, —
  His muse will not surely decline
For one moment to turn from the gay *monde*,
  And sympathize sadly with mine.

Perhaps you 'll consider it silly
  To end with a rascally pun,
But as I have thus done my *billet*,
  Oh, send me back one *billet done!*[2]

[1] Messrs. Planché and Dance, the Beaumont and Fletcher of burlesque.

[2] Query? — An allusion to Mr. William — more commonly called Billy — Dunn, Treasurer of Drury Lane Theatre.

WILLIAM HARNESS.

WILLIAM HARNESS.

Lord Byron.

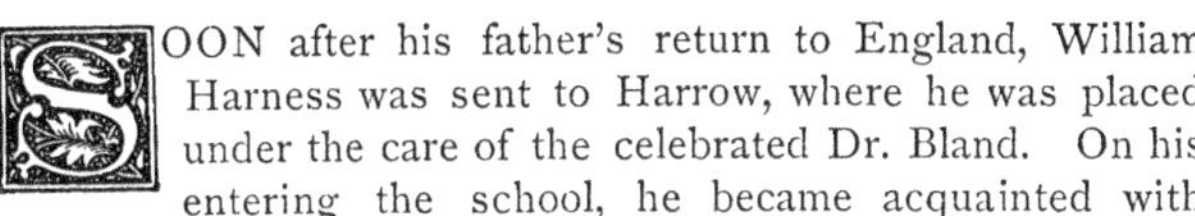

SOON after his father's return to England, William Harness was sent to Harrow, where he was placed under the care of the celebrated Dr. Bland. On his entering the school, he became acquainted with Lord Byron in a manner which was certainly most creditable to the latter. It will be best to give Mr. Harness's own account of this circumstance: —

"My acquaintance with Lord Byron began very early in life, on my first going to school at Harrow. I was then just twelve years old. I was lame from an early accident, and pale and thin in consequence of a severe fever, from which, though perfectly recovered in other respects, I still continued weak. This dilapidated condition of mine — perhaps my lameness more than anything else — seems to have touched Byron's sympathies. He saw me a stranger in a crowd; the very person likely to tempt the oppression of a bully, as I was utterly incapable of resisting it; and, in all the kindness of his generous nature, he took me under his charge. The first words he ever spoke to me, as far as I can recollect them, were, 'If any fellow bullies you, tell me; and I 'll thrash him if I can.' His protection was not long needed; I was soon strong again, and able to maintain my own; but, as long as his help was wanted, he never failed to render it. In this manner our friendship began when we were both boys, he the elder of the two; and it continued, without the slightest interruption, till he left Harrow for Cambridge.

"After this there was a temporary cessation of intercourse. We wrote to each other on his first leaving school; but the letters, as is wont to be the case, became gradually less and less communicative and frequent, till they eventually ceased altogether. The correspondence seemed to have come to a conclusion by common consent, till an unexpected occasion of its renewal occurred on the appearance of his first collection of poems, the 'Hours of Idleness.'[1] This volume contained an early essay of his satirical powers against the head-master of his late school; and very soon after its publication I received a letter from Byron — short, cold, and cutting — reproaching me with a breach of friendship, because I had, as he was informed, traduced his poetry in an English exercise, for the sake of conciliating the favor of Dr. Butler. The only answer I returned to the letter was to send him the rough copy of my theme. It was on the Evils of Idleness. After a world of puerilities and commonplaces, it concluded by warning mankind in general, and the boys of Harrow in particular, if they would avoid the vice and its evils, to cultivate some accomplishment, that each might have an occupation of interest to engage his leisure, and be able to spend his 'Hours of Idleness' as profitably as our late popular school-fellow. The return of post brought me a letter from Byron, begging pardon for the unworthiness he had attributed to me, and acknowledging that he had been misinformed. Thus our correspondence was renewed: and it was never again interrupted till after his separation from Lady Byron and final departure from his country."

[1] The critiques on which called forth *English Bards and Scotch Reviewers*. Byron seems always to have had an unfortunate and irresistible love of satire. Mr. Dyce (in Rogers's *Table Talk*) makes the following reference: "At the house of the Rev. W. Harness, I remember hearing Moore remark that he thought the natural bent of Byron's genius was to satirical and burlesque poetry. On this Mr. Harness observed: 'When Byron was at Harrow, he one day, seeing a young acquaintance at a short distance who was a violent admirer of Bonaparte, roared out: —

'Bold Robert Speer was Bony's bad precursor,
Bob was a bloody dog, but Bonaparte a worser.'

Moore immediately wrote the lines down with the intention of inserting them in his *Life of Byron* which he was then preparing; but they do not appear in it."

Lord Byron thus refers to their early acquaintance at school: "I was then just fourteen. You were almost the first of my Harrow friends — certainly the first in my esteem, if not in date . . . . How well I recollect the present of your first flights! There is another circumstance you do not know; the *first lines* I ever attempted at Harrow were addressed to you."

Such was the commencement of this remarkable friendship. The two boys must have been very dissimilar in disposition as they became such different men. Byron alludes to their difference in conduct when at school; but their characters were not then formed. Moreover, they had several bonds of sympathy; both were fond of poetry and romance; both had warm and affectionate dispositions; both were devoted to study; and both were — lame. When William Harness was little more than an infant, he was playing with and clinging about some curious carving on the posts of an old oaken bedstead which were tied together and lying against the wall. By some unfortunate movement he caused the heavy mass to fall; it came down with crushing weight upon his foot. He never entirely recovered this accident, and he always felt a slight pain in walking; but such was his spirit and perseverance that in after-life he became a good pedestrian.

After the explanation to which Mr. Harness alludes, and Byron's letter of apology, they again became friends. "Our intercourse," writes Mr. Harness, "was renewed and continued from that time till his going abroad. Whatever faults Lord Byron might have had towards others, to myself he was always uniformly affectionate. I have many slights and neglects towards him to reproach myself with; but, on his part, I cannot call to mind, during the whole course of our intimacy, a single instance of caprice or unkindness.

Before leaving England for Greece, in 1809, Byron made a most gratifying request of his friend: —

"I am going abroad, if possible, in the spring, and before I depart I am collecting the pictures of my most intimate schoolfellows. I have already a few, and shall want yours, or my cabinet will be incomplete. I have employed one of the best miniature painters of the day to take them — of course at my own expense, as I never allow my acquaintances to incur the least expenditure to gratify a whim of mine. To mention this may seem indelicate; but when I tell you a friend of ours first refused to sit, under the idea that he was to disburse on the occasion, you will see that it is necessary to state these preliminaries to prevent the recurrence of any similar mistake. I shall see you in time, and will carry you to the limner. It will be a tax on your patience for a week, but pray excuse it, as it is possible the resemblance may be the sole trace I shall be able to preserve of our past friendship and present acquaintance. Just now it seems foolish enough; but in a few years, when some of us are dead, and others are separated by inevitable circumstances, it will be a kind of satisfaction to retain, in these images of the living, the idea of our former selves, and to contemplate, in the resemblance of the dead, all that remains of judgment, feeling, and a host of passions.

"But all this will be dull enough for you, and so good-night; and to end my chapter, or rather my homily,

"Believe me,
"My dear Harness,
"Yours most affectionately,
"BYRON."

After Byron's return from Greece, we find the following proof of his faithful remembrance in one of his letters to his friend: "I have not changed in all my ramblings: Harrow, and of course yourself, never left me, and the

'Dulces reminiscitur Argos'

attended me to the very spot to which that sentence alludes in the mind of the fallen Argive. Our intimacy commenced before we began to date at all, and it rests with you to continue it till the hour which must number it and me with the things that were."

Shortly before Mr. Harness took his degree, he received an invitation to Newstead; and his stay there must have been one of unusual interest and pleasure; this is the account which he gives of his visit.

"When Byron returned, with the MS. of the first two cantos of 'Childe Harold' in his portmanteau, I paid him a visit at Newstead. It was winter — dark, dreary weather — the snow upon the ground; and a straggling, gloomy, depressing, partially-inhabited place the Abbey was. Those rooms, however, which had been fitted up for residence were so comfortably appointed, glowing with crimson hangings, and cheerful with capacious fires, that one soon lost the melancholy feeling of being domiciled in the wing of an extensive ruin. Many tales are related or fabled of the orgies which, in the Poet's early youth, had made clamorous these ancient halls of the Byrons. I can only say that nothing in the shape of riot or excess occurred when I was there. The only other visitor was Dr. Hodgson, the translator of Juvenal,[1] and nothing could be more quiet and regular than the course of our days. Byron was retouching, as the sheets passed through the press, the stanzas of 'Childe Harold.' Hogdson was at work in getting out the ensuing number of the 'Monthly Review,' of which he was principal editor. I was reading for my degree. When we met, our general talk was of poets and poetry — of who could or who could not write; but it occasionally rose into very serious discussions on religion. Byron, from his early education in Scotland, had been taught to identify the principles of Christianity with the extreme dogmas of Calvinism. His mind had thus imbibed a most miserable prejudice, which appeared to be the only obstacle to his hearty acceptance of the Gospel. Of this error we were most anxious to disabuse him. The chief weight of the argument rested with Hodgson, who was older, a good deal, than myself. I cannot even now — at a distance of more than fifty years — recall those conversations without a deep feeling of admiration for the judicious zeal and affectionate earnestness (often speaking with tears in his eyes) which Dr. Hodgson evinced in his advocacy of the truth. The only difference, except perhaps in the subjects talked about,

[1] Afterwards Provost of Eton.

between our life at Newstead Abbey and that of the quiet country families around us, was the hours we kept. It was, as I have said, winter, and the days were cold; and, as nothing tempted us to rise early, we got up late. This flung the routine of the day rather backward, and we did not go early to bed. My visit to Newstead lasted about three weeks, when I returned to Cambridge to take my degree."

Mr. Harness's friendly intercourse with Lord Byron was not interrupted, though carried on under some disadvantages. The poet was prevented from dedicating "Childe Harold" to him, "for fear it should injure him in his profession." And it is evident that in some of his letters Mr. Harness reproved him for his thoughtlessness and dissipation.

"You censure my life, Harness," Byron writes in reply. "When I compare myself with these men, my elders and my betters, I really begin to conceive myself a monument of prudence — a walking statue — without feeling or failing; and yet the world in general hath given me a proud preëminence over them in profligacy!"

"From this time," writes Mr. Harness, "our paths lay much asunder. Byron returned to London. His poem was published. The success was instantaneous; and he 'awoke one morning and found himself famous.' I was in orders, and living an almost solitary life in a country curacy; but we kept up a rather rapid interchange of letters. He sent me his poems as they now appeared in rather quick succession; and during my few weeks' holidays in London we saw one another very often of a morning at each other's rooms, and not unfrequently again in society of an evening. So far, and for these few years, all that I saw or heard of his career was bright and prosperous: kindness and poetry at home, smiles and adulation abroad. But then came his marriage; and then the rupture with his wife; and then his final departure from England. He became a victim of that revolution of popular feeling which is ever incident to the spoilt children of society, when envy and malice obtain a temporary ascendency, and succeed in knocking down and trampling any idol of the day beneath their feet, who may be wanting in the moral courage required to face and out-brave them.

"Such was not the spirit that animated Byron. He could not bear to look on the altered countenances of his acquaintances. To his susceptible temperament and generous feelings, the reproach of having ill-used a woman must have been poignant in the extreme. It was repulsive to his chivalrous character as a gentleman; it belied all he had written of the devoted fervor of his attachments; and rather than meet the frowns and sneers which awaited him in the world, as many a less sensitive man might have done, he turned his back on them and fled. He would have drawn himself up, and crossed his arms and curled his lip, and looked disdainfully on any amount of clamorous hostility; but he stole away from the ignominy of being silently cut. His whole course of conduct, at this crisis of his life, was an inconsiderate mistake. He should have remained to learn what the accusations against him really were; to expose the exaggerations, if not the falsehoods, of the grounds they rested on; or, at all events, to have quietly abided the time when the London world should have become wearied of repeating its vapid scandals, and returned to its senses respecting him. That change of feeling did come — and not long after his departure from England — but he was at a distance, and could not be persuaded to return to take advantage of it.

"Of the matrimonial quarrel I personally know nothing; nor with the exception of Dr. Lushington, do I believe that there is anybody living who has any certain knowledge about the matter. The marriage was never one of reasonable promise. The bridegroom and the bride were ill-assorted. They were two only children, and two *spoilt* children. I was acquainted with Lady Byron as Miss Milbanke. The parties of Lady Milbanke, her mother, were frequent and agreeable, and composed of that mixture of fashion, literature, science, and art, than which there is no better society. The daughter was not without a certain amount of prettiness or cleverness; but her manner was stiff and formal, and gave one the idea of her being self-willed and self-opinionated. She was almost the only young, pretty, well-dressed girl we ever saw who carried no cheerfulness along with her. I seem to see her now, moving slowly along her mother's drawing-rooms, talking to scientific men and literary women, without a tone of emotion in her voice or the faintest glimpse of a smile upon her countenance. A lady who had been on intimate terms with her from their mutual childhood once said to me, 'If Lady Byron has a heart, it is deeper seated and harder to get at than anybody else's heart whom I have ever known.' And though several of my friends whose regard it was no slight honor to have gained — as Mrs. Siddons, Joanna Baillie, Maria Edgeworth, and others of less account, — were never heard to speak of Lady Byron except in terms of admiration and attachment, it is certain that the impression which she produced on the majority of her acquaintance was unfavorable: they looked upon her as a reserved and frigid sort of being whom one would rather cross the room to avoid than be brought into conversation with unnecessarily. Such a person, whatever quality might have at first attracted him — (could it have been her coldness?) — was not likely to acquire or retain any very powerful hold upon Byron. At the beginning of their married life, when first they returned to London society together, one seldom saw two young persons who appeared to be more devoted to one another than they were. At parties he would be seen hanging over the back of her chair, scarcely talking to anybody else, eagerly introducing his friends to her, and, if they did not go away together, himself handing her to her carriage. This outward show of tenderness, so far as my memory serves me, was observed and admired as exemplary, till after the birth of their daughter. From that time the world began to drop its voice into a tone of compassion when speaking of Lady Byron, and to whisper tales of the misery she was suffering — poor thing — on account of the unkindness of her husband.

"The first instances of his ill-usage which were heard, were so insignificant as to be beneath recording. 'The poor lady had never had a comfortable meal since their marriage.' 'Her husband had no fixed hour for breakfast, and was always too late for dinner.' 'At his express desire, she had invited two elderly ladies[1] to meet them in her opera-box. Nothing could be more courteous than his manner to them, while they remained; but no sooner had they gone than he began to annoy his wife by venting his ill-humor, in a strain of bitterest satire, against the dress and manners of her friends.' There were some relations of Lady Byron whom, after repeated refusals, he had reluctantly consented to dine with. When the day arrived he insisted on her going alone, alleging his being unwell as an excuse for his absence. It was summer time. Forty years ago people not only dined earlier than they do now, but by daylight; and after the assembled party were seated at table, he amused himself by driving backwards and forwards opposite the dining-room windows.[2]

"There was a multitude of such nonsensical stories as these, which one began to hear soon after Ada's birth; and I believe I have told the worst of them. No doubt, as the things occurred, they must have been vexatious enough, but they do not amount to grievous wrongs. They were faults of temper, not moral delinquencies; a thousand of them would not constitute an injury. Nor does one know to what extent they may have been provoked. They would, in all probability, have ceased, had they been gently borne with — and perhaps were only repeated because the culprit was amused by witnessing their effects. At all events they were no more than a sensible woman, who had either a proper feeling for her husband's reputation, or a due consideration of her own position, would have readily endured; and a really good wife would never have allowed herself to talk about them. And yet it was by Lady Byron's friends, and as coming immediately from her, that I used to hear them. The complaints, at first so trifling, gradually acquired a more serious character. 'Poor

1 Mrs. Joanna Baillie and her sister.

2 The above gossip all came to me from different friends of Lady Byron.

Lady Byron was afraid of her life.' 'Her husband slept with loaded pistols by his bedside, and a dagger under his pillow.' Then there came rumors of cruelty — no one knew of what kind, or how severe. Nothing was definitely stated. But it was on all hands allowed to be 'very bad — very bad indeed.' And as there was nothing to be known, everybody imagined what they pleased.

"But whatever Lord Byron's treatment of his wife may have been, it could not have been all evil. Any injuries she suffered must have occurred during moody and angry fits of temper. They could not have been habitual or frequent. His conduct was not of such a description as to have utterly extinguished whatever love she might have felt at her marriage, or to have left any sense of terror or aversion behind it. This is evident from facts. Years after they had met for the last time, Lady Byron went with Mrs. Jameson, from whom I repeat the circumstance, to see Thorwaldsen's statue of her husband, which was at Sir Richard Westmacott's studio. After looking at it in silence for a few moments, the tears came into her eyes, and she said to her companion, 'it is very beautiful, but not so beautiful as my *dear* Byron.' However interrupted by changes of caprice or irritability, the general course of her husband's conduct must have been gentle and tender, or it never would, after so long a cessation of intercourse, have left such kindly impressions behind it. I have, indeed, reason to believe that these feelings of affectionate remembrance lingered in the heart of Lady Byron to the last. Not a fortnight before her death, I dined in company with an old lady who was at the time on a visit to her. On this lady's returning home, and mentioning whom she had met, Lady Byron evinced great curiosity to learn what subjects we had talked about, and what I had heard of them, 'because I had been such a friend of her husband's.' This instance of fond remembrance, after an interval of more than forty years, in a woman of no very sensitive nature — a woman of more intellect than feeling — conveys to my mind no slight argument in defense of Byron's conduct as a husband. His wife, though unrelenting, manifestly regretted his loss. May not some touch of remorse for the exile to which she had dismissed him — for the fame over which she had cast a cloud — for the energies which she had diverted from their course of useful action in the Senate,[1] to be wasted in no honorable idleness abroad — and for the so early death to which her unwife-like conduct doomed him, have mingled its bitterness with the pain of that regret?

"But what do I know of Byron? The ill I will speak of presently. Personally, I know nothing but good of him. Of what he became in his foreign banishment, when removed from all his natural ties and hereditary duties, I, personally, am ignorant. In all probability he deteriorated; he would have been more than human if he had not. But when I was in the habit of familiarly seeing him, he was kindness itself. At a time when Coleridge was in great embarrassment, Rogers, when calling on Byron, chanced to mention it. He immediately went to his writing-desk, and brought back a check for a hundred pounds, and insisted on its being forwarded to Coleridge. 'I did not like taking it,' said Rogers, who told me the story, 'for I knew that he was in want of it himself.' His servants he treated with a gentle consideration for their feelings which I have seldom witnessed in any other, and they were devoted to him. At Newstead there was an old man who had been butler to his mother, and I have seen Byron, as the old man waited behind his chair at dinner, pour out a glass of wine and pass it to him when he thought we were too much engaged in conversation to observe what he was doing. The transaction was a thing of custom; and both parties seemed to flatter themselves that it was clandestinely effected. A hideous old woman, who had been brought in to nurse him when he was unwell at one of his lodgings, and whom few would have cared to retain about them longer than her services were required, was carried with him, in improved attire, to his chambers in the Albany, and was seen, after his marriage, gorgeous in black silk at his house in Piccadilly. She

[1] He had made some good speeches in the House.

had done him a service, and he could not forget it. Of his attachment to his friends, no one can read Moore's life and entertain a doubt. He required a great deal from them — not more, perhaps, than he, from the abundance of his love, freely and fully gave — but more than they had to return. The ardor of his nature must have been in a normal state of disappointment. He imagined higher qualities in them than they possessed, and must very often have found his expectations sadly balked by the dullness of talk, the perversity of taste, or the want of enthusiasm, which he encountered on a better or rather longer acquaintance. But, notwithstanding, I have never yet heard anybody complain that Byron had once appeared to entertain a regard for him, and had afterwards capriciously cast him off.

"Now, after these good and great qualities, I revert to the evil of Byron's character and conduct. And here, if he were bad, were there no extenuations, derived from the peculiarities of his position and education, to be pleaded for him? Was he not better, instead of worse, than most young men have proved who were similarly circumstanced? He had virtually never known a father's love, or a mother's tenderness. He was from early childhood wholly cut off from those motives to virtue, and those restraints from vice, which, amid a band of brothers and sisters, grow up around us with the family affections. Home is the only school in which right principles and generous feelings find a genial soil and attain a natural growth. Without a home the boy sees nothing, knows nothing considers nothing, and feels for nothing but himself; and a home Byron never had. The domestic charities and their ameliorating influences were only known to him by name. He was from boyhood his own master; and would it have been strange, if, with strong passions, an untutored will, fervent imagination, and no one with authority to control him, he was sometimes led astray? But during the time he was in London society, what young men were there, with the same liberty to range at will as he, who were less absorbed by its dissipations? Who among them abstracted so much time from the fascinations of the world as he, to study as he studied, and to write as he wrote? I have little doubt, though I don't know it, that in the season of his unparalleled success he was not likely to have been more rigid in his conduct than his companions were in their principles. But it is at least extraordinary that, while thus courted and admired, if his life was as licentious as some have represented, the only scandal which disturbed the decorum of society, and with which Byron's name is connected, did not originate in any action of his, but in the insane and unrequited passion of a woman.

"Byron had one preëminent fault — a fault which must be considered as deeply criminal by every one who does not, as I do, believe it to have resulted from monomania. He had a morbid love of a bad reputation. There was hardly an offense of which he would not, with perfect indifference, accuse himself. An old school-fellow, who met him on the Continent, told me that he would continually write paragraphs against himself in the foreign journals, and delight in their republication by the English newspapers as in the success of a practical joke. When anybody has related anything discreditable of Byron, assuring me that it must be true, for he had heard it from himself, I have always felt that he could not have spoken with authority, and that, in all probability, the tale was a pure invention. If I could remember, and were willing to repeat, the various misdoings which I have from time to time heard him attribute to himself, I could fill a volume. But I never believed them. I very soon became aware of this strange idiosyncrasy. It puzzled me to account for it; but there it was — a sort of diseased and distorted vanity. The same eccentric spirit would induce him to report things which were false with regard to his family, which anybody else would have concealed, though true. He told me more than once that his father was insane and killed himself. I shall never forget the manner in which he first told me this. While washing his hands, and singing a gay Neapolitan air, he stopped, looked round at me, and said, 'There always was a madness in the family.' Then after continuing his washing and his song, as if speaking of a matter of the slightest indifference, 'My father cut his throat.' The contrast between the tenor of the subject and the levity of the expression, was fearfully painful: it was like a stanza of 'Don Juan.' In this instance, I had no doubt that the fact was as he related it, but in speaking of it only a few years since to an old lady [1] in whom I had perfect confidence, she assured me that it was not so; that Mr. Byron, who was her cousin, had been extremely wild, but was quite sane and had died quietly in his bed. What Byron's reasons could have been for thus calumniating, not only himself, but the blood that was flowing in his veins, who can divine? But, for some reason or other, it seemed to be his determined purpose to keep himself unknown to the great body of his fellow-creatures — to present himself to their view in moral masquerade, and to identify himself in their imaginations with Childe Harold and the Corsair, between which characters and his own — as God and education had made it — the most microscopic inspection would fail to discern a single point of resemblance.

"Except this love of an ill-name — this tendency to malign himself — this hypocrisy reversed, I have no personal knowledge whatever of any evil act or evil disposition of Lord Byron's. I once said this to a gentleman [2] who was well acquainted with Lord Byron's London life. He expressed himself astonished at what I said. 'Well,' I replied, 'do you know any harm of him but what he told you himself?' 'Oh, yes, a hundred things!' 'I don't want you to tell me a hundred things, I shall be content with one.' Here the conversation was interrupted. We were at dinner — there was a large party, and the subject was again renewed at table. But afterwards in the drawing-room, Mr. Drury came up to me and said, 'I have been thinking of what you were saying at dinner. I do *not* know any harm of Byron but what he has told me of himself.'"

[1] Mrs. Villiers, Lord Clarendon's mother.
[2] The Rev. Henry Drury.

Mr. Harness's testimony to the good points in Byron s character is especially valuable as it comes from one who was not in the least blinded by the brilliancy of his genius. So delicately sensitive, indeed, was Mr. Harness's nature, that he always, as he confessed, felt Byron's poetry to be a little too "strong" for him. He attributed a large part of Byron's reckless conduct in after-life to the misfortune of his ill-assorted marriage. "It was brought about," he observed, "by well-meaning friends, who knew that Byron wanted money, and thought they were consulting his best interests." He formed the alliance, as is often the case, because other people liked it; but they did not take into consideration how many elements are required to constitute the happiness of sentient human beings. Lady Byron was a person entirely deficient in tact and reflection, and made no allowances for the usual eccentricities of genius. In some periods of our history she might have aspired to a real crown of martyrdom, for she was a Puritan in creed, and an unflinching advocate of her own views. Miss Mitford justly asks, "Why did she marry Byron? His character was well known, and he was not a deceiver!" Possibly she hoped to make an illustrious convert of him, or thought that she might at once share his celebrity and restrain his follies. If so, she greatly overrated her influence, and ignored the perversity of human nature. Byron had a childish weakness for dramatic effect and excitement, and it was his habit to amuse himself at times by indulging in fantastical rhapsodies, full of tragic extravagance. Harness knew these occasions, and merely lapsed into silence, and when the poet found that no one was horrified or delighted, he very soon came to the end of his performance. But Lady Byron was too conscientious, or too severe, to allow the fire thus to die out. She took seriously every word he utteerd, weighed it in her precise balance, and could not avoid expressing her condemnation of his principles and her abhorrence of his language. This fanned the flame, increased his irritation, or added zest to his amusement. Whatever crime she accused him of he was not only ready to admit, but even to trump by the confession of some greater enormity. Few of us have sufficient taste and delicacy for the office of a censor, or sufficient humility to profit by rebuke; but in the present case the difficulties were unusually great. "There can be no doubt," observed Mr. Harness, "that Byron was a little 'maddish.'" He was afflicted with a more than usual share of that eccentricity which so often turns aside the keen edge of genius; but he was amiable, and might have been led, though he would not be driven.

Mr. Harness had no communication with Byron during the latter years of his life. He nevertheless always continued to take a kindly view of the character of his old school-fellow and college friend, and endeavored to make every allowance for his conduct; but at the same time we must not suppose that he permitted any personal feeling to interfere with his sense of right, or to prevent his denouncing the principles advocated in his friend's later writings. We have already noticed his disapproval of Byron's conduct, and as it became more marked, he spoke in stronger language. Their intimacy then ceased, and Byron recklessly abandoned himself to those dissipations which ended in his early death. In 1822, Mr. Harness was appointed Boyle Lecturer by the University of Cambridge; and his duty was "to be ready to satisfy such real scruples as any may have concerning matters of religion, and to answer such new objections and difficulties as may be started." Lord Byron's works were then at the height of their popularity; and as some of them seemed to be exercising a very pernicious influence, Mr. Harness selected for special consideration the poem [1] in which an attempt was made to represent God as responsible for the origin of Sin.

"By a fiction of no ordinary power," he observes, "the rebellious son of a rebellious father is disclosed to the imagination as upon the borders of Paradise, and within the shadowy regions of the dead, holding personal communion with the spiritual enemy of man. Each is represented as advocating the cause of his impiety to the partial judgment of his

[1] *Cain.*

companion in iniquity. Miserable they are ; but still they are arrogant and stern, remorseless and unsubdued by misery. For them adversity has no sweet or hallowed uses. While they make mutual confession of the wretchedness their sin has caused them, they appear to glory in it, as if ennobled by its magnitude and exalted by its presumption. To their licentious apprehensions all excellence appears corrupted and reversed. They call good evil, and evil they call good. Pride is virtue, and rebellion duty. Lucifer is the friend, and Jehovah is the enemy of man ; and while they reciprocate the arguments of a bewildering sophistry, the benevolence of the Deity is arraigned, as if He rejoiced in the affliction of his creatures, first conferred an efficacy on the temptation, and then delighted to exact the penalties of transgression."

Byron had attempted to justify himself by asserting that he had expressed no sentiments worse than those which were to be found in Milton ; but even were this the case (Mr. Harness observed), there would be a peculiar danger in reproducing them in a specious form, and in times when faith was already obscured : "The danger is heightened by the peculiar character of the times. Had the allegations of these malignant spirits been preferred in an age of more general and fervent piety, there had been little peril in their publication. They had only awakened in the breast of the reader a more entire abhorrence of the beings by whom they were entertained and uttered. It was thus in the days of Milton. Every taunt of Satan was then opposed by the popular spirit of devotion, and armed against his cause the deepest and the holiest affections of the heart. But the spirit of those times has past. Zeal has yielded to indifference, and faith to skepticism. We have become so impatient of the restraint of Christianity, and so indulgent to every argument that endows our inclinations with an apology for sin, that few and transient are the feelings of religious gratitude which are offended by the impieties of Cain or Lucifer, and their appeal against the dispensations of Almighty Providence is calmly heard and favorably deliberated ; for, in the skillful extenuation of *their* guilt, we appear to listen to the arguments that soothe us with the justification of our own. There is also a danger in the manner with which these antiquated cavils are revived and recommended. United with the dramatic interest and the seductions of poetry, they obtain a wider circulation. They gain an introduction to the studies of the young; they pass into the hands of that wide class of readers, who only find in literature another variety of dissipation, and who, after having eagerly received the contagion of demoralizing doubts, would indolently cast aside the cold metaphysical essay that conveyed their refutation."

Byron's friendship for Mr. Harness, who even during their intimacy did not scruple to reprove and oppose his principles, was perhaps the most pleasing episode in his private career; and his accusers should know that, during the whole of their correspondence, he never penned a single line to his friend which might not have been addressed to the most delicate woman.

Mary Russell Mitford.

One of William Harness's earliest friends — born at Alresford, in the same woodland district — was Mary Russell Mitford. Their families had long been connected: Dr. Harness gave away Miss Russell, who became Miss Mitford's mother; and it was here that the future authoress passed those happy days — and her earliest years were her happiest — to which she reverted with such fond remembrance in after-life. Here, in the spacious library, lined with her grandfather Russell's books, or in the old-fashioned garden, among the stocks and hollyhocks, she and little William would chase away the summer hours, until the time when the carriage arrived, which was to carry her playmate back to Wickham. A picture taken when she was about six years old enables us to form some idea of her at this time. It represents her with her hair cut short across her forhead, and flowing down at the back in long glossy ringlets, while in her face there is a sedateness and gravity beyond her years, such as we might expect to find in a young lady devoted to study, and celebrated for early feats of memory. William Harness, on the other hand — by two years the younger — was full of joyous and exuberant spirits, with a bright, beaming countenance, a rosy complexion, and a profusion of dark hair which curled and clustered on his open brow.

The following letter from school is interesting from its date, and as showing the early intimacy between William Harness and Miss Mitford : —

"HARROW, 31*st July*, 1808.

"MY DEAR DOCTOR MITFORD, —

"I was impudent enough to invite myself to your house, and you were kind enough to say that I should be welcome ; it was afterwards settled I should come to the races. I am too selfish to let such an opportunity slip, and fully intend to bore you for some time at Grasely. I hope Mrs. Mitford will not turn me out. Will you then, my dear sir, let me know when the races are, and when I shall be least troublesome to you ; for as soon as you appoint I shall come down and harass Miss Mitford to death ! My father and grandmother send their love and compliments to Mrs. and Miss Mitford and yourself. I shall keep all my civil things till we meet.

"Believe me,

"Yours sincerely,

"W. HARNESS."

Mr. Harness observed on this occasion that the Mitfords' mode of living was greatly altered. Dr. Mitford's extravagance had almost consumed the golden gift which the fairies had showered upon his little daughter. A change was visible in the household ; the magnificent butler had disappeared ; and the young Harrow boy by no means admired the shabby equipage in which they were to exhibit themselves on the race-course.

During Mr. Harness's residence at Hampstead, in what may be termed the holiday period of his life, he occasionally indulged his fancy in the composition of short poems, such as were then in fashion, and were considered to add grace and sentiment to the routine of correspondence. In his intercourse with his friends he also found another way of contributing to the entertainment and sociability of those around him. Many of his young lady acquaintances were proficient in acting charades, and found much pleasure in such exercises of ingenuity. As he was known to be a man of taste, he was soon called upon to use his skill for their benefit, and he accordingly planned a somewhat more elaborate performance than they had hitherto tried, by the introduction of a little dramatic scene and dialogue to represent each word. The attempt was successful, and Mr. Harness's charades met with considerable approbation.

Miss Mitford was one of those who were most pleased with his idea, and as she was then writing for the magazines, requested permission to publish some of his charades in "Blackwood." This was granted; for, although Mr. Harness wished to keep them for the use of his own friends, he was unwilling to lose any opportunity of affording pecuniary assistance to his early companion. They accordingly appeared in the year 1826; Miss Mitford adopting Mr. Harness's plans, and developing them with her own facility of expression. "I inclose my charades," she writes to him, "which, in all but their faults, might more properly be called *yours.*" In a letter written at this time, Mr. Harness thus alludes to them, and gives some interesting details about his interview with Deville, the phrenologist: —

"MY DEAR MISS MITFORD, —

"Send me the charades, and I will forward them to 'Blackwood.' I have not a doubt of their doing your opera at Covent Garden, if Charles find it likely to succeed — which, from the nature of the story, must, I should think, be the case. I really think Deville was right about my head; and right, in fact, even when he appeared to be wrong in his description. For instance, he said that I should be offended by *glaring colors*, which is not the case. I have the *eyes of colors*, but am extremely annoyed by colors that don't harmonize, though I am rather fond of strong colors. I forget whether, in my hurry of writing to you, I told you of his extraordinary exposition of the character of my friend Newman's little boy. The child went with me; and Deville having told me the propensities of the child's character, said, 'There is one thing very remarkable in this boy's head; I never saw any English child with the perceptive organs so strongly marked. In general, the English have strong reflection, and the foreigners strong perception; but in this boy there is an exact and beautiful equality subsisting between the two.' His mother is, as you know, a Portuguese. This was an admirable hit.

"By the bye, would it not be better to reserve your charades for your novel? They would take as *new*, and, at the present time, novelty of incident is the very thing that novels want.

"With kindest remembrances to Dr. and Mrs. Mitford.

"Best love,

"Yours ever most faithfully,

WILLIAM HARNESS."

One of these charades formed a complete little drama of the time of the Commonwealth. The word was "Matchlock," and the *personæ* a Puritan's daughter, a Cavalier, and the irritable old Puritan himself. The last of the series published was composed entirely by Miss Mitford. It was on "Blackwood," and gave an exquisite specimen of the authoress's poetic talent, and of her power in describing sylvan scenery.

Miss Mitford in the following letter speaks of her friend's production with her characteristic enthusiasm: —

"THE WIFE OF ANTWERP."

"THREE MILE CROSS, *November 4th*, 1839.

"MY DEAR FRIEND, —

"Let me thank you most sincerely and heartily for the thrice beautiful play. I have read it with equal pride and pleasure — a triumphant pleasure in such an evidence of the sweet and gentle power of my oldest, and, I might almost say, my kindest friend. It breathes the spirit of the old dramatists from first to last, especially of Heywood, whose 'Woman killed with Kindness' is forcibly recalled; but by that sort of resemblance which springs from a congeniality of talent, and makes one say, 'Heywood might have written this, although there is much more of the letter of poetry, more finished and beautiful passages, than can be found in any single play of the 'Prose Shakespeare.' I do not know when I have read a drama which bore such evidence of the author's mind, so good, so pure, so indulgent, so gentlemanly. Lady Dacre told me that it was full of beauty; but I did not expect so much poetry, and I feel sincerely grateful to Mr. Dyce (whom I always liked very heartily on his own account) for rescuing this charming play from the flames. When I said that I had not for a long time seen a drama so full of the author, I fibbed unconsciously, for it is into plays that authors do put their very selves. The character of Kessel is very beautiful and original, and the high-minded Albert and poor, poor Margaret have made me cry more than I can tell. At all events, I rejoice to have it printed. It fixes you in the same high position poetically that you have always occupied socially and professionally. It is a thing for your friends to be proud of, in every sense of the word. If the tableaux go on, I shall come to you for a dramatic scene. Has that book been sent yet? You will be very much pleased with Miss Barrett's ballad, in spite of a little want of clearness, and with Mr. Proctor's spirited poem. In short, it is the only book bearing my name of which I was ever proud; but if we go on I shall be still prouder next year to have you added to my list of poets and friends. What a thing it is, by mere self-postponement and sympathy in the claims of others, to have hidden such a gift! It is just like what your sister does, who — cleverer and better than half her acquaintances — always speaks of herself as nobody.

"God bless you! A thousand thanks for all your kindness. Ever most faithfully yours,

"M. R. MITFORD."

Mr. Harness and Miss Mitford were bound together not only by early associations, but by a mutual geniality of temperament, and a sympathy in each other's tastes and pursuits. Both were ardent lovers of literature, especially of the more social branches of it, and both fully appreciated the powerful influence obtained by the Drama. Miss Mitford had an especial predilection for this kind of composition. "If I have any talent," she writes, "it is for the Drama;" and we can imagine the relief with which she must have flown from the cold cynicism of her father to the kindly encouragement of her early friend, who bade her continue in the path she loved. Nor can we assert that his support was ill-judged, when we read the many noble and touching passages which adorn "Rienzi," and recollect the success it achieved — a success which would have distinguished its author had she never etched a single episode of village life. There may perhaps have been also a kinder motive for Mr. Harness's encouragement; for the theatre then offered better hopes of pecuniary remuneration than any other field of literature.

The affectionate regard which Miss Mitford felt towards her early friend is well shown by the following gratifying offer: —

THREE MILE CROSS, *April* 4, 1837.

"MY DEAR WILLIAM, —

"I have only one moment in which to offer a petition to you. I have a little trumpery volume called 'Country Stories,' about to be published by Saunders and Otley. Will you permit me to give these Tales some little value in my own eyes by inscribing them (of course in a few true and simple words) to you, my old and most kind friend? I would not dedicate a play to you, for fear of causing you injury in your profession; but I do not think that this slight testimony of a very sincere affection could do you harm in that way; for even those who do not allow novels in their house, sanction my little books. Ever affectionately yours,

"M. R. MITFORD."

The dedication was as follows: —

"To
THE REV. WILLIAM HARNESS,
Whose old hereditary friendship
Has been the pride and pleasure
Of her happiest hours,
Her consolation in the sorrows,
and
Her support in the difficulties of life,
This little volume
Is most respectfully and affectionately
Inscribed by
THE AUTHOR."

But although there was such a congeniality in literary taste between Mr. Harness and Miss Mitford, they were at issue on a more important subject. Miss Mitford's views on religion were decidedly "broad," although they would have appeared narrow in comparison with some of the present day. Mr. Harness, as we have seen, was a man of sound doctrine, and faithfully attached to the Church of England, and his friend's views caused some dissatisfaction to his orthodox mind. He desired to bring her round to more correct opinions, and apparently wrote to her on the subject; for we find her, in a letter, tenderly requesting him not to press arguments upon her which could not alter her convictions, and deprecating the discussion of anything which might create a distance between two such early friends.

If there was any person beyond the pale of Mr. Harness's Christian forbearance, that individual was Dr. Mitford. The reckless manner in which he squandered the family property, and his selfishness even to the last, when he became entirely dependent on his daughter's incessant toil, often continued by night as well as by day, would have estranged the affections of any but one

"Whose kind heart refused to discover
The faults which so many could find."

The history of Dr. Mitford's extravagance and folly have been written by Mr. Harness himself. Like other men of his stamp, the doctor seems to have been in turn the impostor and the dupe. Mr. Harness disliked not only his morals, but also his manners, his self-sufficiency and loud talk, and could scarcely understand the amount of filial infatuation which led Miss Mitford to speak of his "modesty" and "excellence."

Notwithstanding Miss Mitford's slavery at the pen, the doctor died considerably in debt; and although her poverty was great, she retained such a filial regard for his memory, that she boldly announces: "Everybody shall be paid, if I sell the gown off my back, or pledge my little pension." In these difficulties a suggestion was made, by those who knew her wide popularity, that a subscription should be set on foot to raise a sum to meet these liabilities. The response to the appeal thus made by Mr. Harness and other friends was more liberal than could have been expected. The following is a letter from Mrs. Opie on this subject: —

"LADY'S LANE, *2d Month, 24th,* 1843.

"MY DEAR FRIEND, —

"I thought I should see thy name on poor dear Miss Mitford's committee. What a sad tale she has to tell! How she has been tried! And what a daughter she has been to a most unworthy father! I know no one like her in self-sacrifice and patient endurance. Surely, under such circumstances, the creditors will take less than their due, and wait for the rest till she can pay it. So few persons like to subscribe to pay debts, that this debt of £800 or £900 will hang, I fear, like a millstone over the subscription. But I forget — this debt paid, she may, perhaps, by the labors of her pen, support herself without help. And I do hope the Queen will double her pension.

"In the meanwhile, I am begging for her. I intend to raise £20, and to get more if I can. I shall ask a sovereign from eighteen persons — I have in hand seven already — and then send the £20 up to some one, or pay it into Gurney's bank, to be remitted to her bankers. In such a case, and in many cases, begging is a Christian duty. She has written to me and sent me the papers to distribute.

"I think she would have gained more by an appeal to the public in the papers, with a list of subscribers ; but she and you and her agents know best what to do. I shall be very sorry if I do not raise £20 or more. How I wish it were as easy for me to serve thy nephew!

"Believe me,

"Much thine,

"AMELIA OPIE."

The sum collected was not only sufficient to cover all the outstanding liabilities, but also to add something to the authoress's narrow income.

During the last two years of her life Miss Mitford's health rapidly declined. Mr. Harness frequently visited her at this time ; and in a letter to a friend shortly before her death she speaks with her old enthusiasm of her early friend : —

"By the way, this most dear friend of mine has been here for ten days — came for one — found himself a lodging, and has stayed ever since, and will stay ten days longer. Did you ever hear of him? . . . . He has every grace and accomplishment — person (even at sixty odd), voice, manner, talent, literature, and, more than all, the sweetest of natures. His father gave away my mother. We were close friends in childhood, and have remained such ever since. And now he leaves the Deep Dene, with all its beauty of scenery and society, to come to me, a poor sick old woman, just because I am sick, and old, and poor ; and because we have loved each other like brother and sister all our lives. How I wish you were here to hear him read Shakespeare, and to listen to conversation that leaves his reading far behind!"

In a note written to himself about this time, and in contemplation of her own approaching dissolution, she observes : —

"You are left, dear friend, to be the one green oak of the forest, after the meaner trees have fallen around you. May God long preserve you to the many still left to grow up under your shade!"

One of the last letters written by Miss Mitford to Mr. Harness, and marked "immediate," contained directions with regard to the publication of her life and correspondence. With characteristic thoughtfulness, she avoids preferring any formal request that might inconvenience her friend or involve him in a laborious and unprofitable undertaking. She does not even express any opinion as to the value of her literary remains, but rather implies a doubt whether any one would think them worth publishing. Finally, however, she gives a list of persons in possession of her correspondence, and observes that no one knew the course of her life better than himself. From the tenor of this letter it is evident that she wished Mr. Harness to write some biographical notice of her; and some conversations which had passed between them confirmed him in this opinion.

Soon after his friend's death, Mr. Harness commenced the task of looking through her letters, but he found the work much more arduous than he had anticipated. Although her habits were in every respect frugal, her favorite economy seemed to be in paper. Her letters were scribbled on innumerable small scraps — sometimes on printed circulars — sometimes across engravings — and half a dozen of these would form one epistle, and had in course of time become confused and interchanged in their envelopes. When we add to this that towards the end of her life Miss Mitford's handwriting became almost microscopic, it can easily be understood that the arrangement of these sibylline leaves was no short or easy undertaking. Mr. Harness worked hard at it, out of affection for his lost friend, but at last he felt that, from failing health, he must either abandon his design or call in to his assistance some person who had more time and energy to devote to its prosecution. Under these circumstances, he applied to Mr. Henry Chorley, a man of well-known literary skill, and one of Miss Mitford's most intimate friends.

In the meanwhile a difficulty arose from a most unexpected quarter. A year before Miss Mitford's death, she made her will, and left her servants K. and Sam her residuary legatees.

It is possible that at that time she thought nothing about her letters, or any life which might be written of her, and felt satisfied that at all events she was leaving everything in the safe custody of her executors.

No literary person would ever dream of committing their private correspondence to the hands of half-educated servants, or indeed to those of any one in whose judgment and ability they had not the fullest confidence. Something seems to have occurred to her mind on this subject at the very last, and, being ignorant of law, she thought a letter to Mr. Harness, her executor, would be in every way a sufficient safeguard.[1] Towards the end of her life, she became very much dependent on her maid, and probably in one of those ebullitions of generosity for which she was remarkable, left her all her little property. On account of the objections raised, Mr. Chorley refused to proceed with the work, unless an arrangement could be made with the Sweetmans. They, on their part, put in exorbitant claims, and Mr. Chorley withdrew, observing that the work would barely remunerate the editor. The undertaking was then relinquished, apparently forever.

Mr. Harness always considered the demands of the Sweetmans to be merely vexatious, as he knew well the wishes of his life-long friend and the entire confidence she placed in him. He was also fully convinced that her servants had no legal claim whatever on any portion of her literary correspondence.

We thus entered upon the work with a flowing sail, and spent two years not unpleasantly in deciphering and arranging the multifarious materials, so as to form an agreeable and continuous narrative of the life of the popular authoress. One great difficulty we encountered spoke favorably for the promise of the book. We had such a redundance of good matter, of clever criticism and graceful description, that we found it very difficult to compress it into anything like readable proportions.

[1] The Sweetmans afterwards filed a bill in chancery against Mr. Bentley and myself. It was dismissed without costs.

The Life of Mary Russell Mitford, commenced in 1866, was three years in progress. In the autumn of 1868 it appeared to be ready, and we offered it to several leading publishers, who all declined it upon different grounds. Even Mr. Bentley, who at first entertained the proposal, afterwards withdrew on receiving an adverse critique. He at the same time observed that if the work were reduced to half its dimensions he might still entertain it. Mr. Harness undertook the abridgment, and, but for my strenuous opposition, would have curtailed his own introductory notices, and omitted the first letter, which is characteristic and interesting from its date. In a few months he resigned his undertaking; he was feeling the weakness inseparable from advanced age; and the careful reduction of six volumes to three required no slight amount of reading and attention. He accordingly placed the further revision of the work entirely in my hands.

Harness at Stratford.

Mr. Harness yielded to few in his enthusiasm for Shakespeare. He was wont to say that his plays contained almost everything. In his early years, inspired with youthful ardor, he made a pilgrimage to the birthplace of the great poet, and although he started with the intention of staying there only four days, he ended by remaining five weeks. He was charmed with the place, and spent his time most enjoyably in exploring the beauties of the country, and in visiting the spots hallowed by the dramatist's memory. He told me that at the close of one long summer day, after returning from a walk to Anne Hathaway's cottage, he took out his volume of Shakespeare, which was his constant companion, and opening it at "King John," became completely absorbed in the tragic story. Time flew by rapidly and unheeded, until warned by his waning lamp, he started up and found that it was past midnight. He went to the window; the stars were shining brightly in the clear sky and shedding their thin light over the old gabled houses and lofty elm-trees; the night was breezeless, and all was shrouded in silence. Suddenly the church clock struck one. The deep booming reverberated through the stillness as though it would awake the spirits of the past; the hour and the scene were alike inspired. Mr. Harness thought how "that great man" might have listened to the same solemn stroke, and recalled the lines: —

> "The midnight bell
> Did with his iron tongue and brazen mouth
> Sound 'one' unto the drowsy race of night." [1]

Mr. Harness found the inscription on Shakespeare's monument in a very imperfect condition. He had it restored at his own expense. Above the epitaph by Ben Jonson is the line: —

> "Judicio Pylium, genio Socratem, arte Maronem,"

the false quantity in which offended Mr. Harness's classical ear, and he proposed to substitute "Sophoclem" for "Socratem." The mistake might have been due to some ignorant copyist; and the genius of Shakespeare seemed as much allied to that of the great tragedian as to that of the philosopher. He much regretted that the original coloring of the bust had not been allowed to remain.

His Edition of Shakespeare.

His edition of Shakespeare was published by Mr. Harness immediately after his appointment to St. Pancras. It had been prepared when he was residing at Hampstead, and had no parochial cure, but only Sunday duty in London. He did not confine himself in his undertaking to merely adding notes to the text of the poet; but also prefixed a Life, which occupied the first volume. This biography was remarkable for its scrupulous impartiality; no such record being in his opinion instructive or valuable, which was not absolutely faithful in all its details, and which did not chronicle the frailties as well as the virtues of its subject. Miss Mitford, in praising the work, says, "I am quite delighted with your edition of Shakespeare. It must do. The 'Life' is like the portrait affixed to it; the old beloved, well-known features which we all have by heart, but

[1] Act iii. scene 3.

inspired with a fresh spirit." She objects, however, to his over-sensitiveness and anxiety to notice all the invidious allegations made against his author's fame. But Mr. Harness thought it unworthy of the character of the great poet to allow him to gain anything by concealment; and speaking of his early days at Stratford, and of the probability that he assisted his father in the unpoetical trade of a butcher, he emphatically rejects "that absurd spirit of refinement which is only too common among the writers of biography, as well as history, and which induces them to conceal or misrepresent every occurrence which is at all of a humiliating nature, and does not accord with those false and effeminate notions so generally entertained respecting the dignity of that peculiar class of composition." He, at the same time, blames the severity with which Shakespeare's early vagaries were punished by Sir Thomas Lucy. "Every contemporary," he says, "who has spoken of our author, has been lavish in the praise of his temper and disposition. 'The gentle Shakespeare' seems to have been his distinguishing appellation. No slight portion of our enthusiasm for his writings may be traced to the fair picture which they present of the author's character. We love the tenderness of heart, the candor, and openness, and singleness of mind, the largeness of sentiment, the liberality of opinion, which the whole tenor of his works proves him to have possessed. His faults seem to have been the transient aberrations of a thoughtless moment, which reflection never failed to correct; the ebullition of high spirits might mislead him; but the principles and the affections never swerved from what was right. Against such a person, the extreme severity of the magistrate should not have been exerted. But the powerful enemy of Shakespeare was not to be appeased; the heart of the Puritan or the game-preserver is very rarely formed of 'penetrable stuff.' Our author fled from the inflexible persecutions of his opponent to seek shelter in the metropolis; and he found friends and wealth and fame where he had only hoped for an asylum. Sir Thomas Lucy remained to enjoy the triumph of his victory, and he yet survives, in the character of Justice Shallow, as the laughing-stock of posterity."[1]

"Shakespeare's first employment in connection with the theatre in London, presents us with a characteristic picture of the times. He was to receive the horses of those who rode to the performance, and was to hold them until the end of the performance. He became, we are told, such a favorite in this office, that every one, when he alighted, called out, 'Will Shakespeare!' and he soon was in such demand that he hired young men to assist him, who would present themselves, saying, 'I am Shakespeare's boy, sir!' That the above anecdote was really communicated by Pope," adds Mr. Harness, "there is no room to doubt."

"But however inferior," he continues, "was the situation which Shakespeare first occupied, his talents were not long buried in obscurity. He rapidly rose to the first station in the theatre, and by the power of his genius, raised our national dramatic poetry, then in its infancy, to the highest state of perfection which it is perhaps capable of reaching."

SHAKESPEARE AS A PLAYER.

Speaking of the characters played by Shakespeare, Mr. Harness draws the following conclusions: "It would appear that the class of characters to which the histrionic exertions of Shakespeare were confined was that of elderly persons — parts rather of declamation than of passion. With a countenance which, if any of his pictures is a genuine resemblance of him, we may adduce that one as our authority for esteeming capable of every variety of expression; with a knowledge of the art which rendered him fit to be the teacher of the first actors of his day, and to instruct Joseph Taylor in the character of Hamlet, and John Lowine in that of King Henry the

[1] (Note by Mr. Harness.) "There can be no doubt that Justice Shallow was designed as the representative of the knight. If the traditional authority of this fact were not quite satisfactory, the description of his coat of arms in the first scene of *The Merry Wives of Windsor*, which is, with very slight deviation, that of the Lucys, would be sufficient to direct us to the original of the portrait."

Eighth; with such admirable qualifications for preëminence, we must infer that nothing but some personal defect could have reduced him to limit the exercise of his powers, and even in youth assume the slow and deliberate motion which is the characteristic of old age. In his minor poems we perhaps trace the origin of this direction of his talents. It appears from two places in his Sonnets that he was lamed by some accident. In the 37th Sonnet he writes: —

'So I made *lame* by Fortune's dearest spite.'

And in the 89th he again alludes to his infirmity, and says, —

'Speak of my *lameness*, and I straight will halt.'

This imperfection would necessarily have rendered him unfit to appear as the representative of any characters of youthful ardor, in which rapidity of movement or violence of exertion was demanded, and would oblige him to apply his powers to such parts as were compatible with his measured and impeded action. Malone has most inefficiently attempted to explain away the palpable meaning of the above lines, and adds, 'If Shakespeare was in truth lame, he had it not in his power to *halt occasionally* for this or any other purpose, the defect must have been fixed and permanent.' Not so! Surely many an infirmity of the kind may be skillfully concealed, or only become visible in the moments of hurried movement. Either Sir Walter Scott, or Lord Byron might, without any impropriety, have written the verses in question; they would have been applicable to either of them. Indeed the lameness of Lord Byron was exactly such as Shakespeare's might have been; and I remember, as a boy, that he selected those speeches for declamation which would not constrain him to the use of such exertions as might obtrude the defect of his person into notice."

Goodness of Shakespeare's Writing.

Mr. Harness was acustomed to say that all that Shakespeare wrote was good, but that many passages were attributed to him which were not authentic. He explains his views on the corruptions of the text in the following words: —

"If Shakespeare still appears to us the first of poets, it is in spite of every possible disadvantage to which his own sublime contempt of applause had exposed his fame, from the ignorance, the avarice, or the officiousness of his early editors. To these causes it is to be ascribed that the writings of Shakespeare have come down to us in a state more imperfect than those of any other author of his time, and requiring every exertion of critical skill to illustrate and amend them. That so little should be known with certainty of the history of his life was the natural consequence of the events which immediately followed his dissolution. It is true that the age in which he flourished was little curious about the lives of literary men; but our ignorance must not wholly be attributed to the want of curiosity in the immediate successors of the poet. The public mind soon became violently agitated in the conflict of opposite opinions. Every individual was called upon to take his stand as the partisan of a religious or political faction. Each was too intimately occupied with his personal interest to find leisure for so peaceful a pursuit as tracing the biography of a poet. If this was the case during the time of civil commotion, under the Puritanical dynasty of Cromwell the stage was totally destroyed; and the life of a dramatic author, however eminent his merits, would not only have been considered as a subject undeserving of inquiry, but only worthy of contempt and abomination. The genius of Shakespeare was dear to Milton and to Dryden; to a few lofty minds and gifted spirits; but it was dead to the multitude of his countrymen, who, in their foolish bigotry, would have considered their very houses polluted if they had contained a copy of his works.

"After the Restoration these severe restrictions were relaxed; and, as is universally the case, the counter-action was correspondent to the action. The nation suddenly exchanged the rigid austerity of Puritanism for the extreme of profligacy and licentiousness. When the Drama was revived, it existed no longer to inculcate such lessons of morality as were enforced by the contrition of Macbeth, the purity of Isabel, or the suffering constancy of Imogen; but to teach modesty to blush at its own innocence, to corrupt the heart by pictures of debauchery, and to exalt a gay selfishness and daring sensuality above all that is noble in principle and honorable in action. At this period Shakespeare was forgotten. He wrote not for such profligate times. His sentiments would have been met by no correspondent feelings in the breasts of such audiences as were then collected within the walls of the metropolitan theatres, composed of men who came to hear their vices flattered, and of women masked, ashamed to show their faces at representations which they were sufficiently abandoned to delight in. The jesting, lying, bold intriguing rake, whom Shakespeare had rendered contemptible in Lucio, and hateful in Iachimo, was the very character that the dramatists of Charles's time were painting after the model of the court favorites, and representing in false colors as a deserving object of approbation. French taste and French morals had banished our author from the stage, and his name had faded from the memory of the people. Tate, in his altered play of "King Lear," mentions the original, in his dedication, as an obscure piece. The author of the "Tattler," in quoting some lines of "Macbeth," cites them from the disfigured alteration of D'Avenant. The works of Shakespeare were only read by those whom the desire of literary plunder induced to pry into the volumes of antiquated authors, with the hope of discovering some neglected jewels that might be clandestinely transferred to enrich their own poverty of invention; and so little were the productions of the most gifted poet that ever ventured to embark on the varying waters of the imagination known to the generality of his countrymen, that Otway stole the character of the Nurse, and all the love-scenes of "Romeo and Juliet," and published them as his own without the slightest acknowledgment of the obligation or any apprehension of detection. A better taste returned; and when, nearly a century after the death of Shakespeare, Rowe undertook to superintend an edition of his Plays, and to collect the memoirs of his life, the race had passed away from whom any certain recollections of the great national poet might have been gathered, and nothing better was to be obtained than the slight notes of Aubrey, the scattered hints of Oldys, the loose intimations which had escaped from D'Avenant, and the vague reports which Betterton had gleaned in his pilgrimage to Stratford."

The Globe Theatre.

The following sketch by Mr. Harness of the manner in which the performances of the theatre were conducted, affords an interesting picture of the times: he was always fond of characteristic details: —

"The 'Globe' and the play-house in 'Blackfriars' were the property of the company to which Shakespeare was himself attached, and by whom all his productions were exhibited. The 'Globe' appears to have been a wooden building, of a considerable size, hexagonal without and circular within; it was thatched in part, but a large portion of the roof was open to the weather. This was the company's summer theatre, and the plays were acted by daylight. At the 'Blackfriars,' on the contrary, which was the winter theatre, the top was entirely closed, and the performances were exhibited by candle-light. In every other respect the economy and usages of the houses appear to have been the same, and to have resembled those of every other contemporary theatre.

"With respect to the interior arrangements there were very few points of difference between our modern theatres and those of the days of Shakespeare. The terms of admission indeed were considerably cheaper; to the boxes the entrance was a shilling; to the pit and galleries only sixpence; sixpence also was the price paid for stools upon the stage; and these seats, as we learn from Dekker's 'Gull's Hornbook,' were peculiarly affected by the wits and critics of the time. The conduct of the audience was less restrained by the sense of public decorum, and smoking tobacco, playing at cards, eating and drinking, were generally prevalent among them. The hour of performance also was earlier; the play beginning at first at one, and afterwards at three o'clock in the afternoon. During the time of representation a flag was unfurled at the top of the theatre, and the floor of the stage (as was the case with every floor at the time from the cottage to the palace) was strewn with rushes. But in other respects, the ancient theatres seem to have been very nearly similar to those of modern times; they had their pit, where the inferior class of spectators, the 'groundlings,' vented their clamorous censure or approbation; they had their boxes, to which the right of exclusive admission was hired by the night for the more wealthy and refined portion of the audience; and there were again the galleries or scaffolds above the boxes, for those who were content to purchase inferior accommodation at a cheaper rate. On the stage, the arrangements appear to have been nearly the same as at present; the curtain divided the audience from the actors, which at the third sounding — not indeed of the bell, but of the trumpet — was withdrawn for the commencement of the performance. With regard to the use of scenery, it is scarcely possible, from the very circumstances of the case, that such a contrivance should have escaped our ancestors. All the materials were ready to their hands; they had not to invent for themselves, but to adapt an old invention to their purposes, and at a time when every better apartment was adorned with tapestry; when even the rooms of the commonest taverns were hung with painted cloths: while all the essentials of scenery were continually before their eyes, we can hardly believe our forefathers to have been so deficient in ingenuity as never to have conceived the design of converting the common ornaments of their walls into the decorations of their theatres. Mr. Gifford, who adheres to Malone's opinion, says, 'A table, with a pen and ink thrust in, signified that the stage was a counting-house; if these were withdrawn, and two stools put in their places, it was then a tavern;' and this might be satisfactory as long as the business of the play was supposed to have been passing within doors; but when it was removed to the open air, such meagre devices would no longer be sufficient to guide the imagination of the audience, and some new method must have been adopted to indicate the place of action. After giving the subject considerable attention, I cannot help thinking that Steevens was right in rejecting the evidence of Malone, and concluding that the spectators were, as at the present day, assisted in following the progress of the story by means of painted and movable scenery." [1]

Mrs. Siddons.

It must be remembered that, in the days in which Mr. Harness wrote, the legitimate drama had not yet been superseded by extravagant and ephemeral representations. A charge of pedantry might have been brought against the stage with more justice than one of frivolity. The theatres, of which there were but two, were not places for idleness and dissipation, but for study and intellectual enjoyment. There were then no stalls ; nor did the pit offer that cheap rate of accommodation which has tempted managers to introduce performances of a broad and tawdry character. Moreover, the lovers of Shakespeare could then have their taste gratified to an extent which has since been impossible. The works of the great dramatist were rightly represented by the combined talent of the Kemble family. Under them, the stage became a source of high moral, as well as artistic, instruction. Never, since the days of classic Attica, had the drama struck so deeply the finer chords of the human heart ; and the well-read volume was as frequent in the pit as was the white handkerchief in the gilded tiers. So jealous at this time were the audience of the fame of the great dramatist, that I have been told that the omission of a single line, or even of a word, would call forth an immediate expression of disapproval. The proud sovereign of this assemblage of high-born women and scholarly men was no less a person than Mrs. Siddons, who seems to have enjoyed a celebrity verging upon adoration. At her appearance enthusiastic applause rang through the crowded house. None who had not seen her could ever realize the impression she made. As she walked the stage

[1] This opinion is confirmed by the ancient stage directions. In the folio Shakespeare, of 1623, we read 'Enter Brutus, *in his orchard;*' 'Enter Timon, *in the woods;*' 'Enter Timon, *from his cave.*'

like one of Nature's queens, all could understand the dignity of motion implied in Virgil's expression: —

"Incessu patuit dea."

Campbell speaks of "her lofty beauty, her graceful walk and gesture." And when we add to this the charm of her flexible and expressive voice, we cannot be surprised at the admiration she awakened. Few who saw her ever forgot her. Crabbe Robinson used to say that he prided himself on three things; he had been intimate with Goethe, he had made a walking tour with Wordsworth, and *he had seen Mrs. Siddons.* Mr. Harness could not be less deeply impressed by one who so eloquently interpreted his favorite oracle; and as might have been expected, he regarded her performance from a critical point of view. "Her high judgment watched over her qualifications." "It was not merely her appearance that gave her such power," observed Mr. Harness, "she owed much to her persevering industry. She admitted to me one day, in reply to a question, that, although it might sound egotistical for her to say it, she did not think that there would be again such an impersonation of Calista [1] as her own, taking into consideration the voice, the use of the stage, and above all the laborious study." On a later occasion, when he was referring to the excellence of her intonation, she observed that over-exertion in large theatres had injured her power of expression, which was much greater in her earlier days. The perfection at which she had arrived in her art, and the skill with which she equaled Nature, may be estimated from a reply made to Mr. Harness by a well-known critic, when he observed that Mrs. Siddons had played her part with spirit on the previous night. "Yes," returned his friend, "but I never before saw her so much like an actress."

Mr. Harness related the following anecdote in which the conduct of the great actress was very characteristic. He was dining at Lord Lonsdale's, and among the company were Mrs. Siddons and Mr. and Miss Edgeworth. Mr. Edgeworth, who

[1] A part in *The Fair Penitent* for which she was celebrated.

was sitting next to Mrs. Siddons, Sam Rogers being on the other side of her, observed after dinner, "Madam, I think I saw you perform Millamont thirty-five years ago." "Pardon me, sir." "Oh! then it was forty years ago; I distinctly recollect it." "You will excuse me, sir, I never played Millamont." "Oh, yes, ma'am, I recollect." "I think," she replied, turning to Mr. Rogers, "it is time for me to change my place," and she rose with her own peculiar dignity.[1]

Prospero's Island.

Mr. Harness objected much to the over-inquisitive spirit which some critics have evinced in the study of Shakespeare. In a review in the "Quarterly" of "Hunter on the 'Tempest,'" in which he blames the writer for his persistent endeavors to define the localities mentioned in that play, he writes as follows: —

"The island was called into existence by a far more potent magician than even Prospero; and 'like the baseless fabric of a vision' melted 'into thin air,' leaving 'no rack behind,' with a deep and solemn sound of funeral music, on the 23d April, 1616, the day when that mighty master died. After the departure of Prospero and Miranda, it was never visited again by any human creature. The unearthly inhabitants possessed it altogether till the hour of its dissolution. They were then variously dispersed. Caliban, clinging to one of the largest logs which Ferdinand had so industriously piled up, but which had never been 'burnt,' was floated on it in safety to the coast of Algiers. Ariel, with all his subtle company, the 'elves of hills, brooks, standing lakes and groves,' clapping their tiny hands, and singing 'Where the bee sucks' in sweetest melody and fullest chorus, flitter away delighted to meet the spirit of the great magician from whose fancy they had derived their life and being, and to pour forth their gratulations around him as he ascended on his upward way to regions more bright and

[1] This incident is said, by Crabbe Robinson, to have occurred at Mr. Sotheby's; but there was some confusion in his mind on the subject. It was related to him by Mr. Harness.

pure and ethereal than any to which they even 'in their pride of flight' could venture to aspire. Since that happy hour they have all dwelt in harmony together in one of the fairest and most secluded valleys of 'Araby the Blest.' We know the spot; but for worlds we would not be wicked enough to deliver them over in their merry ignorance to the tender mercies of the commentators. Were we to let fall the slightest hint of the position of their melodious home, we are well aware that Mr. Hunter or Mr. Rodd, or both those gentlemen together, would start off to Rotherhithe to-morrow morning, would hire a steamer and go paddling away in a cloud of thick black smoke in pursuit of them; and having reached the spot, they would, without the least sense of compunction, gather the sweetest blossoms that Ariel ever sucked his honey from, and crush them between the leaves of their *hortus siccus;* they would hunt down the innocent spirits themselves; they would scare them with unearthly sounds; they would catch them with bird-limed twigs and butterfly nets, run pins through their delicate bodies, fix them to the bottoms of glazed boxes, and bear them away in triumph to be deposited as curiosities among the natural history shelves of the British Museum."

Macready lost, as he said, £2,000 a year, owing to an article written by Mr. Harness in the "Quarterly." So much weight had his critiques with the public of the day.

THE KEMBLES IN AMERICA.

The following letters are interesting as giving an account of the Kembles' visit to America:—

To the Rev. William Harness.

"BOSTON, *Sunday, May 5th*, 1833.

"Do not imagine that I have any intention of letting you forget me, my dear Mr. Harness, or that I mean to delegate to newspapers, and such like unsatisfactory channels of information, the task of keeping my recollection alive with you. I certainly have suffered a tolerably long interval to escape since the writing of my first epistle; but that it did not follow from thence that I never meant to write to you again, *this* is proof. If I were to ask you all the questions I should like answered with regard to things in general, and particularly in my poor dear little country, I might fill my letter with one huge note of interrogation, and leave you to answer all that is 'being, doing, and suffering' in England; but I rather think some account of ourselves might be more satisfactory to you; and so, according to your noble and poetical friend, 'Here goes!' (By the bye, his Life by Moore is a terrible pity; why could n't his works be left to speak for him? They are his best record after all.)

"We are all in excellent health, except that my father is lame and cross, D—— sleepy and cross, and I purely cross, and nothing else. With regard to my father's lameness, he caught it — or, rather, it caught him — by the calf of the leg, in the act of springing off the stage after me, in Benedick. 'T is an accident of no great importance — a sprain or fracture of one or two of the smaller fibres in the leg, which makes him go a little haltingly just now, but is not likely to inconvenience him long. As for all the other ailments, that is the crossness, 't is owing to a bitter bleak east wind, which is the only air that blows in Boston, and keeps us all in a state of misanthropy and universal dissatisfaction. Perhaps, under these circumstances, I had better have deferred writing to you; but, had I waited till the wind changed its quarter, I must have waited till we returned to New York; for Boston is the abiding place of the east wind.

"Our houses, wherever we go, are very fine; our business most successful. The people and places vie with each other in kindness and civility to us; and as for me, I am so praised, so admired, so courted, and so flattered, that I am thrown into the depths of humility, sometimes, when I come to consider my own unworthiness; and only fear that at last I shall acquire such an idea of my own excellence, importance, and admirableness that I shall come to the conviction that 'the world is mine oyster.' Seriously, I am sometimes perplexed at the universal kindness and almost affection that is expressed towards me, when I cannot help feeling that indeed I have done nothing really to deserve it. However, thank God for it! And as for the desert, why perhaps it is with me as with the man who said he did not know whether he could play on the fiddle or not, for he 'd never tried.

"Boston is a Yankee town, which I dare say is as much as you know about it; but, sir, 'tis moreover the wealthiest town in the Union; 't is, sir, the most *belles-letterish* and blue town in the Union; 't is, sir, the most aristocratic town in the Union, and decidedly bears the greatest resemblance to an English town of any I have seen. The country round it, too, is more like a bit of the old land than anything I have yet seen; and, though some of the wild romantic scenery round Philadelphia enchanted me very much, the white clean cottages, the blossoming apple-trees and flowering garden-plots of the villages round this place have recalled England more vividly, and given me more pleasure than anything I have yet seen. The society is a little stiff; they have, unfortunately, a reputation in this good town for superior intellect, and are proportionately starched and stupid. However, to have known Webster, and even Audubon, is in itself something; and though Channing has been obliged by ill-health to leave Boston for the South, I trust yet to have the privilege of knowing him — who, I think, reflects more honor on his native city than all its other superiorities put together.

"We act every night here but Saturday. I grumble dreadfully at this hard work — not because it tires me, but because I am idle and like two holidays in a week. However, when I consider that every night lost is a large sum of money lost (for our profits are very great) I am willing to give up my laziness, so long as the work is not too much either for my father or myself. I take an amazing quantity of exercise on horseback; 't is meat and drink and sleep to me, and affords me, moreover, the best opportunity of seeing the country, which one never does well in a carriage; and 't is quite entertaining to see how, before I have been a fortnight in a place, all the women are getting into riding-skirts and up upon horses. I have received ever so many thanks for the improved health of the ladies here who, since my arrival, are all horseback-mad; and I truly think a good shaking does a woman good in every way.

"I have acted several new parts since I have been in this new world; Katherine, the Shrew, which I do pretty well, Bizarre, which I also do pretty well, but particularly the dancing — Violante in 'The Wonder,' which I do worse than anything that can be seen, and Mary Copp in 'Charles the Second,' which I do very fairly well, leaving out the singing. Bianca seems to be my favorite part with the public, in tragedy, and Julia in the 'Hunchback,' in comedy. I hear Knowles has written another play with a magnificent woman's part. Of course we shall have it out here before long; I am curious to see it.

"I have seen Washington Irving several times since I have been in this country. He is idolized here, and talks of settling himself in some little sunny nook on the Hudson — that broadest, brightest river in the world. He is very delightful, a most happy, cheerful, benevolent, simple person. His absence of seventeen years from this country has produced changes in it which seem to fill him with amazement and admiration. And, indeed, 't is a most marvelous country! It stands unparalleled under every aspect in which it can be considered, and presents one of the most interesting and extraordinary subjects of contemplation that the eye of a politician, or the more extensive gaze of a philosopher, can scan. A land peopled, as this has been, by the overflowings of all other lands; to the south colonized by the adventurous but thrifty younger branches of noble families of England, and in great measure also by men whose vices and crimes, as well as their utter poverty, drove them to find shelter away from the society whose laws they had outraged; to the north, again, this new world owing its first civilized inhabitants to the purest and loftiest spirit of Freedom — the holiest and most steadfast spirit of Religion (emanating from England, too); and all having received their first dawn of civilization from bodies of men differing from each other in object, in religious faith, in country and lineage: a whole continent thus strangely reclaimed from utter savageness, and in the process of a century and a half becoming, from a desolate and utter wilderness, a great political existence, taking a firm and honorable station among the powers of the world. A land abounding in cultivation, civilization, populous towns, full of wealth, of business, of trade, of importance; vast ports receiving the flags of every nation under Heaven; to see huge ocean steamboats carrying hundreds of people to and fro every hour along the Hudson, the St. Lawrence, the Mississippi, whose waters, a hundred years ago, were never visited but by the Indian canoe; to see forests felled, and towns arising, railways and canals traversing and connecting what were wild tracts of interminable wood and waste; to see life, and all its wonderful arts and sciences, reclaiming these vast solitudes to the uses of man and the purposes of civilized existence: this mighty operation which is at this instant going on under our very eyes makes this country one of great interest, of admiration, of anxious observation to all the world. 'T is a marvelous country indeed!

"Bless my soul, I did n't mean to be cross[1] to you, because that 's an infliction! Don't you wish that you and I wrote better hands? Pray, dear Mr. Harness, if you have time to spare, write to me again; it pleases me to hear from England, and it pleases me to hear from you.

"For I am very truly, and with great regard,

"Yours,

"FANNY KEMBLE."

To the Rev. W. Harness.

"NEW YORK, *24th April*, 1834.

"MY DEAR FRIEND,

"When I left England I promised I would write to you, and I am ashamed that I have so long neglected to redeem my promise; but I rely upon your good-nature to excuse me, al-

[1] The last page of the letter is crossed.

though I confess I hardly deserve forgiveness. Fanny, I know, has already told you all that we have seen and done ; so that you have not been left in ignorance of our proceedings by my sin of omission. Pray, which are considered more deadly by divines, sins of omission, or sins of commission ? You will not have time to answer me on this point before we meet ; therefore, I must seek for information from my friends of the cloth in this hemisphere — Dr. Wainwright or Dr. Channing : both learned men and pious Christians. Wainwright, with whom I am better acquainted than I am with Channing, seems to me more of a man of the world ; he mixes with general society, and is a well-bred, liberal clergyman, an Episcopalian, and likely to become the next Bishop of Boston. Channing, you know, is a Unitarian, a mild, engaging person in discourse, an eloquent and impressive preacher in the pulpit. Wainwright is a good preacher, too ; he has much more physical power than Channing, but in my opinion is far his inferior in point of intellect.

"So much for the leaders in *your* profession. For those in mine, you are almost as well acquainted with their merits as I am. Mr. Booth, as well as Mr. Hamblin, you must have seen in England ; and Mr. Forrest you will probably see, for report says he is to visit London. He is in person of Herculean proportions, fitter, in appearance, for a drayman or a porter than an actor. I have seen him but in two parts, Pierre, which he acted indifferently well ; the other, Oroloosa, an Indian ; in the representation of which characters he has acquired his reputation. There was an American of the name of Scott, whom I preferred, in the same tragedy ; but he is thought by his countrymen very inferior to Forrest. There are two favorite actresses, too, not very distinguished for talent. Miss Vincent and Miss Clifton : the latter is a very tall but beautiful girl.

"We hope to find you and your dear sister at home when we reach London. We did intend to sail from New York on the 16th of June, but for the advantages of a superior ship and a more agreeable captain, we have been induced to postpone our departure until the 24th of June: so pray look out for the arrival of the *United States*, commanded by Captain Holdritch. How happy Fanny's friends will be to see her once more before she is married, won't they? The legitimate drama will have another chance, I hope, of resuscitation; and we shall both at least take leave of the British stage in a manner worthy of the house of Kemble!

"God bless you! give my affectionate regard to your dear sister; and believe me, my very dear friend, unalterably yours,

"C. KEMBLE.

"Fanny has told you of the irreparable loss we have sustained by the death of her aunt. May all our deaths be as peaceful and as happy!"

THE KEANS.

Mr. Harness took little interest in the drama of the present day. Low comedy and scenic effects were his aversion; and he was wont to say that acting was now a debased art. He still knew a few of the elder members of the histrionic profession, and especially Charles Kean, for whom he had a great personal regard. He remarked how much he had done to raise the social character of the stage, and was deeply affected when he was sent for to attend his friend in his last hours. He had an equal esteem for Mrs. Kean. Referring to her kindness and good-nature, he said that she took great interest in the little children who came to act in the pantomimes, and that she used to teach them their Catechism between the pieces, thus endeavoring to compensate for their loss of regular instruction. Mr. Harness's schools, like many others in London, suffered much from the withdrawal of little pupils in the winter. On first entering his school at Knightsbridge, after the Christmas holidays, he inquired why the attendance was so small? "Because, sir," replied the teacher, "so many of the children are gone to be angels!"

"Memorials of Catherine Fanshawe."

One of the undertakings of Mr. Harness's later years was the preparation, for private circulation, of the "Memorials of Miss Catherine Fanshawe." This lady had been one of his most intimate friends, and had even proposed to make him her heir, but he refused the offer, averring that he could not endure the thought that he should in any way benefit by her death. He was often wont to say that he could not understand the desire which some persons evinced to obtain legacies; for, as he well observed, it was impossible to receive one without incurring the loss of a friend more valuable than any money thus acquired. Miss Fanshawe accordingly only made him the bequest of her etchings and manuscripts, which he gladly accepted. From these Mr. Harness compiled a small volume of "Memorials," to rescue her memory from the oblivion which threatened it. Those who have only heard of her in connection with the riddle on the letter H, have little idea of the range of her endowments or the elegance of her taste. Mr. Harness speaks with affectionate remembrance of "her varied accomplishments, her acute perception of the beautiful, her playful fancy, her charming conversation, her gentle and retiring manners, her lively sympathy with the sorrows and the joys of others, and, above all, her simple piety;" and he observes that she was a cherished member of that society, not very extended, but intimately united by a common love of literature, art, and science, which existed in London at the close of the last and the opening of the present centuries, and which, perhaps, "taken for all in all, has never been surpassed."

Miss Fanshawe's poems and sketches evince a considerable appreciation of humor. One of the latter, representing an evening party some eighty years since, with two politicians gesticulating before the fire-place, surrounded by a languid knot of fops and dandies, while the ladies are left to themselves, dozing and yawning behind their fans at the other end of the room, might, but for the quaintness of costume, remind us of many similar festivities at the present day. But Miss Fanshawe's great success lay in her delineation of children, of whose varying moods and expressions of countenance she seems to have possessed an admirable perception. Many charming groups of them are here photographed from her sketches.

The celebrated riddle by which Miss Fanshawe is best known arose, Mr. Harness said, from an accidental conversation at the Deep Dene. Mr. Hope was at the time entertaining with his usual liberality a number of eminent and literary friends, and in the course of the evening some remarks turned the conversation upon the letter H, and the unworthy treatment it received in the centre of metropolitan civilization. The party retired soon afterwards, but the subject of discussion had touched Miss Fanshawe's ingenious fancy, and while others slept her mind was busily employed. Next morning at breakfast she brought down the poem and read it to the delighted and astonished guests: —

"'T was whispered[1] in heaven, 't was muttered in hell,
And echo caught faintly the sound as it fell;
On the confines of earth 't was permitted to rest,
And the depths of the ocean its presence confessed.
'T will be found in the sphere when 't is riven asunder,
Be seen in the lightning, and heard in the thunder.
'T was allotted to man with his earliest breath,
Attends at his birth, and awaits him in death;
Presides o'er his happiness, honor and health;
Is the prop of his house and the end of his wealth.
In the heaps of the miser 't is hoarded with care,
But is sure to be lost on his prodigal heir.
It begins every hope, every wish it must bound,
With the husbandman toils, with the monarch is crowned.
Without it the soldier, the seaman may roam,
But woe to the wretch that expels it from home!
In the whispers of conscience its voice will be found,
Nor e'en in the whirlpool of passion be drowned.
'T will not soften the heart; but, though deaf be the ear,
It will make it acutely and instantly hear.
Yet in shade let it rest, like a delicate flower;
Ah! breathe on it softly — it dies in an hour."

[1] Mr. Harness said that the original commenced: —
"'T was in heaven pronounced."

Those lines thus first introduced were soon well-known and admired throughout the country, and from their style and curious felicity were attributed to Byron, the popular poet of the age. They afterwards crept into some foreign editions of his works, and are even at the present day often ascribed to him.

One of the odes in this volume records the lecture delivered by Sydney Smith on "The Sublime," and the gay dresses and toilettes of his fair audience. There is much wit and elegance in the poem, which is after the manner of Gray; but it was only suggested by Miss Fanshawe, and written by Miss Berry. (Mr. Harness often met this lady in society; she received the sobriquet of Black-berry from her dark eyes, and to distinguish her from her sister, who received the uncomplimentary title of Goose-berry).

The following specimen of Miss Fanshawe's humorous talent was much admired by one of the late Prime Ministers: —

SPEECH OF THE MEMBER FOR OLDHAM.

"Mr. Cobbett asked leave to bring in very soon
A Bill to abolish the sun and the moon.
The Honorable Member proceeded to state
Some arguments used in a former debate.
The heavenly bodies, like those upon earth,
Had, he said, been corrupt from the day of their birth;
With reckless profusion expending the light,
One after another, by day and by night.
And what classes enjoyed it? The upper alone,
Upon such they had always exclusively shone:
But when had they ever emitted a spark
For the people who toil underground, in the dark —
The people of England, the miners and borers,
Of earth's hidden treasures the skillful explorers?
But their *minds* were enlightening; they learn every hour
That discussion is knowledge, and knowledge is power.
Long humbled and crushed, like a giant they rise,
And sweep off the cobwebs that darken the skies;
To sunshine and moonshine their duties assign,
And claim equal rights for the mountain and mine.
  Turn to other departments. High time to inquire
What abuses exist in air, water, and fire.
Why keep up volcanoes? that idle display!
That pageant was all very well in its day;

But the reign of utility now has commenced,
And wisdom with such exhibitions dispensed.
When so many were starving with cold, it was cruel
To make such a waste of good fire and fuel.
As for Nature, how little experience had taught her
Appeared in the administration of water.
Was so noble a capital duly employed?
Or was it by few (if by any) enjoyed?
Poured on marshes and fens which were better without,
While pasture and arable perished for drought;
When flagrant injustice so often occurs
Abler hands must be wanted and younger than hers;
Not to speak of old Ocean's insatiable needs,
Or of seas so ill-ploughed they bear nothing but weeds.
At some future day he perhaps should be able
To lay the details of their cost on the table.
At present, no longer the House to detain,
He 'd confine his remarks to the subject of rain.
Was it wanted? A more economical plan,
More equably working, more useful to man,
In this age of improvement might surely be found,
By which all would be sprinkled, and none would be drowned.
He would boldly appeal to the nation's good sense,
Not to sanction this useless, enormous expense.
If the wind did but shift, if a cloud did but lower,
What millions of rain-drops were spent in a shower?
Let them burst through the shackles of wind and of weather,
Do away with the office of rain altogether;
Let the whole be remodeled on principles new,
And consolidate half the old funds into *dew*.

. . . . . .

He hoped that the House a few minutes would spare
While he offered some brief observations on air.
Not the sun nor the moon, nor earth, water, or fire,
Nor Tories themselves when with Whigs they conspire,
Were half so unjust, so despotic, so blind,
So deaf to the cries and the claims of mankind,
As air and his wicked prime minister, wind.
Goes forth the despoiler, consuming the rations
Designed for the lungs of unborn generations!
What a waste of the elements made in a storm!
And all this comes on in the teeth of Reform!
Hail, lightning, and thunder, in volleys and peals!
The tropics are trembling, the universe reels;
Come whirlwind and hurricane, tempest, tornadoes,
Woe! woe! to Antigua, Jamaica, Barbadoes!
Plantations uprooted, and sugar dissolved;
Rum, coffee, and spice in ruin involved;

And while the Caribbees were ruined and rifled,
Not a breeze reached Guiana, and England was stifled!
  Rate all that exists at its practical worth —
'T was a system of humbug from heaven to earth!
These abuses must cease — they had lasted too long;
Was there anything right? Was not everything wrong?
The crown was too costly, the Church was a curse;
Old Parliaments bad, Reformed Parliaments worse;
All revenues ill-managed, all wants ill-provided;
Equality, liberty, justice derided!
But the people of England no more would endure
Any remedy short of a Radical cure.
Instructed, united, a nation of Sages
Would look with contempt on the wisdom of ages;
Provide for the world a more just legislature,
And impose an agrarian law upon Nature."

Masters and Servants.

Mr. Harness had a great affection for tried and faithful servants; so much so that he erected a stained glass window in his church to the memory of his aged nurse. He loved to recall the times when servants and masters lived together as members of the same family, with mutual respect and common interests; and in a passage in which he deplores the change which has now taken place, he sketches a pleasing picture of their former confidential relations: "Worldly circumstances used not to sever classes. A little more than fifty years ago, when Crabbe the poet resided for some time in the house of Mr. Tovell, a gentleman of considerable landed property in Suffolk, he found the drawing and dining rooms only opened on state occasions, and the family generally living with the domestics in the old-fashioned kitchen; where, while the master of the house read his book or his newspaper by the capacious fireside, the lady sat at a little round table superintending the work, and working with the maids. In this manner kindly feelings were naturally produced; civilization was diffused by intercourse; and the science of house management acquired by the servant at the hall was carried with her on her marriage to make the comfort of her husband's cottage. In houses of a higher rank, there were always some domestics who had lived long enough in the family to be considered as a part of it; who held a confidential place in the regard of the lord or lady; and who formed a connecting link between them and the menials — every one of whom, perhaps, was born on the estate; while a knowledge of the merits or demerits, the weal or woe, of all was maintained by the superintendence of that most important but now obsolete member of every large establishment, the chaplain. This tie of friendly care on the one hand, and of attached dependence on the other, has been gradually loosened. Instead of it, there has grown up, between master and servant, a cold, unsympathizing, incommunicable distance — an obstinate, impenetrable reserve — which exists in no other country, which every really Christian heart feels it painful to keep up, and which no one of ordinary good-nature could think of maintaining towards a dog or a cat that he happened to come as frequently in contact with. By such a state of things both parties are losers; the master and the mistress, perhaps, the most. It may be taken as a rule without exception that the members of a family cannot live long in a state of indifference towards each other. If they are not united by feelings of regard, they will be severed by feelings of enmity. If the master takes no care to attach his domestics by words and acts of kindness, they very soon begin to look upon him with an evil eye, to lose all concern for his interests; and if they abstain from defrauding him themselves, they rejoice in the success of the cheat by which he is defrauded. It is only latterly that all the links of good feeling between the higher and lower members of the same household have been broken asunder. They used to be bound together by a joint interest in the younger branches of the family. Some years ago, there still remained the old footman, or the gray-headed groom, or the trusty nurse-maid to whom the children could be safely given in charge — who loved the children, and were loved by them in turn. But now, these are exploded. What is wanted is the restoration of an humbler, kindlier, freer manner of intercourse between manufacturers and their men, farmers and their laborers, masters of families and their domestic servants. I hardly know a more disgusting piece of hypocrisy than that which I see at the present day so constantly exhibited, when some arrogant woman of fashion, who treats her country neighbor with supercilious incivility, her less exclusive relatives with the coldest indifference, and her domestics with a most withering stiffness, passes by all the legitimate objects of her kindness, and goes out of her way to lavish her factitious sympathy and capricious interest on the unknown inmates of some garret or cellar of a London alley."

State of the English Bible.

On some Church questions Mr. Harness was in advance of his age — especially with regard to the revision of the Bible. Writing in the "Edinburgh Review" he notices "the mischief that has been inflicted on the sense of the inspired writings by the mode of breaking them up into chapter and verse;" and, speaking further of the translation, he observes that the phrase of the Hebrew language is retained to a most confusing extent. He cites such instances as the following, "the covenant of salt," meaning "a friendly contract." "They are crushed in the gate," for "they are found guilty in a court of justice." "The color of the lips," for "praises and thanksgivings," "I have given you cleanness of teeth," meaning "extreme scarcity." "Such are," he observes, the sort of Hebraisms of which Selden says, "what gear do the common people make of them?" He also objects to the combination of all the books of Scripture into one volume, rendering it either small in type or inconvenient in size. "If a man would fain take his evening walk into the fields, with the Prophecies of Isaiah as his companion, it is no light grievance to him that he must either forego his inclination, or carry along with him at the same time the Law of Moses and the History of the Jews, the Psalms of David and the Proverbs of Solomon."

Edward Irving.

One of the most remarkable circumstances connected with Mr. Harness's cure in St. Pancras was, that he was brought into close proximity with the celebrated Edward Irving, who was then attracting many followers. The Scotch church was on the opposite side of Regent Square, and the performances which took place in it were so distasteful to Mr. Harness, and led astray so many weak brethren, that — although with great reluctance, for he disliked polemical discussions — he preached a sermon (afterwards published) in which he pointed out the utter groundlessness of Mr. Irving's pretensions.

He showed how different were the unintelligible rhapsodies of the Irvingites from that divine gift of foreign languages which was so necessary for gospel missionaries in the early centuries. "There is nothing," he observes, "so frugal as Providence. What! persons inspired to speak languages unknown to others and unintelligible to themselves! As a blessing, a gift, a grace, an illumination from the Almighty to his saints, there is nothing parallel to this to be met with in the whole range of the Scriptures; and, as a punishment, a blindness, and a curse upon his enemies, it surpasses even the malediction against the people of Babel." In a letter to a friend, in which he reiterates his commendation of the sober, steady teaching of the Church of England, Mr. Harness observes, "Edward Irving told me several times that he could not understand why he met with no such true Christians as in the *orthodox* Church of England. He used the word 'orthodox' in the sense of anti-Calvinistic. And even when we were standing talking in Regent Square, on one side of which his church stood, and mine on the other, he said, pointing first to his own, and then to mine, 'I don't know how it is I have no such humble, quiet Christians *here* as you contrive to assemble about you *there!*' That cannot be a bad system which works such effects."

The influence which Mr. Irving exerted, not only over a large section of the laity, but also over some of the clergy, is thus casually alluded to in a postscript to a letter from Dr. Milman to Mr. Harness: "Can you send me a good, steady humble-minded curate? I have just parted with one after three months, who will be a follower of Irving in three more

— the acting of the Strand Theatre with the reasoning faculties of St. Luke's; *d'ailleurs*, a good kind of young man."

Harness's Early Reminiscences.

Mr. Harness's recollections formed an interesting link between several generations of literary men. As a child he had known Joseph Warton, whose brother, the celebrated poet, had been acquainted with Pope; who, in turn, could remember to have seen Racine walking in his red stockings in Paris. Sir George Beaumont told him that when at Rome he had spoken to the donkey-man who had accompanied Claude and Gaspar Poussin on their sketching excursion to Tivoli. In his youth he remembered Dr. Parr — his snappish wit, and the long pipe he smoked after dinner; the latter causing him especial astonishment, as smoking was then rare and unfashionable.

Paley.

He might also have known Paley, but his information about him was probably derived from some of the tutors at Christ's College, to which the great apologist had himself belonged. Mr. Harness had several little anecdotes illustrative of Paley's homely manners and rough humor. At the first visitation he attended, after his preferment to the archdeaconry, he dined in company with a large assemblage of clegymen, all of whom were eager to hear his observations. He remained silent, to their great disappointment, until the second course was served. At length the great man spoke; every ear was strained. What was his oracular utterance? "I don't think these *puddens* are much good unless the seeds are taken out of the raisins!" At another banquet, shortly after his preferment, he found himself exposed to an unpleasant draft of air. "Shut that window behind me," he called out to one of the waiters, "and open one lower down, behind one of the curates!"

Crabbe.

Later than these was Crabbe, the poet, who after publishing "The Library," "The Village," and other poems, disappeared from public sight in a country living for two-and-twenty years, and was generally supposed to be dead, until he revived again in the "Register" in 1807, and reëntered London literary circles in 1813. Mr. Harness greatly admired his poems: perhaps he appreciated them the more because they referred so much to country parish life. He particularly noticed the beauty of a little story in the "Tales," where an heiress is prevented by a rich aunt from marrying a man of inferior position. She by degrees forgets him, and becomes entirely engrossed with the accumulation of money. Her lover, on the other hand, becomes poorer, and is at last an inmate of an almshouse. He reminds her of her promise, which she disowns.

"He shares a parish-gift; at church he sees
The pious Dinah dropped upon her knees;
Thence, as she walks the streets with stately air,
As chance directs, oft meet the parted pair;
When he, with thickest coat of badgeman's blue,
Moves near her shaded silk of changeful hue;
When his thin locks of gray approach her braid,
A costly purchase made in beauty's aid;
When his frank air, and his unstudied pace,
Are seen with her soft manner, air, and grace,
It might some wonder in a stranger move,
How these together could have talked of love."

Crabbe visited Edinburgh in 1822, when the festivities in honor of the arrival of George the Fourth drew together such a brilliant assemblage of rank and talent. Scott was too much engaged to do the honors for all his distinguished friends, and assigned some of them to Lockhart, who, to afford mutual gratification, introduced Crabbe to Brewster. Next day, to his consternation, Crabbe observed, "That Dr. Brewster seems an agreeable man — what is he?" and Brewster, on meeting Lockhart, inquired, "By the way, who was that old clergyman you brought to see me? Did you say his name was Crabbe?"

HARNESS AND SCOTT.

In the opening article of the "Quarterly," for January, 1868, a review appeared of the "Life of Scott," written by

Dean Milman, and towards the end of it was the following reference: "Proofs of the veneration in which all classes held him greeted Scott wherever he went. Twice on the occasion of the coronation of George the Fourth this was shown in a remarkable way. The Rev. Mr. Harness, the accomplished friend of Mrs. Siddons and Lord Byron, describes that, while he was standing in Westminster Hall, a spectator of the coronation feast, he observed Sir Walter trying, but in vain, to make his way through a crowd to a seat which had been reserved for him. 'There 's Sir Walter Scott,' said Mr. Harness; 'let 's make way for him.' There was no need for more; the throng pressed itself back so as to make a lane for Scott, and he passed through without the slightest inconvenience." Milman was writing from memory, and Mr. Harness told me that the facts were not quite accurately given in this account. Scott had been in Lord Willoughby's box, but had left it, and on returning found it full of ladies. He was accordingly left without a seat, and while looking hopelessly about was seen by Harness from the balcony, who immediately beckoned to him; and all the people, when they heard who he was, compressed themselves to make room for him. He said, however, that they were very anxious to know whether he was quite sure that he *was* Sir Walter Scott.

Few persons who heard him speak could have doubted Scott's nationality; it could not have been said with justice that Scott —

> "Hung
> On the soft phrase of Southern tongue."

His accent, on the contrary, was so broad that Mr. Harness said he sometimes could not understand him without difficulty. One day when they had been talking of "Lucia di Lammermuir," which had lately appeared, he changed the subject by observing, "Weel! I think we 've a'most had enow of that chiel." Literature, according to Scott's account, was much better paid then than it is at present; for on a friend asking him to subscribe to assist a poor author, he refused to comply, asserting that he knew no one worthy of the name — except

Coleridge — who was not making from £500 to £12,000 a year.

COLERIDGE.

Mr. Harness used occasionally to visit Coleridge when the latter was staying with Mr. Gillman, the apothecary-doctor, at Highgate. The poet originally went there to recover his health, which he had broken down by over-indulgence in opium. He placed himself there under a sort of voluntary restraint, and strict orders were given by Mr. Gillman that no drugs of any kind were to be allowed him. Coleridge, missing the stimulant to which he had been long accustomed, pined and languished under the restriction; he abandoned his pen and sank into utter despondency. One day a large roll of papers came to the poet from the publisher, and on Mr. Gillman's visiting him in the evening he found him an altered man; Coleridge was himself again, full of animation and energy, and busily employed in writing an article for the forthcoming "Review." The change was so sudden and remarkable that the doctor's suspicions were aroused. He instituted inquiries and found that a roll of opium had, at the poet's entreaty, been inclosed in the packet which had arrived that morning from the publisher.

Eminent literary men have often been remarkable for the fertility of their conversation, and their powers in this respect have not unfrequently been used without due restraint and discrimination. Coleridge was no exception to this rule; he would continue to talk on in an unbroken flow, and connect his arguments and observations so adroitly that until you had left him you could not detect their fallacy.[1] Mr. Harness called on him one day with Milman, on their return from paying a visit to Joanna Baillie. The poet seemed unusually inspired, and rambled on, raising his hands and his head in the manner which Charles Mathews so cleverly caricatured; and

[1] Wordsworth and Rogers called on him one forenoon in Pall Mall. He talked uninterruptedly for two hours, during which time Wordsworth listened with profound attention. On leaving, Rogers said to Wordsworth, "Well! I could not make head or tail of Coleridge's oration: did you understand it?" "Not a syllable," replied Wordsworth. Sometimes, however, his conversation was admirable.

asserting, among other strange theories, that Shakespeare was a man of too pure a mind to be able to depict a really worthless character. "All his villains," he said, "were bad upon good principles; even Caliban had something good in him." Coleridge, in his old age, became a characteristic feature in Highgate. He was the terror and amusement of all the little children who bowled their hoops along the poplar avenue. Notwithstanding his fondness for them — he called them 'Kingdom-of-Heaven-ites' — his Cyclopean figure and learned language caused them indescribable alarm. Sometimes he would lay his hand on the shoulders of one of them and walk along discoursing metaphysics to the trembling captive, while the rest fled for refuge and peeped out with laughing faces from behind the trees. "I never," he exclaimed one day to the baker's boy — "I never knew a man good because he was religious, but I have known one religious because he was good."

Lamb.

We can scarcely mention Coleridge without being reminded of his friend and school-fellow, Charles Lamb. On reading the life of this author, lately published by Barry Cornwall, Mr. Harness observed that it must surprise every one how such a clever man as Lamb could have said so few good things. He was chief jester to the "Morning Post," and, though it by no means follows, he was a man of undoubted wit. Mr. Harness remembered many bright bits of fun which from time to time sparkled in his conversation. On one occasion, an old lady was pouring into his ear a tirade, more remarkable for length than substance, when, observing that the essayist was fast lasping into a state of oblivion, she aroused him by remarking in a loud voice, "I 'm afraid, Mr. Lamb, you are deriving no benefit from my observations!" "Well, Madam!" he replied, recollecting himself, "I cannot say that I am; but perhaps the lady on the other side of me is, for they go in at one ear and out of the other."

Elliston, the actor, a self-educated man, was playing cribbage one evening with Lamb, and on drawing out his first card, exclaimed, "When Greek meets Greek, then comes the tug of war." "Yes," replied Lamb, "and when *you* meet Greek you don't understand it."

Sheridan.

Among the distinguished persons with whom Mr. Harness was acquainted, he not unfrequently met the celebrated Sheridan. He was present at some of the sumptuous entertainments with which the dramatist regaled his friends, and remarked that, although his guests denounced his extravagance, they never refused his invitations. Sheridan was not devoid of that vanity which so often accompanies talent. On one occasion, at a Theatrical Fund Dinner, he made a very high-flown speech in which he spoke of himself as being "descended from the loins of kings!" "That is quite true," said Dr. Spry, who was sitting next to Harness; "the last time I saw his father,[1] he was the King of Denmark."

Sheridan's solictor found his client's wife one day walking up and down her drawing-room, apparently in a frantic state of mind. He inquired the cause of such violent perturbation. She only replied "that her husband was a villain." On the man of business further interrogating her as to what had so suddenly awakened her to a sense of that fact, she at length answered, with some hesitation, "Why, I have discovered that all the love-letters he sent me were the very same as those which he sent to his first wife!"

Rogers.

The poet Rogers was a more intimate friend. He was one of those few instances in which talent is found united with wealth and energetic labor. In his literary work he was most persevering; so much so that he spent no less than seventeen years in writing and revising "The Pleasures of Memory." The hasty slip-shod style of the present day was not to his taste. Rogers, like Byron and his compeers, aimed at producing finished pieces; and though they sometimes thus confined their eagle-flight, they at least avoided an ignominious fall to the

[1] He was an actor.

ground. But Rogers was not only a wealthy banker and rural poet; he had also a keen sense of humor, and there was something in the deadness of his countenance and the dryness of his manner which seemed to give additional point to his sarcasms. Mr. Harness said that many of his most telling hits seemed to have little force, when related under different circumstances. Some, however, the reader will, as I imagine, be able to understand without any oral interpretation. Rogers's dwelling was "a cabinet of Art," and he kept a model bachelor's household; his servants consisting of three men and one woman. When one of the former who had been a long time in his service, died, a kind-hearted friend called to condole with him on the loss he had sustained. "Well!" exclaimed Rogers after listening for some time to his expressions of sympathy, "I don't know that I feel his loss so very much, after all. For the first seven years he was an obliging servant; for the second seven years an agreeable companion; but for the last seven he was a tyrannical master."[1]

Speaking of France brought him to the following story, to which he gave considerable effect: "An Englishman and a Frenchman had to fight a duel. That they might have the better chance of missing one another, they were to fight in a dark room. The Englishman fired up the chimney, and, by Jove! he brought down the Frenchman! When I tell this story in Paris," observed Rogers, "I put the Englishman up the chimney!"

Mr. Harness had many other little interesting scraps about Rogers. The poet greatly disliked writing letters of condolence, and when he had that melancholy duty to perform, he generally copied one of Cowper's. Lord Landsdowne once spoke to him in congratulatory terms about the marriage of a common friend. "I do not think it so desirable," observed Rogers. "No!" replied Lord Landsdowne, "why not? His friends approve of it!" "Happy man!" returned Rogers,

[1] The poet seems to have been somewhat unfortunate in his servants. On one occasion when in the country, his favorite groom, with whom he used to drive every day, gave notice to leave. Rogers asked him why he was going and what he had to complain of? "Nothing," replied the man; "but you *are* so dull in the buggy."

"to satisfy all the world. His friends are pleased, *and his enemies are delighted!*"

Moore was a friend of Rogers, and also of Mr. Harness; but I seldom heard the latter speak of him, except with reference to Byron, and to his having asked for information and letters which might be of use in the "Life" he was compiling. Speaking of Moore's taste for biography, and the number of Memoirs he had composed, Rogers one day cynically observed, "Why, it is not safe to die while Moore 's alive!"

Washington Irving.

Among the American friends of this literary coterie, Washington Irving may be mentioned, though he was scarcely to be called an American, inasmuch as his father was an Englishman, and his mother a Scotchwoman. He was often in this country, as his brother was a merchant in Liverpool; and when he visited London, he usually breakfasted with Mr. Harness, and dined with Rogers. Alluding to the vanity and self-appreciation of young America, not unnatural in a rising nation, Mr. Harness told me that a friend of his spoke in the following manner of a play he had lately written: "I wrote a tragedy last winter — and a very good one it was; and my father said he wished to read it, and I allowed him; and *he* said it was a very good one. And he said he should like to go over it with me, word for word, and line for line; and we went over it word for word and line for line; and he said he should like to show it to Washington Irving, and so he did; and *he* thought it was very good, and he said he should like to go over it with me word for word and line for line. And so we did, *and it was beautiful to observe the difference between that old man and me!*"

Theodore Hook.

At Mrs. Siddons's receptions, Mr. Harness became acquainted with Theodore Hook, who was then in general request in fashionable and literary society. He was an accomplished musician, and almost as remarkable for his *improvisa-*

tore talent as for his brilliance in repartee. Wherever he happened to be present, he was looked upon as the wag of the party, and his love of merriment sometimes caused him to indulge in pleasantries which, though sufficiently harmless in themselves, verged too closely upon the limits of propriety. One evening, Mr. Harness, who shared the prejudices then entertained about waltzing, observed to Theodore that he was glad to hear that he disapproved of the new dance. "Well, I don't know about that," returned his friend, "'t is a mere matter of feeling."

When Theodore was travelling along the south coast, he arrived in the course of his journey at Dover, and alighting at the Ship Hotel, changed his boots, ordered a slight dinner, and went out for a stroll through the town. Returning at the appointed time, he was surprised to find the whole establishment in confusion. A crowd had collected outside the door — the master of the house was standing at the foot of the stairs with two candles in his hands, and on Theodore's entrance, he walked backwards before him, and conducted him into the principal saloon, where all the waiters were standing, and a magnificent repast had been provided. The wit was much amused at the dignity to which he had been promoted; but, being an easy-going fellow, made no scruples, and sitting down, did full justice to what was set before him. Next day he signified his intention of departing, and ordered a coach; when, to his astonishment, a carriage-and-four drove up to convey him to his destination. He inquired, with some apprehension, what he was to pay for all this grandeur, and was no less astonished than gratified on receiving the answer, "Nothing whatever, your Royal Highness." He was never more thoroughly mystified; but the next night, on taking off his boots, which he had bought ready-made just before he went to Dover, he found "H. S. H. the Prince of Orange," written inside them. They had been originally made for the Prince, who was then in England, suing for the hand of Princess Charlotte, and notice had been given that all his expenses while in the country should be set down to the charge of the government.

Lydia White.

Among those most celebrated for their hospitalities during Mr. Harness's earlier residence in London, was Miss Lydia White. She kept a "menagerie," and was herself not the least remarkable specimen it contained. Brave in paint and plaster — a wonderful work of art — she underwent all the labor necessary to produce the grand effect, not from any vanity or affectation, but from motives of pure benevolence. "Were I," she observed, "to present myself, as I naturally am, without any of these artificial adornments, instead of being a source of pleasure, and perhaps amusement, to my friends, I should plunge them into the profoundest melancholy." This considerate lady was not only fond of clever conversation, but sometimes herself joined in the tournament of wit. Mr. Harness remembered many sallies of playful nonsense which he had heard from her; one of those he preserved was the following: On the return of Charles X. to Paris, Talma was engaged to play "Sylla;" but he looked so much like Napoleon, that he was ordered to put on a curly wig. "Why," said Lydia, "were he to do that, we should hardly know Scylla from Charybdis."

On another occasion, at one of her small and most agreeable dinners in Park Street, the company (most of them, except the hostess, being Whigs) were discussing, in rather a querulous strain, the desperate prospects of their party. "Yes," said Sydney Smith, "we are in a deplorable condition; we must do something to help ourselves; I think we had better sacrifice a Tory Virgin." This was partially addressed to Lydia White, who at once catching and applying the allusion to Iphigenia, answered, "Well, I believe there is nothing the Whigs would not do *to raise the wind!*"

Henry Hope.

Among Mr. Harness's more intimate friends, the name of Henry Hope should not be omitted. This celebrated millionaire, the author of "Anastasius," and the unfortunate hero in the picture of "Beauty and the Beast," was unremitting in his kindness and hospitality towards the young clergyman. He frequently invited him to stay at the Deep Dene, and here Mr. Harness found himself surrounded by all the talent and wealth of England. The tone of the conversation sometimes amused him much; as when Rothschild observed to Hope that a man must be "a poor scoundrel who could not afford to lose two millions;" or replied to a nobleman who said he must be a supremely happy man, "I happy! when only this morning I received a letter from a man to say that, if I did not send him £500, he would blow out my brains!"[1] Mr. Hope had a tutor for his sons at the Deep Dene. One day, when Mr. Harness was staying there, he found this gentleman pacing up and down the room in the most distressing agitation of mind. "Is there anything the matter?" inquired Mr. Harness, anxiously. "The matter!" he replied, "I should think there was! Three of the worst things that can possibly happen to a man: I 'm in love — I 'm in debt — and I 've doubts about the doctrine of the Trinity!"

Mr. Hope died in 1831. The night after his death Mr. Harness dreamed that he saw Lord Beresford's country residence in an unusual state of commotion. He woke up with the impression that some death or other great calamity had happened there: and though he afterwards thought lightly of the matter, he determined, as he was going in that direction, to call at Lord Beresford's in Duchess Street, on his way home. On arriving there, he found the blinds down, and the house shut up; and upon inquiring, the gate-porter told him that Mr. Thomas Hope had died the day before at Bedgebury Park. Mr. Harness had not known that his friend was either ill or in England. Mr. Hope left Mr. Harness his literary executor.

1 The demands made upon the great are certainly most extraordinary. I remember the late Archbishop Sumner telling me that a man wrote to him to send him immediately £500, as it would save him from "some unpleasant complications." It was to be directed to X. Y. Z., Post Office, Bristol.

SERJEANT TALFOURD.

It was through Miss Mitford's introduction that Mr. Harness became acquainted with Serjeant Talfourd. He had been a Reading boy — a pupil of Dr. Valpy's — and the authoress felt an admiration for his talents even greater than that she entertained for everything else of worth which emanated from her "Belford Regis." He was one of those many *protégés* for whom she predicted a successful career; and when, in after-years, her prophecy had proved true, she often stayed on a visit at his house in London. One of these occasions was shortly after the production and favorable reception of the serjeant's well-known play of "Ion." Miss Mitford was also herself at the zenith of her fame. "Rienzi" had run for fifty nights at Drury Lane; and the attention she received, and the crowds of visitors she attracted, kindled a flame of jealousy in the breast of the rival author. Some complaints of his unreasonable conduct towards her may be found in her letters at this period. It was, perhaps, natural that a man who had just written a successful play should feel a little proud of his bantling; but the serjeant seems, in this respect, to have altogether exceeded the bounds of moderation. One morning at breakfast, during Miss Mitford's visit, he opened a newspaper and came upon a review depreciating his beloved play. This brought matters to a crisis. He loudly inveighed against the injustice of the critic; and on Miss Mitford's endeavoring to pacify him, by remarking that it was really not so severe, and that she should not have felt so much had the strictures been made on her "Rienzi," "Your 'Rienzi,' indeed!" replied the serjeant contemptuously; "I dare say not! That is very different!" I have even heard it stated that the dissension on this subject became so unpleasant that Miss Mitford packed up her boxes one morning and drove away to Mr. Harness's. The serjeant may, perhaps, be pardoned, for his affection for "Ion" was deep and constant. On one occasion, when Dickens was calling on Rogers at Broadstairs, he observed, "We shall have Talfourd here to-night." "Shall we?" returned the poet; "I am rejoiced to hear it. I hope he will come and dine; but how do you know he is coming?" "Because 'Ion' is to be acted at Margate, and he is never absent from any of its representations."

There was as much careless freedom in Talfourd's household as in that of most men of genius. Goldsmith himself could not have desired a more entire absence of conventionality. One day, when Mr. Harness was dining at their house in company with several judges, the serjeant and Mrs. Talfourd sat throughout dinner each with a cat in their lap. On another occasion, Mrs. Talfourd requested him to carve a chicken which was placed before him. He essayed to comply, but on his making the attempt the bird spun round and shot off the dish. Mr. Harness, who was a little timid in society, was much perturbed by this misadventure; but on examining the cause of it, he found that he had been given a fork with only one prong! "Will you be so good as to cut that tart before you," said the hostess to another guest. "Certainly, if you desire it," was the reply; "but perhaps you are not aware that it has not been in the oven?"

A Dinner at Thackeray's.

The name of Dickens brings us to that of his great contemporary, Thackeray; with regard to whom Mr. Harness appeared to entertain some prejudice. He thought his Bohemianism and the general tone of his writings exercised an injurious influence on the rising generation. His first personal experience of the novelist was certainly not calculated to remove this impression. Thackeray invited him to dinner, and Mr. Harness accepted with delight, promising himself a rich intellectual feast at the house of a man of such literary reputation. He was gratified in one respect, for when he arrived he found learning and talent most ably represented. The party at dinner was large, and while the ladies remained the conversation wandered softly among flowers and wine and airy compliments. At length the movement came — the flutter of fans and silks — and the gay *cortége* of youth and beauty made its way to the upper world. The light element had now passed away; the hour had arrived; and Mr. Harness looked forward to such a discussion as should surpass the days of yore. Now was the time for sharp repartee and for the settling of accounts between rival wits — for the cut and thrust and skillful parry. He settled himself in his chair, prepared to take his part if necessary, and kept his eyes and ears open, so as not to lose a single word or gesture. "Do you smoke?" inquired the host. "Smoke?" Mr. Harness had never been guilty of such an offense against social morality. In his day, tars and bargemen were the only smokers — except Dr. Parr — and he retained all the old prejudices against such an imitation of chimney-pots. He would as soon have thought of going to carouse at a public-house as of smoking in the dining-room after dinner. "Smoke, sir? I do not." But his firm refusal had no effect whatever on the epicurean company by which he was surrounded. Cigars and tobacco were placed upon the table; punch and negus followed; and the observations which were made during the rest of the sitting consisted only of such instructive remarks as "Pass the box," and "Fill up!"

DR. MILMAN.

Dr. Milman, who was for a long period Vicar of Reading, before he became Dean of St. Paul's, was one of Mr. Harness's and Miss Mitford's earliest friends. Speaking of his celebrated poem, Mr. Harness observed that one day he found Mr. Murray in an unusual state of disquietude and indignation. "Would you believe it," demanded the publisher, "Milman has written to ask me for an additional sum for the second edition of the 'Fall of Jerusalem?' Why, it was I who made that poem." "You?" repeated Mr. Harness in much astonishment; for although Mr. Murray was an excellent man of business, he could never have been accused of being in the least degree poetical — "you made the 'Fall of Jerusalem?'" "Yes," maintained the publisher stoutly. "I should like to know what that poem would have been if I had not brought it out in an octavo form?" Mr. Murray sent the MS. of "Philip van Artevelde" to Milman and Harness for their opinions as to its prospects of success. Both, strange to say, were unfavorable to it. Mr. Harness said he never knew a book look so different in print from what it did in manuscript. There was to the last much sympathy and intercourse between these remarkable brother clergymen.

A Prison Chaplain.

On our conversation turning one day upon the fact that clergymen generally were destined to witness but small results from their labors, Mr. Harness remarked that allusion had been made to the same subject previously when he was visiting a prison chaplain. Mr. Harness asked him whether his ministry had been attended with success. "With very little, I grieve to say," was the reply. "A short time since I thought I had brought to a better state of mind a man who had attempted to murder a woman and had been condemned to death. He showed great signs of contrition after the sentence was passed upon him, and I thought I could observe the dawnings of grace upon his soul. I gave him a Bible, and he was most assiduous in the study of it, frequently quoting passages from it which he said convinced him of the heinousness of his offense. The man gave altogether such a promise of reformation, and of a change of heart and life, that I exerted myself to the utmost, and obtained for him such a commutation of his sentence as would enable him soon to begin the world again, and as I hoped with a happier result. I called to inform him of my success. His gratitude knew no bounds; he said I was his preserver, his deliverer. 'And here,' he added, as he grasped my hand in parting, 'here is your Bible. I may as well return it to you, *for I hope that I shall never want it again.*'"

Some of Harness's Anecdotes.

A country rector, coming up to preach at Oxford in his turn, complained to Dr. Routh, the venerable Principal of Maudlin, that the remuneration was very inadequate, considering the travelling expenses, and the labor necessary for the composition of the discourse. "How much did they give you?" inquired Dr. Routh. "Only five pounds," was the reply. "Only five pounds?" repeated the doctor. "Why, I would not have preached that sermon for fifty."

At a dinner party a somewhat dull couple, who affected literature, informed their friend that they were going to visit the city of Minerva. Mr. Harness, who happened to be sitting next to the humorous Jekyll, heard him mutter to himself, "To the Greeks — foolishness."

The Bishop of Derry was disputing with a Roman Catholic priest about purgatory. "Well, my lord," replied the priest in conclusion, "you may go farther and fare worse."

Jones, the tailor, was asked by a customer who thought much of his cut, to go down and have some shooting with him in the country. Among the party was the Duke of Northumberland. "Well, Mr. Jones," observed his Grace, "I 'm glad to see that you are becoming a sportsman. What sort of gun do you shoot with?" "Oh, with a double-breasted one, your Grace," was the reply.

Speaking of Brummell, Mr. Harness remarked that many of the dandies of his time were men of wit, and not mere clothes-horses. He remembered a party standing to admire a sunset where the orb of day was departing in a golden glory. "Does it very well, does n't he?" observed Brummell. On another occasion Brummell was walking with a friend past the newly erected bronze statue in Hanover Square. "Well," said his friend, "I never thought Pitt had been so tall a man." "Nor so green a one," added Brummell. Belvoir Castle was at that time very famous for its hospitalities. So large was the number of invitations that people used to come and go almost without the knowledge of the duke. When one set had left, another succeeded as a matter of course, without waiting for any formal invitation. Brummell was among those who enjoyed these privileges. On one occasion a friend went down to Belvoir, and as usual applied for an apartment. "There are none vacant," replied the housekeeper. "None vacant!" returned the dismayed visitor; "how can that be? I know that Mr. Brummell came up to town yesterday." "Yes, sir," replied the lady, "*but he took the key along with him.*"

Having consorted with so many of the most brilliant wits for half a century, Mr. Harness had heard so many racy sayings, that it was difficult to produce any *jeu d'esprit* which seemed to him really original. On one occasion (when he had been dining in company with the Bishop of Oxford and Mr. Gladstone) I inquired how he enjoyed his privilege, and what was the character of the intellectual banquet? "Well," he replied, "after dinner the gentlemen began to relate anecdotes, and, to say the truth, I don't think I ever heard so many stale 'Joe Millers' in my life."

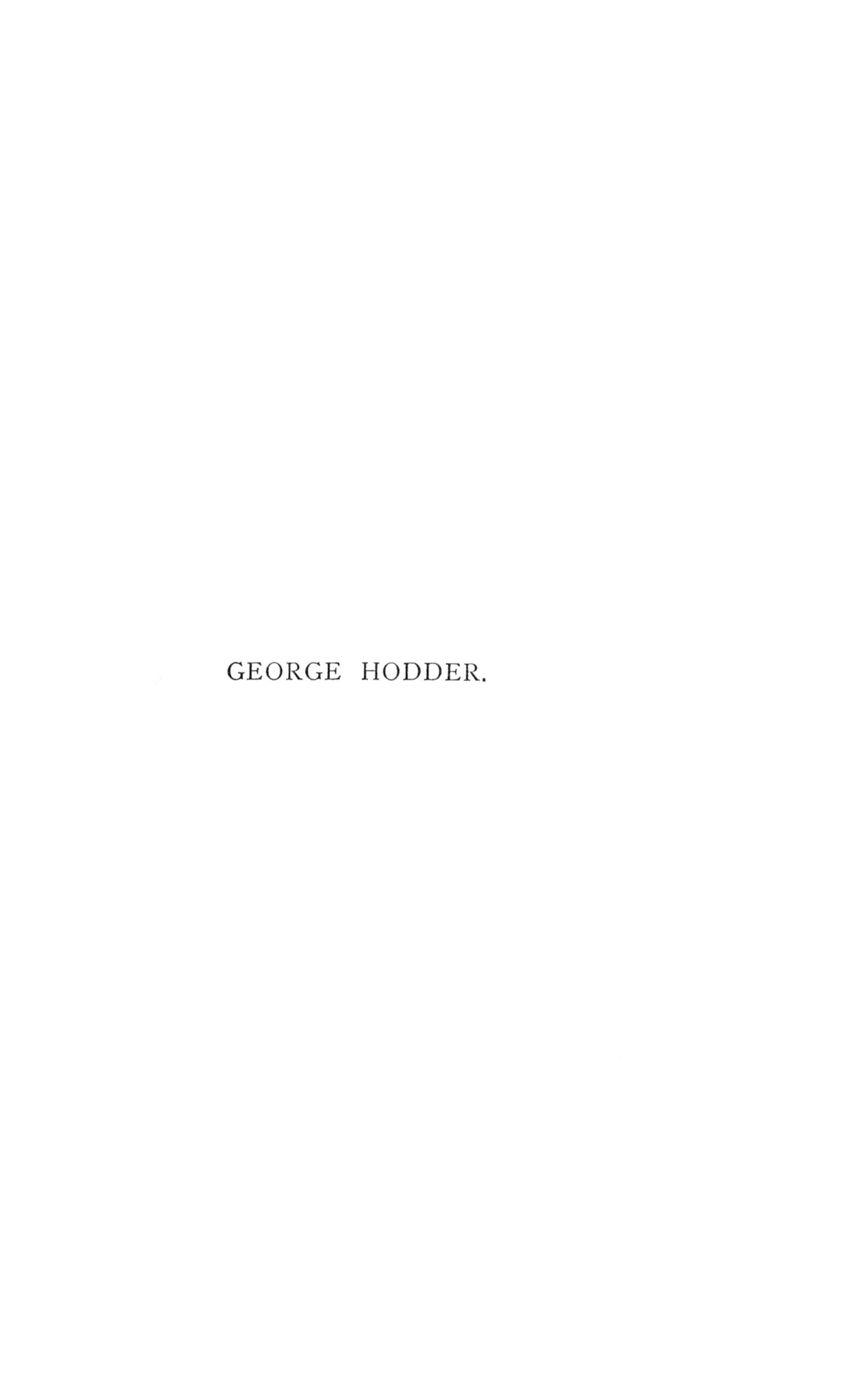

GEORGE HODDER.

GEORGE HODDER.

DOUGLAS JERROLD.

EIGH HUNT, in his memoir of Lord Byron, speaks of the first time he ever saw the poet; but he recalls the fact in a manner which critics have not hesitated to condemn as at variance with good taste. I hope, therefore, that when I mention the circumstances under which I first saw the late Douglas Jerrold I shall only be recording an incident which the great wit himself, or his biographer and son, William Blanchard Jerrold, would hardly fail to smile at good-humoredly.

I had, a few months previously, become the intimate associate of Henry Mayhew, who has long since gained for himself a well-known name in the roll of literary worthies, and who had but just achieved a privilege he had long sought, namely, that of being admitted to the friendship of Douglas Jerrold. Henry Mayhew was then living next door to the Colosseum, in Albany Street, Regent's Park, and was constantly engaged in experiments with an electric battery, which were fraught with some danger, and once had the effect of producing an explosion, which created no little alarm amongst the neighbors. In order to be well protected against the mischievous influence of the chemicals used in his scientific investigations, he was accustomed to wear an entire suit of some black material, highly glazed and loosely made. On one occasion he had asked me to come to his house to see some of his experiments, and I too gladly availed myself of the invitation, though I had no idea at the time that I (a mere stripling under twenty years of age) should then have the gratification of meeting an author whose writings in the "New Monthly Magazine" I had read admiringly, and whose plays I was bold enough to think (as, indeed, I still think) were among the most charming productions of our dramatic literature. To my great delight, however, I had not been in the room many minutes before I was introduced to Douglas Jerrold, who was flitting about with that peculiar restlessness of eye, speech, and demeanor, which was among his most marked characteristics. I confess I was not surprised to find him a man of small stature, as I had heard before that his proportions were rather those of Tydeus than of Alcides; but I was a little astonished when I saw in the author of "Black-eyed Susan," "The Rent-Day," and "The Wedding Gown" (all of which pieces and many others he had then produced), an amount of boyish gayety and a rapidity of movement which one could hardly expect from a writer who had risen to high rank as a moralist and censor.

As a matter of course, a friendly interchange of jokes took place; for Henry Mayhew, though young, had shown, by his farce of "The Wandering Minstrel," and other kindred works, that a keen sense of wit and humor was among his intellectual qualities; and after a few satirical allusions on Jerrold's part to what he obviously thought the visionary nature of Henry Mayhew's occupation, he turned suddenly upon the ambitious experimentalist (whose highly polished clothing had caused him much amusement), and exclaimed, "Why, you look like an advertisement of Warren's blacking!"[1] It is not for me to say whether this little *jeu d'esprit* was of the most brilliant order of joking, but I am at least bound to state that the rapid flash produced its natural effect, and no one laughed more heartily than Jerrold himself; for it was a doctrine of

[1] This *mot* has been published by Blanchard Jerrold in his *Wit and Opinions of Douglas Jerrold;* but inasmuch as he received it from me, I shall not be accused of plagiarism; and I give it precisely as it occurred.

his, as it was of Charles Lamb, that a man had a perfect right to laugh at his own jest.[1]

From that time forth I saw much of Douglas Jerrold, and few had better or more frequent opportunities of observing the kindliness of his nature, and the pleasure he took in performing offices of friendship for literary aspirants in whom he felt an interest. As to his many good sayings, so slight was his estimate of their possible effect, that even friendship seemed to have no charm against the shaft, and hence it became a stereotyped phrase that Jerrold was always "bitter" — an accusation which gave him so much pain that he more than once, in his writings, made it the subject of earnest deprecation. Against this charge of bitterness his son aptly vindicates him. He says: "Although Douglas Jerrold often said bitter things, even of his friends, this bitterness never lost him a friend; for to all men who knew him personally, he was valued as a kind and hearty man; he sprang ever eagerly to the side even of a passing acquaintance who needed a kindness. He might possibly speak something keenly barbed on a grave occasion; but his help would be substantial and his sympathy not the less hearty. For with him a witty view of men and things forced itself upon his mind so continually and irresistibly, and with a vividness and power so intense, that sarcasm flashed from his lips even when he was deeply moved. He knew that his subjection to the dominant faculty of his mind had given him a reputation in the world for ill-nature; and he writhed under this imputation, for he felt how little he deserved it." It is quite unnecessary for me to confirm this statement by any words of my own, but I shall select from a correspondence which is now before me two letters of Jerrold's in order to show how tenderly considerate he was for the feelings of a friend under the most delicate circum-

[1] Shakespeare expresses himself to a different effect, when he says: —

> "A jest's prosperity lies in the ear
> Of him that hears it, never in the tongue
> Of him that makes it."
>
> *Love's Labor's Lost.*

stances. Moreover, the letters are strongly characteristic of Jerrold's laconic and forcible style. The first is an answer to an invitation I had just sent him to be present at my wedding, and is as follows : —

"*September 22d*, 1852.

"DEAR GEORGE, — Don't you put yourself out of your way to be embarrassed by too many visitors. I'll see you when you come back, in your bran-new fetters. Meanwhile, I wish you both all happiness. "Yours faithfully,

"D. JERROLD."

The second letter is dated in March, 1857, four years and a half afterwards, and refers to the death of my dear wife : —

"DEAR GEORGE, — I have just heard from my daughter of your terrible bereavement. Believe me that I sympathize with you most deeply. Though knowing personally but too little of your dear wife, I know enough to feel that your loss must be dreadful. But sorrow is the penalty we pay for life. For the sake of the dear child you must bear up and wrestle with your affliction.

"Believe me sincerely yours,

"DOUGLAS JERROLD."

That Jerrold's friends were many is sufficiently proved by the fact that in the various social clubs he established or assisted in establishing he always had the support and coöperation of men who knew him for his private worth as well as his public usefulness, and who were glad to belong to a society of which he was, by universal consent, the head and front. Not that he ever assumed to himself a dominating position, or that he wished it to be supposed that he possessed any special power of attraction in his personal characteristics ; but he was essentially, as he called it, a "clubable man," and had the faculty of promoting good fellowship to an extent which few men have been able to inspire. Of the clubs he set afloat and gave names to, within my own recollection, I particularly call to mind those which he christened respectively "Hooks and Eyes" and "Our Club" — the former holding its weekly meetings at the "Albion," in Russell Street, Covent Garden, and the latter at Clunn's, in the Piazza, Covent Garden.[1] Of the members of those clubs (one of which grew out of the other) there are many still living who will gladly vouch for the fact that he tuned the first instrument in the band — that he gave the key-note to their joviality, and that the company continued to look up to him as the ruling spirit in their social revels. Apropos of clubs, it may be here stated that Jerrold was so pleased with the success of his "Chronicles of Clovernook," and so impressed with the poetic sound and the lasting popularity of the name — "Clovernook!" — that although it can scarcely be called more than a fragment, he often declared his belief that it had a better chance of reaching the hands of future generations than the rest of his books. Sharing in this conviction, and wishing to pay a tribute to his father's memory, Blanchard Jerrold, some few years after his death, endeavored, in conjunction with a select body of friends, to raise a sum of money, in shares, to purchase a freehold in the country, within a few miles of London, for the purpose of establishing a rural retreat, in the shape of a club (to be called "the Clovernook"), to which its members might resort when anxious to escape from the cares and responsibilities of London life. The prospectus of this club I have not before me at the present moment, but having been its honorary secretary, I have in my possession several letters referring to it, and I transcribe a portion of one of them, because it emanates from a gentleman who was well qualified to form a judgment upon the subject. The letter is from John Cordy Jeaffreson, the author of "Crewe Rise," "Olive Blake's Good Work," "A Book about Doctors," etc. He says: —

"The Clovernook Club has my warmest wishes for its

[1] Many years before this period Jerrold was an active member of a club, called "The Mulberries," which was held at the Wrekin Tavern, in the neighborhood of Covent Garden, and in which a regulation was established that "some paper, or poem, or conceit bearing upon Shakespeare should be contributed by each member," the general title being "Mulberry Leaves."

success, and I hope one day to be a member of it. I also fully appreciate the compliment paid me by its promoters in placing my name on the committee; but I cannot, without knowing more exactly than I do at present the pecuniary arrangements and prospects of the undertaking, consent to be a shareholder. Although I am a literary man, I have not said 'Good-by' to Caution and Prudence, and do not wish to render myself liable to be called upon to pay a large sum for expenses during the first or second year of the Club's existence — and yet in this unpleasant position I may find myself if I join in the responsibilities of an affair the probable durability of which I know nothing about. On one occasion, and one only, Mr. —— invited me to join the Club, and I then stated that I heartily approved the scheme, and should like to be a member, but, as I was very likely going ere long to India, I did not think I should invest in a share."

Whether Mr. Jeaffreson's sly allusion to the fact that, *although* he was a literary man, he was not without caution and prudence, produced any immediate effect with intending members and shareholders need hardly be stated here; suffice it that the promoters of the scheme saw that it would be difficult to obtain the desired support from the only persons to whom they could wisely and conscientiously appeal, and therefore they very properly abandoned it before any material expense was incurred.

It was at the two clubs above mentioned — the "Hooks and Eyes" and "Our Club" — that Douglas Jerrold was known to have said many of the best things that are recorded of him; but as the great majority of these have been published in "The Wit and Opinions of Douglas Jerrold," I need not now seek them out, although it is not to be supposed that the son was enabled to string together *all* the gems that reflected the flashing light of his father. The indefatigable literary explorer, Mr. John Timbs, has devoted several pages of his book on "Club Life" to a chapter on "Douglas Jerrold's Clubs," in which he has adroitly introduced much of the rich fruit that fell around the table when Jerrold was present. In point of fact, the wise and witty sayings of Jerrold have found so many chroniclers, in various shapes and forms, that it would perhaps be in vain to give any important instances which would not at once lead to the exclamation, "I have seen *that* before!"

As a specimen of the singularly laconic style of Jerrold's letters — a style which he has been heard to say, jocularly, that he adopted because he felt, when writing a private epistle, he was "not going to be paid for it" — the following note, received from him a few days before Christmas Day, may be appropriately quoted: —

"SUNDAY EVENING. — Putney.

"DEAR HODDER, — Will you dine with me on Xmas Day?

"Yours truly,

"D. J."

The recollection of my long intercourse with Douglas Jerrold brings to my mind so many agreeable pictures in which he forms the most prominent figure, that I am tempted to dwell for a short time longer upon this part of my task, and to relate such of my experiences as relate especially to himself, unconnected, except in a small degree, with other men of literary distinction.

One of my earliest and most agreeable reminiscences of Jerrold brings me to a period which at once suggests many occurrences of peculiar interest (as will presently be seen) to those who, in their estimate of public characters, would gladly acquire some knowledge of their private tastes and virtues. It was in the year 1841; and Jerrold had for some time domiciled himself and his family at a snug little villa at Boulogne, in the Rue D'Alger, Capécure, which, as "all England" knows (for all England is supposed to be familiar with Boulogne), is on "the other side of the water" from the town proper; his motive for residing in France being to educate his children — two girls (the elder of whom afterwards became Mrs. Henry Mayhew) and three boys. William Blanchard Jerrold, the eldest son, was at that period a rosy-cheeked stripling of about fourteen years of age; and I am glad to think that, as time passed away, my acquaintance with him ripened into a substantial and enduring friendship. Jerrold had often written to friends in London, apprising them of the comfortable quarters he was housed in, and inviting them to partake of his hospitality. Amongst those who were thus favored was myself, and I well remember the cordial terms in which the invitation was conveyed, and the many temptations held out to me to undergo "the perils of the Channel" for the first time. The prospect of a fortnight's sojourn under the roof of such a companion as Douglas Jerrold was much too tempting to be resisted; and the pleasure I felt was enhanced when I received a letter from him, stating that, if I came on a given day at a specified time, the tide would enable me to arrive at Boulogne at an hour when he could meet me on the port. I went by "long sea," as it was called — that is to say, by steamboat direct from London Bridge to the harbor of this picturesque and enlivening watering-place. The day was a Sunday in the month of August, and the vessel reached its destination between two and three o'clock in the afternoon. The weather was lovely in the extreme, and the port was thronged with people, all more or less anxiously looking for the arrival of the boat. The scene was altogether the most perfect instance of cheerful bustle and animation I had ever witnessed; and I was disposed to wonder how it was that, in the midst of so much attractive excitement, an author could find sufficient repose for the due exercise of his brain; for Jerrold was at that time engaged in many important literary undertakings.

Long before I was enabled to leave the deck of the vessel, I descried, to my infinite delight, Jerrold standing as near to the landing-place as the crowd would permit him; and the moment he saw me he gave me such a "sweet smile of welcome" that I could but feel what a care-dispelling visit fortune had placed in store for me. Then came the hearty shake of the hand, and the joke — far, far indeed from a "bitter" one — and the delay during the tedious ceremony at the custom-house; for in those days the passport system was carried out with the most provoking determination. Arrived at Jerrold's dwelling he exclaimed, as we entered, placing himself in a sort of theatrical attitude, "The bandit's haunt! Let us see what fare we have within!" I very soon found, however, that his habits were by no means of a melodramatic cast, and that he was surrounded by every comfort, not to say luxury, which could be desired by a contented and united English family abroad. His children were home from school that day, and I was much impressed by the pride and pleasure he seemed to feel in introducing them, and in pointing out jocosely their several characteristics.

He occupied himself "at his desk" (as he always expressed it when speaking of his mental employment) in the morning; and in the afternoon he was ready for a walk along the sands, or an excursion into the market-place to amuse himself with the fruit-vendors, or for a jaunt into the country to one of the many attractive little villages which lie within a few miles' distance of Boulogne. A dip in the sea — his native element, as he sometimes called it — was a relaxation to which he was especially addicted; but he did not care to indulge it where the multitude were wont to assemble for the same object. On one occasion I was walking with him at sunset along the beach, in the outskirts of the town, when the tide was unusually low, and the sands were as smooth and unruffled as a drawing-room carpet. The charm of the weather seemed to absorb Jerrold's attention, for the evening was as calm and placid as the countenance of a sleeping infant, and he made frequent allusions to the atmosphere, which, he said, was such as he had never experienced "out of France." At length, fixing his eye upon the almost motionless sea, and inhaling the fresh air as if he were sipping nectar, he suddenly exclaimed: "How lovely the water looks! Egad, I'll have a dip!" and in scarcely more time than is occupied by the pantomime-clown in making his inevitable "change," he stuck his stick in the sand, placed his hat upon the top and his clothes around it, and ran into the water with a nimbleness which he could hardly have surpassed in the midshipman days of his youth.

During this visit to Douglas Jerrold, I made the acquaintance of Mr. and Mrs. Alfred Wigan, the now celebrated, but then comparatively unknown, dramatic artists, who had been living for some weeks at Boulogne, and with whom I enjoyed a daily companionship.

Mr. and Mrs. Wigan were frequent guests at the house of Douglas Jerrold, who entertained a strong opinion in regard to the dramatic capabilities of the former, and was resolved to promote his advancement by every means at his command, although up to that period Mr. Wigan had really done nothing to indicate the possession of that histrionic power which he has since displayed. During his stay at Boulogne, Jerrold wrote that most charming of serio-comic dramas, "The Prisoner of War," and also the comedy of "Gertrude's Cherries," in which he introduced a character called Alcibiade Blague (a Frenchman speaking broken English), which he had studiously designed for Alfred Wigan, and was resolved that no one but that gentleman should play it. The piece was ultimately produced at Covent Garden Theatre, but with a degree of success which can only be pronounced moderate, although it was brimful of the characteristic charms of Jerrold's dramatic muse, and Mr. Wigan achieved high distinction by his personation in the part so generously assigned to him.[1] "The Prisoner of War," which was produced at Drury Lane Theatre in February, 1842, met with a different fate, for it proved to be one of the most entertaining and effective pieces that ever came from Jerrold's pen, comprising as it did a delightful admixture of comedy and pathos, and being performed by such artists as Mr. Phelps, Mr. James Anderson, Mr. Hudson, Mr. Selby, Mr. Morris Barnett, Mr. George Bennett, Mr. Keeley, Mrs. Keeley, Miss Fortescue, Mrs. C. Jones, Mrs. Selby, etc. It is not a little singular that, proud as Jerrold was and had reason to be of this admirable work, he never saw it played — at least during its first season; but he always expected, he said, that the result

[1] It is difficult to conceive why this piece, with many others of the same author's productions, including *The White Milliner*, *The Heart of Gold*, etc., has not been published in the collected edition of Jerrold's comedies and dramas.

would prove as gratifying as it did ; for the sentiment was homely and truthful, and there were two characters in the piece — Peter Pall Mall and Polly Pall Mall, brother and sister — represented by Mr. and Mrs. Keeley, which were sufficiently diverting to insure a successful ordeal for even a less meritorious work.

The reference to this drama in particular naturally leads to the consideration of Douglas Jerrold's dramas in general ; and I cannot but think it a source of national regret that such thoroughly original and legitimate productions as "Time Works Wonders," "Bubbles of the Day," "The Rent Day," "The Schoolfellows," "The Housekeeper," "The Wedding Gown," "Doves in a Cage," "The Prisoner of War," "Retired from Business," etc., should not be occasionally revived on the metropolitan stage, for the charm of reading them is so great that one yearns to see them assume a substantial form and color. Setting aside the more important plays in five acts — "Time Works Wonders"[1] and "Bubbles of the Day" — it has always appeared to me that Jerrold's dramatic works are the best efforts of his genius, combining as they do the most concise and salutary plots, and an infinite knowledge of the secret springs of character, with the most terse, yet impressive dialogue ; and it is certainly sad to think that "Black-Eyed Susan" (the extraordinary merit of which, strange to say, he could never be induced to admit) should be the only one of his pieces which holds its due position before the public, while encouragement is given to a class of composition which never did, and never can, belong to the "literature" of the drama. Jerrold's dramas still "live," but, unhappily, not in the full knowledge of those who would rejoice in becoming more practically acquainted with them than they can possibly be through the unaided process of *reading*.

To return to the domiciliary habits of Jerrold at his little cottage at Boulogne-sur-Mer. In the simplicity of his heart

[1] When Jerrold first told me he had finished this comedy he called it "School-girl Love," and I made free to remark that I did not think the title sufficiently imposing for a five-act play.

(for it is a trite proverb that the greatest minds can find pleasure in the smallest diversions) he had a most amiable predilection for giving juvenile parties — that is to say, parties consisting of his two daughters and certain of their school companions ; and on those occasions he included in the programme of the evening's amusement "acting charades," in which the principal performers were himself, Mr. and Mrs. Wigan, and M. Bonnefoy, the preceptor of his three boys. With what impulsive delight he entered into the spirit of those entertainments may be imagined by those who are not unmindful of the energy he displayed when subjecting himself to the ordeal of the stage ; and they may also conceive the intelligent zeal and earnestness with which Mr. Wigan (who was then patiently awaiting the chance of showing the "metal" that was in him) performed his part in the extempore representations. But the greatest charm of all to be found in those merry *soirées* was gathered from the graceful agility of the juvenile ladies, who would commence a dance in the drawing-room and continue it in the garden, under the light of the moon — "sweet mistress" of the ceremonies, as she was "of the sky." The entire bevy of young damsels being dressed in white muslin, the effect of their evolutions, as they tripped round the green sward at the back of the house, was certainly suggestive of a scene from one of those ever-captivating fairy stories, which are the delight of age no less than of youth, and which, it is hoped, may always recur to us at our seasons of rejoicing. Many years have elapsed since those happy times, and I have often reverted to them with a memory full of gratitude for the enjoyment I then experienced, and have asked myself the question "Will such days or nights ever come to us again?" Or is it that, by some singular ordination of Providence, we are prone to look at the past with a higher sense of thankfulness than at the present? In any case, I shall ever be keenly alive to the conviction that at no period of my career have I partaken of more unalloyed pleasure — more innocent and healthful amusement, than I enjoyed under the "roof-tree" of Douglas Jerrold, at Boulogne-sur-Mer.

Some years afterwards Jerrold rented a cottage in the neighborhood of Herne Bay; and there also I received, under similar circumstances, his most agreeable hospitality; but, blessed as he was with all those domestic comforts which sufficed to gratify his moderate aspirations, the absence of that picturesque element belonging to the French watering-place prevented his indulging that perfect *abandon* which he felt under the sunny skies of the Pas de Calais. Still he was ever the most pleasant and attentive of hosts, as Mrs. Jerrold was the most thoughtful and considerate of housewives; and it was noticeable that, so cunningly did the former arrange his few hours' work by rising early in the morning, that he never seemed absent from his guests, who were often somewhat numerous at that time. Plans would be arranged daily for drives or pedestrian excursions to Margate or Canterbury, or to some sequestered nook lying far away in the country; and on those occasions Jerrold would infuse new life into the party, by his never-ceasing glee, and by the rapidity with which he seized every possible opportunity of "tuning his merry note" to the utterance of a jest or anecdote that sprang out of the conversation, or from some fleeting material which his quickness of perception had enabled him to discover by the wayside.

One of the most agreeable and most memorable of the excursions now referred to was a jaunt by private conveyance to Whitstable, the object being to eat oysters fresh from the sea. The party on that occasion consisted of Jerrold, John Leech, Henry Mayhew (who was then engaged in the preparation of an English dictionary on a very elaborate scale, and had taken up his abode in a quiet, rural spot, with a view to pursuing his labors), Kenny Meadows, and myself. The oysters were pronounced to be such as "nobody" had ever tasted before; and as they were supplied to us at less than half the cost that they have reached of late years, the quantity consumed was sufficient to justify a general recourse to some obviously-smuggled Schiedam, which caused us all to smack our lips with approving gusto, and which found such charms for one of the party (who shall not be described by name), that he achieved the feat of imbibing, on the return journey, under a scorching July sun, the contents of a full flask. And he lives to tell the tale! That he did not present himself at dinner that day may well be believed; and much did he lose by his absence, for Jerrold was in one of his most humorous moods, and managed without any abnormal effort to keep the table in a roar; but, it must be confessed, at the expense of our valiant spirit-drinker, whose prowess had rendered every allusion to his name a source of unavoidable merriment. It was during Jerrold's residence at Herne Bay that he conceived and planned many of the best-known emanations from his pen, including "The Chronicles of Clovernook," already referred to; and other attractive contributions to the "Illuminated Magazine," which had been started not long previously under his auspices and those of Mr. Ebenezer Landells, the engraver. The duty of sub-editor was assigned to me, and in that capacity I was called upon to be the medium of communication between the artists and the authors, and to supply the former with wood-blocks as well as subjects for their work. The practical responsibility of arranging the contents of each number also devolved upon me; and, as this brought me in contact with contributors who preferred addressing me to inflicting their correspondence upon the editor, Douglas Jerrold, I often received letters which possessed an interest beyond that of the passing moment. I copy the following as an example of the unreserved manner in which a writer will place his confidence in one who, if he does not occupy the "editorial chair," has immediate access to it. The letter is from a gentleman who had already published two successful novels, and has since written others of corresponding ability and power: —

"NOTTINGHAM, *May* 2, 1844.

"DEAR SIR, — Will you be kind enough to ascertain whether the last story I sent to Mr. Jerrold is acceptable or not? I observe myself absent again this month, or you would not have been troubled. But the fact is I am one of those unlucky dogs to whom the pen is a dependence, — precisely the same thing, you know, as saying my life hangs on a thread ; and, therefore, it is of importance to me — that is to the extent of the bread-basket — to avoid delay as far as possible in the publication of such papers as may have the luck to meet with approval, or, if not, to have them returned as early as may be convenient.

" I feel entire reliance upon Mr. Jerrold's kindness and consideration for my excuse in making these remarks, because he knows too well how much, at the very best, must be endured by any one like myself and thus situated. But whether, on that account, we deserve any more consideration than your happy and flourishing amateur penman, who feels sufficiently paid by seeing himself in print, is a question upon which, of course, I can offer no opinion.

" Believe me, very sincerely yours,

" CHARLES HOOTON."

As I could not always be present when Jerrold was arranging the contents of the number for the ensuing month, his practice was to send me word by letter the names of the articles he had chosen, and which he desired should be next in order of publication. The following will serve to convey some idea of the fairness with which he dealt out his opinions upon papers submitted to his editorial judgment. It will be seen that the letter refers to an illness from which I was then recovering, and to other matters of a personal nature, but the main object of his writing was to direct my attention to a decision he had come to respecting contributions he had received for the " Illuminated Magazine."

" *September* 9.

" MY DEAR HODDER, — I write after hard morning's work, so write *short*. I 'm happy to hear you 're recovering. I have no doubt that among us we shall be able to make you some little amends if the San. [Sanatorium] should fail.[1]

" ' The Dwellings of the Poor ' goes in this month. Hoskins *not at all*.

[1] The Sanatorium, or Home in Sickness — an institution of which I was then secretary.

"If you return in about ten days, 't will be time enough for index. The Mag. is rising. I have been worked to death for 'Punch,' having it all on my shoulders, Mark,[1] à Beckett, and Thackeray being away. Nevertheless, last week it went up 1,500.

"Yours ever truly,

"D. J."

Some of the best papers that Jerrold ever wrote for serial publications appeared in this periodical: "Elizabeth and Victoria" (a comparison between the social customs and vices of the two reigns); "The Order of Poverty;" "The Old Man at the Gate;" "The Two Windows;" "The Folly of the Sword;" and, above all, "The Chronicles of Clovernook," which he composed under the disadvantage of seriously impaired health. During the progress of that work he was attacked by rheumatism in so aggravated a form that I frequently saw him propped up in bed while he prepared a chapter which the printer's boy was waiting below to receive; and it was really touching to observe the patient endurance he betrayed when engaged in an occupation which necessarily increased the pain he was suffering. Whether his sensibilities were quickened by the sad condition he was reduced to, or whether his mind had become so thoroughly imbued with the subject he was treating, that even pain could not prevent his fulfilling his purpose, it is not for me to say; but certain it is that during that long and severe illness the most poetical thoughts ever kindled in the brain of Jerrold were laid before the world. The body was weakened by suffering, but the light within was unquenched, and the results of his mental vigor at that crisis forcibly illustrate the truth of a theory which he advocated, whenever he heard of any extraordinary achievement by a contemporary whose advanced age would seem to render such achievement impossible — that "Genius never dies."

Indeed, so weak and emaciated had poor Jerrold become at that time that many of his friends began to have serious mis-

[1] Mark Lemon, the editor.

givings as to his ultimate recovery; but (as he was often heard to exclaim in after-days) he took counsel with himself one morning as he endeavored to rise in his bed; and when he thought of what he had done, and what he hoped to be still capable of doing, he said, "No — I am *not* going to die." That he uttered these words with the same emphasis and vigor which characterize the ejaculations of Uncle Toby in the "Story of Lefevre" can hardly be suggested; but he was certainly a man of stern resolve; and he felt that his health gave signs of improvement, and that he was not doomed to end his days thus prematurely. But whether his health had improved or not, such was the dominant force of his will that he determined to undergo the ordeal of the cold-water cure at Great Malvern; and he allowed himself to be carried from his bed to the conveyance that was in readiness to remove him from his home. He was absent, I think, about three weeks; and on his return his health, though not perfectly restored, was much invigorated, for the root of the disease seemed to have been destroyed, and he was capable of resuming his literary labors and the editorship of the "Illuminated Magazine," which, as he had reason to believe, was "rising" in circulation.

The principle upon which this magazine was conducted afforded an illustration among the many which came within my knowledge of the exceptional readiness shown by Jerrold to allow young authors, who had never before "seen themselves in print," to make their *début* under his editorial auspices. There are many writers now holding prominent positions before the public whose names were totally unknown, either to fortune or to fame, until Douglas Jerrold, with a vivid appreciation of the merit that was in them, gave them an opportunity of starting on the career they aspired to. The pages of the "Illuminated" were generously thrown open to "all comers" whose contributions presented sufficient evidence of talent to Jerrold's discriminating eye; and, what is more, he permitted them to affix their names to their articles if they were so disposed, for he could not see the justice of one all-powerful writer keeping his own name prominently forward while those of his *collaborateurs* were suppressed.

The "purpose" of the "Illuminated Magazine," as stated by Jerrold in a preface to the first volume, is thus described: —

"It has been the wish of the proprietors of this work to speak to the MASSES of the people; and whilst sympathizing with their deeper and sterner wants, to offer to them those graces of art and literature which have too long been held the exclusive right of those of happier fortunes."

That the magazine contained many articles especially adapted to the "masses" can scarcely be averred, nor was Jerrold's style of writing (at least in those days, when he had not yet thrown himself into the arena of newspaper controversy) such as could be said to appeal successfully to the comprehension of the "great uneducated;" but his heart and sympathies kept him their firm champion, although his nature was so fastidious that his friends were often known to say to him, "Jerrold, you 're a thorough aristocrat in the main."

The magazine came into existence in the month of May, 1843, and terminated its career at the close of the third volume (each volume extending over a period of six months). The final number contained the following: —

"POSTSCRIPT BY THE EDITOR.

"With this number closes the third volume of the 'Illuminated Magazine,' and with it close the duties of the present editor. In the progress of his task he has received so much pleasure and encouragement from the sympathies and best wishes of many, that he cannot lay down the pen without thus formally acknowledging them. Trusting that the brevity with which this is done will not impugn its sincerity, the editor — as editor — bids his readers a respectful farewell; but not without the hope of again meeting them in these pages.

"DOUGLAS JERROLD.

"*Sept. 27th.*"

The limited career of this work was doubtless owing to its unwieldly size, for it can scarcely be supposed that a monthly periodical, whose page presented almost as many superficial inches as that of the "Illustrated London News," would be regarded as a convenient form for the ultimate operation of binding. The work was admirably printed; the illustrations were engraved by E. Landells, and designed by the best artists of the day in this branch of the pictorial art, including Kenny Meadows, Leech, Hine, Prior, Harvey, Henning, Gilbert, etc.; the letter-press comprised some of the most readable productions of the day, both in poetry and in prose, and, above all, one of the leading attractions was the series of papers by the editor, under the title of "Chronicles of Clovernook," which, as previously stated in this volume, Jerrold estimated as his masterpiece in descriptive and imaginative writing. It is abundantly clear, therefore, that the cause of its downfall must not be looked for in the contents, but in the unwillingness of the reading world to be diverted from the more handy magazines to which it had become familiarized.

Not very long after the extinction of the "Illuminated Magazine," Messrs. Bradbury and Evans (who by this time had so allied themselves to Jerrold that he seldom published anything except under their auspices) produced a monthly periodical, bearing Jerrold's name as the editor, with a desire to resume, as far as possible, the same character of articles for which the former work was especially distinguished. The new publication was called "Douglas Jerrold's Shilling Magazine," and, when all preliminaries were settled, he addressed me the following note in reference to Dr. Hitchman, whose name I recall with much satisfaction: —

'*Nov. 11th*, '44.

"DEAR HODDER, — I arrived back last night. My object in now writing is that you should speak to Mr. H. (I forget his name), the surgeon of Sanatorium, telling him that I have a magazine coming out on the 1st of January (the thing is *decided*), and that I shall be very glad if he will furnish an article of the same nature to his last. The matter must be of the *present day*, and social in its application.

"Yours truly,

"D. J."

I need not say that the wish of my correspondent was strictly obeyed by me, and also, I believe, by the learned doctor.

In the new magazine, which in point of size was the very opposite of the "Illuminated," Jerrold published his "St. Giles and St. James," "Twiddlethumb Town," and "The Hedgehog Papers;" but as I was in no way associated with him in regard to the periodical, I shall not attempt to enlarge upon its characteristics, further than to draw attention to a somewhat romantic incident which I communicated to him, and which it was his intention to introduce into that work if its career had not been prematurely brought to a close. It was some time after the "Shilling Magazine" was projected that a now deceased sister of mine, having lost her husband in one of the Indian wars, was about to return to this country. She had made her way from the seat of warfare to Calcutta, there to embark on one of the steamers leaving that city. Hearing, however, that a sailing vessel, under the command of one of her brothers, Captain Charles Hodder, was shortly to arrive at Madras, she prolonged her stay at Calcutta, and ultimately made her way to the former city. There she was detained several weeks, as she was resolved to return to England in her brother's ship, and the money she expended in consequence of the delay was actually a matter of serious consideration, seeing that she had not long lost her husband, and that she would not be able to complete her pecuniary arrangements until her arrival in London.

At length came the day of sailing, and my sister (who had her only child with her, a boy some twelve months old) was the sole female passenger; but she was so overjoyed at the idea of returning home under the care and guidance of her own brother, that she was fully reconciled to her position, and indeed she felt some little compensation for the sad bereavement she had lately sustained. One evening, while still skirting the Coromandel coast, the vessel struck upon a reef, and my brother found that she was doomed to be a total wreck. Hastening down to his sister's cabin, and throwing his arms round her neck, he exclaimed, "Margaret, the ship's ashore, and I am a ruined man!" She never murmured, nor gave way to those hysterical shrieks in which the tender sex too often seek relief in their misfortunes, but affectionately embraced her brother, and implored him to hope for the best. She then placed what money she possessed at his disposal, and begged that he would resort to it in case of need. Nor did she dream of deserting him, but was heroically resolved to remain with him whatever might betide. It was, however, unadvisible that she should continue on board that night, as there appeared to be no chance of saving the vessel, and the probability was that early in the morning the whole of the crew would be compelled to abandon her. The lady was therefore conveyed ashore with her child, and she lay on the beach all night under the shelter of a capacious umbrella. She had taken with her a necessary supply of provisions, and, from what I understood at the time, the natives endeavored to steal them, for at break of day my brother, in surveying the spot by the aid of his telescope, saw his sister belaboring some two or three black fellows with a formidable weapon she held in her hand. But this is only a single instance of the courage and determination she displayed after the melancholy catastrophe, for the abandonment of the vessel was found to be inevitable, and my sister's exemplary fortitude was of great service to her brother in the strait to which he was unhappily reduced. So completely had she fixed her mind upon reaching England with him, that she accompanied him by the overland route (as he was compelled to expedite his return in order to relate the particulars of the wreck to the owners of his vessel), and played a Christian woman's part towards him until she saw him in safety at her own fireside in London. On my recounting this little story to Jerrold some time afterwards, while sitting *tête-à-tête* with him at the Café de l'Europe, in the Haymarket, I found I had touched a chord in his sensitive heart; and when I came to the close, he exclaimed, thumping his hand upon the table, as was his wont when his enthusiasm was aroused, "By G—d! that woman 's a heroine! There 's a sister for a brother to be proud of!" He then begged me to sketch out the details of the adventure upon paper; and I speedily did so. But, for the reason I have already described, his rendering of the story never appeared in print.

I have spoken of the agreeable intercourse I enjoyed with Douglas Jerrold on the occasion of my first visit to Boulogne —a seaport which, although it has been almost the fashion to regard it as an English rather than as a French watering-place, is, to all intents and purposes, as much a constituent part of the great empire of France as any other town lying between the straits of Dover and Paris. At the period just referred to I had no thought of anything beyond pleasure and recreation; but many years subsequently I visited the same country again with my friend, under circumstances which partook chiefly of a business character. In such high esteem was the name of Jerrold held as the writer of the "Q" articles, which formed the political element of "Punch," that in the beginning of the year 1848 some few gentlemen of small capital tempted him to sanction the starting of a weekly journal in the liberal interest, under the title of "Douglas Jerrold's Weekly Newspaper," himself, of course, the editor; and the revolution which drove Louis Philippe from the throne occurring shortly afterwards, it was suggested that a powerful impetus might be given to the undertaking by Jerrold visiting Paris, and writing in the midst of the popular disturbances a series of articles from ocular demonstration.

All arrangements being made for his departure, he proposed that I should accompany him, with a view to assist him by collecting material for the exercise of his pen; and we arrived in Paris a few days after the outbreak of the revolutionary movement. To describe the state of Paris at that extraordinary crisis would indeed be idle, as the details have long become matter of universal history. But I feel bound to revert to that period because it affords me an opportunity of exhibiting a new phase of Douglas Jerrold's character, though at the same time I should state that the son has recorded in the biography already referred to — chiefly indeed from information supplied by myself — some particulars of the father's visit to the French capital. On our arrival in that metropolis many of the streets were rendered totally impassable by the barricades which had been raised throughout the city. The insurrectionary fury had been partially spent; but the whole populace was in a most disorganized condition; and so imminent was the danger of an *émeute* arising, that the National Guard were in arms at all hours of the day and night, and the peaceful portion of the citizens were constantly disturbed by the sounding of the *rappel.* In all the public places flags and placards were exhibited, presenting such inscriptions as "*Vive la Réforme,*" "*Vive la Garde Nationale.*" "*A bas le Roi!*" "*A bas Guizot!*" "*Vive le peuple!*" etc., while the universal cry was "*Liberté, Egalité, Fraternité.*"

Amongst the many excitements in which the people indulged was that of planting, in the most frequented streets, "trees of liberty," some of which manifested a disposition to grow, but the great majority were so choked by the surrounding paving-stones that they vainly struggled to exist. All this was abundantly visible to us during the first twenty-four hours of our stay in Paris; and Jerrold, having once satisfied his eyes as to the general condition of the city, would not have been at all sorry had he been compelled to return home on the day after his arrival. On the second day he sat down in an uncomfortable corner of our private sitting-room, in, if I remember rightly, the Hôtel Bedford, and penned a long letter for his paper; but gave little or no proof that he was writing from the scene of action. I saw, when he had dispatched his parcel, that he had embarked in an enterprise which was not likely to yield a return commensurate with the outlay, and in the few subsequent attempts he made to fulfill his mission it was evident that his mind was not in his work. "After all," he more than once exclaimed, "I might just as well do this in Cheapside or Fleet Street;" and on my reminding him that I had accompanied him to Paris for the sole purpose of collecting "facts" for him, and that I was most willing to carry out that object, he said, somewhat angrily, "D—n the facts! I don't want facts." Whereupon I expressed my regret that I had ever left London, as I did not like the idea of being useless to him; and many a time, when I hastened back to the hotel after spending some hours in gathering valuable information, and thought I should please him by describing what I had seen or learnt, he received me with coldness, and emphatically declined to accept my proffered aid. I frequently reminded him that he had not yet delivered the letters of introduction, which he possessed, to Lamartine, Ledru-Rollin, and other influential persons, either in connection with the Provisional Government, or with some important public department; but he always evaded the subject, and said he was in no hurry to perform a task which he detested.

At length I found that he had abandoned all further idea of acting in the character of a "special correspondent" for his own paper, resting content to supply himself with a few miscellaneous incidents of a cursory nature, and retaining them until he should be seated at his own desk at Putney Common, where he then resided. In short, he was blessed with so many "aids to reflection" and enjoyment in his own English home that he could not brook the discomfort of writing in "strange nooks and corners," without the accustomed implements of his calling, and far removed from those domestic influences which he often confessed quickened his impulses and chastened his understanding. The work he had embarked in was totally unsuited to him, and it was really grievous to notice the expression of his countenance, as, morning after morning, the post brought him a letter from his *locum tenens* in London, Mr. Frederick Guest Tomlins, complaining of his shortcomings, and urging him to return, or to act in a manner more worthy of his ambition and of the known reputation he bore. He felt himself, however, in the position of an irresponsible agent, and he thought it would have been just as little worthy of him to attempt that which he knew he could not successfully accomplish as to neglect the duty altogether; but at the same time he was reluctant to return to England until he had been absent a sufficient time to show that, at least, he had *tried* to fulfill the trust reposed in him. His plan, therefore, was to pass the morning in reading the French newspapers, and thus laying in a stock of material, either for his paper or for his weekly contributions to "Punch," and to devote the remainder of the day to sauntering about the Boulevards, choosing a restaurant to dine at, and visiting a theatre in the evening.

In ordering his dinner his great fancy was for *quelque chose appétissante*, as he called the lighter form of *entrées*, and a bottle of Tavel — the latter because he said it was "the Frenchman's port," and it was lighter and dryer than our own. It must be confessed, however, that the bent of his genius did not lie in the direction of gastronomy; and though he well knew the difference between a *gourmand* and a *gourmet*, he had not the skill to order a dinner with a due regard to economy, either in reference to money or food, and the result was that the former was often unnecessarily expended, and the latter was much more plentiful than *recherché*. He had every desire to vary his place of entertainment; but if he could not procure his favorite Tavel he would not go a second time to a restaurant where that almost-exploded wine was disregarded. Although proud to be thought an Englishman, it was a source of annoyance to him to be treated as one, and he was apt to resent as an indignity any allusion to his being of the family of "John Bull." One day he essayed his taste and skill at the Café Riche, which was on a somewhat more extensive scale than the restaurants he generally patronized, and upon his asking for the *carte du jour*, the waiter roused his anger to a high pitch by saying, "*Il y a du bon rosbif aujourd'hui.*" "Don't come to France to eat roast beef," he curtly replied: "Plenty of that at home." And he never dined at the Café Riche again.

Thus the same spirit of discontent continued to pervade his actions during the few remaining days of his sojourn in the French metropolis; and it was by no means decreased as the morning of his departure drew near; for then he began to reproach himself for not having delivered his letters of introduction. I observed that his mornings were often disturbed by visits from John Poole, the author of "Paul Pry," who had for many years been living in Paris; and although Jerrold never distinctly told me the object of his seeking him, it was evident from the manner of the latter, and from a few broken sentences he muttered, that there was some cause for coldness between them. "Poor Poole!" he exclaimed one day, after receiving a visit from him; "he has not made the best of his chances in life." At another time he observed that Poole was never known to *say* a good thing; but that if an idea struck him in society he would "book it for his next magazine article." Amongst others who sought Jerrold's acquaintance in Paris was the Rev. Francis Mahony ("Father Prout"), and I had the gratification of meeting the two men at a little dinner-party at the residence of Mr. Thomas Frazer,[1] the correspondent of the "Morning Chronicle," on the Boulevard des Capucines. Even on that occasion it was noticeable that Jerrold was ill at ease, and was not much disposed to talk upon the subject which at that period naturally absorbed the attention of the community. Indeed, he constantly reflected, both in society and when alone, that his visit to Paris had involved a loss of time and money, and that, on his return home, he should not receive that hearty welcome from his fellow-workers on the newspaper which his public position would otherwise have led him to expect. When the morning came for his departure — about a fortnight after his arrival — he openly acknowledged that his mission to Paris had been a failure; and as he was arranging his portmanteau, he took therefrom a small packet, and, throwing it into the fire, said, "There are my letters of introduction!"

[1] This is the kind-hearted man alluded to by Thackeray in his *Ballad of Bouillabaisse*: —

"There's laughing Tom is laughing yet."

Although, as I have already shown, Jerrold's character at that time did not appear in a light quite so amiable as his friends could have wished, I had many a *tête-à-tête* with him which contributed much to my enjoyment, for Jerrold never shone to better advantage than when he was talking worldly wisdom to those who were glad to profit by what he taught them. Indeed, as a rule, he was an acceptable monitor, and did not give his advice in a patronizing or dictatorial spirit, but seemed to make himself tolerably sure that his words would at least be cheerfully received, if not, perhaps, fully acted upon. It was during our stay in Paris that he said some of those "good things" which have since bestrewn the paths of literature, and as they have now become the common property of the reading and the talking world, I shall avoid the risk of repetition by quoting only one or two of his bits of wisdom, which might, not inaptly, come under the category of "advice to young men." Talking of marriage, he said he would never advise a man to choose a wife on account of her intellect any more than for the sake of her money. "As to myself," he added, "since I have been married I have never known what it is to turn down my own socks." Speaking of young authors allowing their names to appear amongst the contributors to various publications at one and the same time, instead of concentrating their energies upon some work of an enduring character, he said, "Don't scatter your small shot." In allusion to the vice of getting into debt, he remarked that a man must be forgiven for procuring meat and bread upon credit, "but he has no right to do this sort of thing in the same way" (pointing to a bottle of wine which stood before him). On my telling him that I had just attempted a little story in verse, and that I should be glad if he could recommend it for publication, he said, "Why not *walk*, and tell the same thing in prose?" He once told me a little story, which, as it seems to have escaped the notice of those who have written about him, although it may possibly be known in some shape, I shall introduce here, especially as Jerrold used to say that the incident came within his own experience. A passenger, well-to-do in the world, had fallen overboard at sea, and his life was saved by an Irish sailor who jumped in after him. As a reward for the trifling service which his preserver had rendered him, the generous passenger presented Paddy with sixpence! Whereupon the sailor, looking him full in the face, and scanning him from head to foot with a smile of supreme contempt, exclaimed, in a rich Hibernian brogue, "Be jabers, it 's enough!"

On the occasion of the first performance of Jerrold's comedy of "Time Works Wonders," I had the good fortune to occupy a seat in his private box, and I well remember his feeling of delight, at the close, when he contemplated the success he had achieved. A party of his friends had arranged to sup together at the Bedford Hotel, Covent Garden, and as we walked thither from the Haymarket Theatre I offered him my hearty congratulations, for I had never witnessed a "first night" which was more fruitful in agreeable results than that of "Time Work Wonders." Arrived at the door of the hotel, I could not help repeating the gratification I felt at the author's well-merited triumph, when Jerrold, turning his eye full upon me, and smacking his chest with his hand, exclaimed, with a degree of exultation which was most natural under the circumstances, "Yes; and here 's the little man that 's done it!"

"Time Works Wonders" was indeed a work for the author to be proud of, for we have had no piece in modern times so bristling with wit, so varied in character, and, withal, so interesting yet simple in plot, as this really admirable comedy. Why it should so long have remained unrevived is a question which I fear involves some reflection upon those of our managers who are guided by a desire to encourage the "legitimate drama"—a phrase which, I take it, is intended to signify the drama of intellect, as contradistinguished from the unhealthy creations of a vitiated taste.

As the offspring of eminent men must be admitted to bear a degree of interest in the eyes of the public proportionate to that which attaches to their parents, I may here take the opportunity of introducing some further mention of Douglas

Jerrold's family, my object being to show that he was keenly alive to the necessity for seeing his children occupy a favorable position in the world. Edmund Douglas, his second son, received an appointment in the Treasury from Lord John Russell, and was afterwards transferred to an office in the Commissariat. Thomas Serle Jerrold (godson of Mr. T. J. Serle, the dramatist), the third son, was placed under the care of Mr. Paxton (afterwards Sir Joseph) at the Duke of Devonshire's estate at Chatsworth, with a view to his learning the art of gardening; and it was during young Tom's apprenticeship that his able instructor made his design for the Great Exhibition Building in 1851. On the opening of the Great Northern Railway to that part of the world where Chatsworth is situated, I was instructed by the editor of a paper with which I was then connected, to take the journey, and to describe such objects of interest as might appear on the route, and particularly to direct my attention to the beauties of the Duke of Devonshire's seat. I placed myself under the guidance of Mr. Paxton, who received me with great courtesy, and after pointing out to me all the principal charms of the garden grounds, conducted me at length to a spacious conservatory which he had designed, and which was then approaching completion. It was built exclusively of iron and glass, and when Mr. Paxton had described the improvements it embraced over other structures of the like kind, he said he was then finishing a design upon the same principle for the contemplated building in Hyde Park. Having led me up a steep flight of stairs into an office in the garden, where several young men were engaged in preparing architectural plans, he called my attention to the drawing he had spoken of, and said, "That 's the design I intend for the Great Exhibition." — "But surely you 're too late," I observed; "for the designs have already been sent in, and are now being exhibited." "I don't mind that," he replied, "they must have this. Look at the economy of it, and consider how short a time will be required to erect the building." The result is far too widely known to need another word from me; but I have recalled the circumstance because the newspaper article

I wrote at the time contained the first public mention that was ever made of the Great Exhibition building of 1851.

It was in the following year that Edmund Jerrold received his appointment in the Commissariat, and as he was under orders to proceed to Canada, his father and mother gave a little ball in his honor on the eve of his departure. Being a young gentleman of somewhat graceful proportions, and not a little proud to exhibit himself to the best advantage, he wore his uniform on the occasion, and was of course a very conspicuous object during the evening. In short, his glittering appearance was almost calculated to monopolize the attention of the lady visitors ; and his father being anxious that he should distinguish himself in some way beyond that of displaying his elegant costume, hoped, when his health was proposed, as it was in due course, after supper, that he might make a speech which would be considered "an honor to his family." When Edmund rose, champagne-glass in hand, to express his acknowledgments, he seemed so full of confidence, and presented so bold a front to the assembled guests, many of whom were standing in clusters around the room, that his father must have thought he had a son of whose oratorial powers he should doubtless one day be proud. The young officer, however, had scarcely got beyond the words "Ladies and gentlemen, for the honor you have done me," ere he suddenly collapsed, and resumed his seat ! Never was astonishment more strangely depicted upon the human countenance than it was upon that of Jerrold at this singular fiasco on the part of his hopeful son. He was literally dumbfounded, but at length he exploded with a sort of cachinnatory splutter — not to call it laughter — and looking round the room, in doubt as to where he should fix his gaze, he murmured "*Well!*" Amongst the guests on that evening was Dr. Wright, Jerrold's medical attendant, and that gentleman had selected as his partner in a dance Miss Mary Jerrold, our host's youngest daughter. The Doctor being "more than common tall," and the young lady being rather short, but not of very minute proportions, their combined appearance produced a somewhat ludicrous effect as they waltzed round the *salon*, and Jerrold, suddenly catching a glimpse of them, exclaimed, "Hollo! there's a mile dancing with a mile-stone!"

An interesting period in the life of Douglas Jerrold was the fiftieth anniversary of his birthday, which he resolved to celebrate with all the honors due to such an occasion. The day was the 3d January, 1853, and Jerrold received at his dinner-table, in the Circus Road, St. John's Wood, a large number of his most intimate friends, including the proprietors and contributors to "Punch" — Mr. Charles Knight (whom he held in very high esteem), Mr. Hepworth Dixon, Mr. E. H. Baily, R. A., the eminent sculptor, and a few others, including myself, who were better known to friendship than to fame. Jerrold was in remarkably good health and spirits, and treated the allusions that were made to the occasion of the meeting in a tone of hilarity which rendered the question as to "ages" matter of jocular rather than sentimental import. The evening was indeed one of the merriest I ever passed in the society of Douglas Jerrold, and so gratified was Mr. Baily, who was the Nestor of the party — being, indeed, in his seventy-fifth year — that he said he should gladly commemorate the event by making a bust of Jerrold, and presenting a cast of it to every one present. The bust was executed in marble, and is now in the possession of the family, who not only regard it as one of the most poetically conceived works which modern sculpture has produced, but seldom speak of it without calling to mind the interesting occasion which gave rise to it. So admirable is it as a likeness, and so graceful as a composition, that I am constrained to say, in common with others similarly situated, that I was sadly disappointed that Mr. Baily was unable to carry out his promise to its full extent.

In the month of May, 1857, Jerrold was stricken with his mortal illness; and saddening indeed was the effect upon his club-mates and his dearest friends, as day by day they found their hopes for his recovery becoming fainter and fainter. Every conceivable attention was paid to him, both by the members of his household and by the physicians — Dr. Cleveland, Dr. H. G. Wright, and Dr. Quain — to whom his case was intrusted; but he expired in the beginning of June. By a melancholy coincidence, I chanced to arrive at his chamber-door at the very moment that the family were leaving the room after seeing him breathe his last; and Mrs. Jerrold having begged me to enter, I was much impressed by the picture that presented itself. All had quitted the room with the exception of Mr. Copeland, the brother-in-law of Douglas Jerrold, then the proprietor of the Theatre Royal, and the Royal Amphitheatre, Liverpool. That gentleman was leaning over the body of his departed friend and relative, and looking at his countenance with the most profound attention, while he struggled in vain to conceal the grief that oppressed him. For some minutes Mr. Copeland and I remained the sole watchers over the corpse, and when, after giving vent to the feelings which literally overpowered me, I at last contrived to tear myself from the house, I could not possibly dismiss the reflection from my mind that the place which Douglas Jerrold had so many years held in my memory and esteem was never likely to be supplied.

The funeral of my lamented friend took place at Norwood Cemetery, on a bright morning in the month of June, and the spot chosen for his interment was in close proximity to the grave of his boy-friend and literary associate, Laman Blanchard. Those who were present on that mournful occasion — and they were indeed numerous — can never forget the extraordinary interest which attached to the event. Long before the time fixed for the arrival of the funeral *cortége*, the burial-ground was absolutely thronged with gentlemen celebrated in literature, the drama, and fine arts. Indeed, it would have been difficult to mention the name of any person well known to those three professions who was not there to take part in the generous tribute that was being paid to one who had, by the unaided force of his genius and will, successfully climbed

"The steep where Fame's proud temple shines afar."

The coffin was of plain oak, and was borne upon an open car, on each side of which were the initials "D. J." In the mourning coaches which followed it were seated Mr. Blanchard Jerrold and Mr. Thomas Serle Jerrold (Douglas Jerrold's eldest and youngest sons), Mr. Copeland (his brother-in-law), Mr. Henry Mayhew (his son-in-law), and the three medical gentlemen who had attended the deceased in his last illness. The pall-bearers were Mr. Charles Dickens, Mr. W. M. Thackeray, Mr. Charles Knight, Mr. Horace Mayhew, Mr. Mark Lemon, Mr. Monckton Milnes, M. P. (now Lord Houghton), and Mr. Bradbury (of the firm of Bradbury and Evans), all of whom wore on their arms crape rosettes embroided with the initials "D. J." As the coffin was being conveyed to the chapel, some hundreds of gentlemen followed in procession, and amongst these should be mentioned the names of John Leech, Shirley Brooks, John Tenniel, Tom Taylor, Percival Leigh, Samuel Lucas (at one period reviewer of books in the "Times"), W. Bayle Bernard, John Baldwin Buckstone, T. Sydney Cooper, R. A., George Cruikshank, Peter Cunningham, Augustus Egg, R. A., John Forster, James Hannay, William Hazlitt, J. A. Heraud, Charles Kenney, E. Landells, Charles Landseer, R. A., Thomas and George Landseer, E. Lloyd (the proprietor of "Lloyd's Weekly Newspaper," which bore the name of Douglas Jerrold as editor for the last five years of his life), Daniel Maclise, R. A., Kenny Meadows, John Oxenford, Sir Joseph Paxton, Albert Smith, E. M. Ward, R. A., Benjamin Webster, Erasmus Wilson, Forbes Winslow, E. Moxon, etc. A glance at these names, which form but a very small proportion of the vast assembly gathered together at the spot, will furnish a conspicuous proof of the various interests and pursuits represented on that sad morning ; and it may be safely affirmed that few have been the funeral ceremonies where those who attended them were influenced by feelings of more unfeigned regret than were manifested at the obsequies of Douglas Jerrold.

THE ORIGIN OF "PUNCH."

The projector of "Punch" was unquestionably Henry Mayhew, and, although the fact may not be regarded by its thousands of readers as a matter of very grave importance, I shall offer no excuse for briefly dwelling upon it, because doubts have been expressed, not only amongst the uninformed, but amongst those who might be supposed to be acquainted with the subject, as to the individual to whom the merit is justly due. The question has repeatedly been brought upon the *tapis* in every-day conversation; and it has been quite amusing to note the self-confident manner in which quidnuncs and that aggressive class of people who may be called the know-everything section of the community, have described circumstantially all the particulars of the "identical meeting" at a tavern near Drury Lane, at which "Punch" was started! The *starting* of "Punch" was undoubtedly the result of many meetings; but its *origin* was the result of Mr. Mayhew's personal cogitations, as already stated; and, not to say it vain-gloriously, it happened that I was the first individual to whom he mentioned the idea, simply because I was the first individual he saw (that is, in whom he could be expected to confide) on the day he disclosed it to his friends.

Henry Mayhew was then (the summer of 1841) living in the neighborhood of Charing Cross; and as I chanced to be a near neighbor of his, an arrangement had been come to by which I should visit him every morning; and I well remember that, for several weeks, we commenced the day at an early hour, in order that we might study "Euclid" together. One morning, on entering his sitting-room, I found Mayhew in unusually high glee (although his spirits were seldom at a low ebb), and I instinctively came to the conclusion that, as he was constantly bent upon the discovery of some "new notion," he was now about to exhibit his creative power under circumstances of an exceptionally propitious character. "I 've a splendid idea!" he exclaimed, with an impulsive eagerness which showed that he had been anxiously wishing for the opportunity of opening his mind upon the subject. "What, *another!*" I exclaimed. "Delighted to hear it! What is it?" — or words to the like effect. "A new comical periodical," said Mayhew. "You know the French 'Charivari,' don't you?" "Yes," was the reply. "Well, my idea is to start a similar thing, called "Punch, or the London Charivari." "Good!" said I. And we forthwith proceeded to draw up a list of the names of artists and contributors whom Mayhew suggested should be asked to associate themselves with the undertaking. The name of Gilbert à Beckett (an old friend and *collaborateur* of Mayhew's in his works of a humorous and satirical character) was the first on the list, and then followed those of Douglas Jerrold, Mark Lemon (with whom Henry Mayhew was then in daily communication), Sterling Coyne, W. H. Wills, H. P. Grattan, and others. Suddenly, he or I, or both (but it is by no means material to the issue, as the lawyers have it), remarked that there was a clever fellow rejoicing in the *nom de plume* of "Paul Prendergast," who had recently shown much force of humor in "The Comic Latin Grammar, and who was then engaged in writing "The Comic English Grammar." To ascertain his baptismal name was the first step necessary; and we soon found it to be Percival Leigh, and that he was living in Chapel Place, Oxford Street.

It was arranged that Mayhew should write to Douglas Jerrold, and that I should assist him in obtaining the coöperation of the chosen writers and artists to whom we could insure easy access; but, above all, I was to seek out "Paul Prendergast," and offer him such terms as might tempt him to enroll his name among the contributors. I had no difficulty in seeing him (though he was busily occupied at his desk at the time), and on my telling him the object of my mission, he very prudently said he had certain scruples about embarking in a publication without knowing something of its characteristics, and that he should be glad to have an opportunity of glancing at a copy before he could undertake to write for it. It could not be disputed that this somewhat uncommon piece of caution was perfectly reasonable; but when I took my departure I felt fully assured in my own mind that, as Mr. Leigh's reputation was yet to be established, and as his literary capacity appeared especially to indicate a quaintness of humor which must find a convenient outlet for its expression, his name would ere long be included among the adherents to "Punch." Meanwhile, he conferred with his friend John Leech, who had illustrated his "Comic Latin Grammar," and the result was that "Paul Prendergast" and John Leech made their joint obeisance to Mr. Punch in the fourth number of his work, in an article called "Foreign Affairs" — the letter-press by the former, and the pictorial design (representing types of continental character, as seen in the neighborhood of Leicester Square) by the latter.

But our immediate business is with the initiation of the weekly periodical, some particulars of the birth of which cannot be otherwise than interesting, if not important, to a large portion of the public, hundreds of whom have been familiar with the work from its very commencement. Not much time had elapsed ere all preliminaries were settled, and the contents of the first number agreed upon. Archibald Henning (long since passed away) was to be the chief illustrator, and Ebenezer Landells was to have the superintendence of the engraving department. The principal contributors to No. 1 were Gilbert à Beckett, Sterling Coyne, W. H. Wills, H. P. Grattan, Mark Lemon, and Henry Mayhew, the last two being joint editors. The frontispiece on the "wrapper" was drawn by Henning, as was also the large cartoon (which, as it was the period of a general election, represented a group of "Candidates under different heads"); and the miscellaneous "small cuts" were executed, if I remember rightly, by an artist named Brine. The printer was Mr. Joseph Last, then of Crane Court, Fleet Street, who, together with Mr. Landells, was a shareholder in the speculation. The original prospectus of the work was as follows: —

WILL BE OUT SHORTLY,[1]

And continued every Saturday,

(*Size of the Athenæum,*)

PRICE THREEPENCE.

A NEW WORK OF WHIT AND WHIM,

Embellished with Cuts and Caricatures.

TO BE CALLED

PUNCH;

OR,

THE LONDON CHARIVARI.

This *Guffawgraph* is intended to form a refuge for destitute wit — an asylum for the thousands of orphan jokes — the superannuated Joe Millers — the millions of perishing puns, which are now wandering about without so much as a shelf to rest upon! It will also be devoted to the emancipation of the Jew *d'esprits* all over the world, and the naturalization of those alien JONATHANS, whose adherence to the truth has forced them to emigrate from their native land.

The proprietors feel that the "eyes of Europe" will be upon them — that every visible animal, like our political patriots, will look out for

NO. 1.

"PUNCH" will have the honor of making his first appearance in this character on SATURDAY, JULY 17, 1841; and will continue, from week to week, to offer to the world all the fun to be found in his own and the following heads: —

POLITICS. — "Punch" has no party prejudices; he is Conservative in his opposition to Fantoccini and political puppets, but a progressive Whig in his love of *small change* and a repeal of the union with public *Judies.*

[1] Under this line was a small wood-cut, representing Lord Melbourne, Lord John Russell, and Lord Morpeth, who were then in office (the first being Prime Minister), but were expected to be "*out* shortly."

FASHIONS. — This department will be conducted by Mrs. J. Punch, whose extensive acquaintance with the *élite* of the areas will enable her to furnish the earliest information of the Movements of the Fashionable World.

POLICE. — This portion of the work will be under the direction of an experienced nobleman — a regular attendant at the various offices — who, from a strong attachment to "Punch," will be in a position to supply exclusive reports.

REVIEWS. — To render this branch of the periodical as perfect as possible, arrangements have been made to secure the critical assistance of John Ketch, Esq., who, from the mildness of the law, and the congenial character of modern literature, with his early associations, has been induced to undertake its *execution.*

FINE ARTS. — Anxious to do justice to native talent, the criticisms upon Painting, Sculpture, etc., will be confided to one of the most popular artists of the day — "Punch's" own immortal scene-painter.

MUSIC AND THE DRAMA. — These will be amongst the most prominent features of the work. The Musical Notices will be written by the gentleman who plays the mouth-organ, assisted by the professors of the drum and cymbals. "Punch" *himself* will DO the Drama.

SPORTING. — A prophet has been engaged! He will foretell not only the winners of each race, but also the "VATES"[1] and colors of the riders.

The FACETIÆ will be contributed by the members of the following learned bodies: —

The Court of Common Council and the Zoölogical Society.

The Temperance Association and the Waterproofing Company.

The College of Physicians and the Highgate Cemetery.

The Dramatic Authors' and the Mendicity Societies.

The Beefsteak Club and the Anti-Dry Rot Company.

[1] The name assumed by a Mr. Harrison, at that time the sporting correspondent of a daily paper.

Together with original humorous and satirical articles, in verse and prose, from all the

FUNNY DOGS WITH COMIC TALES.

LONDON:

PUBLISHED FOR THE PROPRIETORS BY R. BRYANT,

AT "PUNCH'S" OFFICE, 3, WELLINGTON STREET, STRAND;

Where all communications (prepaid) for the Editors should be forwarded.

At length came the day of publication. It was Saturday, July 17, 1841 (for the system of issuing periodical works in anticipation of the date was not then the prevailing practice as it has since become), and Mr. Mayhew's thoughts and attention were directed, with inevitable anxiety, to the publishing office, from a desire to ascertain the progress of the "circulation." If the aforesaid Mr. Bryant be still extant, he will, doubtless, remember how frequently and eagerly Mr. Mayhew, or myself — sometimes both — applied to him to know the state of affairs in his all-important department. In short, it may be frankly stated that Mayhew and I walked up and down that part of the Strand leading from Wellington Street towards St. Clement's Church the greater part of the afternoon, discussing the prospects of the new undertaking, and the former congratulating himself upon the success it was likely to achieve, as we continued to obtain fresh intelligence in respect to the number of copies disposed of.

As to the ultimate success of the work, it is only necessary for me to say that it struggled on manfully and cleverly for many months (its momentary dissolution being daily predicted by alarmists and "Job's-comforters"), but from the unfortunate obstacle caused by the want of capital, its promoters fell into difficulties, and, in order to save it from bankruptcy, the property was disposed of to Messrs. Bradbury and Evans, the present printers and proprietors, for a sum little exceeding the amount of Mr. Punch's liabilities, Mr. Landells still holding a small share, which, however, was soon bought up by the new authorities, and Mr. Lemon retaining the editorship, with Mr. Mayhew (who had yielded that post to him) as his auxiliary in the discharge of the somewhat essential duty of "thinking and suggesting."

From the above statement it is pretty clear that "Punch" was *not* projected at a tavern near Drury Lane Theatre, or at a tavern near anywhere else; that nobody but Henry Mayhew was the actual *originator* of it; and that the earliest contributors to it did *not* comprise one half, or even one fourth, of the names which those, who delight in relating all they do *not* know, have been pleased to number among its fathers and godfathers and its multitude of literary offspring.

The following lines, which appeared in "Punch" in the month of January, 1843, and were written by Percival Leigh, are amply sufficient to indicate, at least to those who know something of Greek and Latin, the locality of Mr. Punch's symposia, and even the name of the hostelry where they took place: —

SODALITAS PUNCHICA, SEU CLUBBUS NOSTER.

POEMA MACARONICUM, VEL ANGLO-GRÆCO-CANINO-LATINUM.

Sunt quidam *jolly dogs*, *Saturday* qui nocte frequentant
Antiqui *Στέφανον*, qui stat prope mœnia Drurî,
Βουλόμενοι saccos cum *prog* distendere *rather*,
Indulgere jocis, necnon Baccho atque *tobacco*;
In mundo tales non *fellows* ante fuere:
Magnanimûm heroum celebrabo carmine laudes,
Posthac illustres ut vivant omne per ævum.
Altior *ἐν Στέφανῳ* locus est, *snug cosy* recessus;
Hîc *quarters* fixêre suos, conclave tenent hîc,
Hîc dapidus cumulata gemit *mahogany* mensa.
Pascuntur variis; *roast beef* cum *pudding of Yorkshire*
Interdum; *sometimes* epulis queis nomen agrestes
Boiled leg of mutton and trimmings imposuere.
Hic *double X* haurit, *Barclay and Perkins's* ille;
Nec desunt mixtis qui sese potibus implent
Quos "*offnoff*" omnes consuescunt dicere *waiters*.
Postquam exempta fames *grubbo*, mappæque remotæ,
Pro cyathis clamant, qui *goes* sermone vocantur
Vulgari, *of whisky*, *rum*, *gin*, *and brandy*, sed et sunt;
Cœlicolum qui *punch* ("erroribus absque") liquore
Gaudent; et pauci vino quod præbet Oporto,
Quod certi *black-strap* dicunt *nick*nomine Graii.
Haustibus his *pipi*, communis et adjiciuntur
Shag, Reditus, Cubæ Silvæ, *Cheroots* et Havannæ.

"Festinate viri," *bawls one*, "nunc ludite verbis:"
Alter "Fœmineum Sexum" propinat, et "*Hurrah!*"
Respondent, *pot-house* concusso plausibus omni.
Nunc similes veteri versantur *winky* lepores
Omnibus, exiguus nec, Jingo teste, tumultus
Exoritur, quoniam summâ nituntur opum vi
Rivales ἄλλοι *top-sawyers* ἔμμεναι ἄλλων.
Est genus ingenui lusûs quod nomine *Burking*
Notum est, vel *Burko*, qui claudere cuncta solebat
Ora olim eloquio, pugili vel forsitan isto
Deaf Un, vel *Burko* pueros qui *Burxit*; at illud
Plausibus aut fictis joculatorem excipiendo,
Aut *bothering* aliquid referentem, constat, amicum.
Hôc parvo excutitur multus conamine risus.
Nomina magnorum referam nunc pauca virorum:
Marcus et Henricus,[1] *Punchi* duo lumina magna,
(*Whacks* hic Aristotelem, Sophoclem *brown walloppeth* ille)
In *clubbum* adveniunt; Juvenalis [2] et advenit acer
Qui veluti *Paddywhack for love* contundit amicos;
Ingentesque animos non parvo in corpore versans
Tullius;[3] et Matutini qui Sidus *Heraldi* est
Georgius;[4] Albertus Magnus;[5] vesterque Poeta.[6]
Præsidet his Nestor,[7] qui tempore vixit in Annæ,
Creditur et vidisse Japhet, non *youngster* at ullus
In *chaff*, audaci certamine, vinceret illum.
Ille jocos mollit dictis, et pectora mulcet,
Ni faciat, *tumblers*, et *goes*, et pocula *pewter*,
Quippe aliorum alii jactarent forsan in aures.

An important accession to the pictorial strength of "Punch" was realized in the introduction of Mr. H. G. Hine, who made his *entrée* in the pages of that periodical in the month of September following the date of its commencement. Mr. Hine had been known to Mr. Landells through his illustrations to the "Cosmorama" and other publications; and although he was professedly a landscape-painter, and had no more experience of drawing *on* the wood than a stanch teetotaler has of drawing wine *from* it, he was at once thrust into a prominent position as an artistic contributor to "Punch's" columns. His chief speciality consisted in the grotesque ideas which he developed, with much facility, in the small cuts; but he soon

1 Mark Lemon and Henry Mayhew. 2 Douglas Jerrold.
3 J. H. Tully, the composer.
4 G. Hodder (at that time connected with the *Morning Herald* newspaper).
5 Albert Smith. 6 Percival Leigh. 7 Henry Baylis.

proved himself capable of greater things, and it is not a little remarkable that he executed the whole of the illustrations to "Punch's" first Almanack, with the exception of the border pieces, which were the work of Hablot Browne. Mr. Hine has long since abandoned the duties of a comic artist for the more congenial pursuit to which he originally intended to devote his talents, and he is now a conspicuous member of the Institute of Painters in Water Colors — his charming representations of *downy* scenery, dotted with sheep, and relieved by little villages which would seem to have dropped into pleasant valleys designed expressly to receive them, being always amongst the chief attractions of its annual exhibitions.

Mr. Birket Foster, another "knight of the brush," rather than of the pencil, also made certain contributions — though not many — to the early numbers of "Punch;" but they were of a character which showed him to be eminently *un*fitted for the task of delineating *facetiæ*. He was, however, a pupil of Mr. Landells at the time, and it was natural that the latter should test his qualities by every means at his command; but Mr. Foster did not suffer many years to elapse ere his name became famous in a very different branch of art to that which "Punch" would have marked out for him, and I have referred to him in this place merely by way of showing the diversity of artists whose works have ornamented the pages of the favorite periodical. Among the earlier illustrators, besides those already mentioned, were Alfred Crowquill, Newman, Lee, Hamerton, John Gilbert, William Harvey, and Kenny Meadows. The first frontispiece, as I have stated, was by Archibald Henning; the second was by Harvey; the third by Gilbert; the fourth by Meadows — the practice during the first few years of "Punch's" existence being to commence a new wrapper with each succeeding volume; until at length Richard Doyle appeared upon the scene, and it was thought that the grotesque, yet graceful contribution which he supplied was far too good to be thrown aside at the expiration of six months. The proprietors of the work, therefore, very wisely caused Mr. Doyle's frontispiece to be stereotyped, and it now remains, with certain modifications, the permanent tableau on the outer covering of "Punch."

It will be seen from the above enumeration of names that, in the early stages of Mr. Punch's career, he gave encouragement to artists who evinced no qualifications for humorous art; but the frequent changes he made led to a state of things which showed that he was only desirous to place the right man in the right place. It certainly could not be said that William Harvey, the graceful and poetical illustrator of "Knight's Pictorial Shakspere," was ever intended for a "Punch" artist; and as to John Gilbert (also an able illustrator of the great poet), so impressed was Douglas Jerrold with the solid character of his academic forms and imposing outlines that he exclaimed, "We don't want Rubens on 'Punch'!" When Mr. Tenniel first associated himself with the popular periodical, it was generally thought that his abilities were of too classic an order for the duty he had undertaken; for it will be remembered that this gentleman executed one of the cartoons for the Houses of Parliament (an allegory of Justice), which gained a prize at the exhibition in Westminster Hall; and that he once represented on the walls of the Royal Academy a striking picture of "Adam and Eve in Paradise." Such un-*Punch*-like subjects as these, and such un-*Leech*-like treatment as they required and received, were by no means suggestive of comicality in the artist; but Mr. Tenniel had too much confidence in the pictorial strength he possessed to feel that he need limit himself to a particular sphere; and hence he persevered with his pencil, until in time he became inoculated, as it were, with a sense of humor which has not been subordinate to, but has served to stimulate, his graphic powers. It may be remarked that Mr. Tenniel's introduction to "Punch" was in consequence of Mr. Doyle's withdrawal from the scene of his many successes; and it is no secret to state that, by the course adopted by the latter, he sacrificed a handsome income, rather than remain attached to a publication which had satirized the religion he professed.

Horace Mayhew.

As I have incidentally mentioned the name of Horace Mayhew, I may here state that I made his acquaintance, through his brother Henry, some two years before the date of "Punch's" birth, at which latter period he was absent on a tour in Germany. It chanced, however, that he returned to this country before the first volume was completed, and in the course of a week or two he became an acknowledged contributor to the work, and was afterwards appointed sub-editor. That appointment he held for some considerable time, and in the discharge of his duties was a medium of communication between the writers and the artists; but the office was eventually abolished as unnecessary, and has never since been filled up. Horace Mayhew's close connection with "Punch" brought him to educate his mind for the particular form of literature to which that periodical belongs, and he was not only the suggester of many subjects (as, for example, "The Female Robinson Crusoe") which were handed over to the treatment of others more experienced than himself, but was the author of several popular works of a humorous kind, including "Letters Left at the Pastrycook's;" "Model Men," "Model Women," and "Model Couples;" "Change for a Shilling," etc., together with a remarkable piece of graphic drollery, illustrating "The Tooth-ache" in a variety of stages, from the commencement of the disorder to the final extraction of the offending member. This was published in the elongated roller form, and the designs, as well as the descriptive letterpress at the foot of each, were supplied by the author himself; but were afterwards drawn upon wood by the great George Cruikshank, who, however, declared that his rendering of the subject, although it might be somewhat more artistic, rather detracted than otherwise from the singular merit of the originals. As I have been from the period of my first knowledge of Horace Mayhew on terms of uninterrupted friendship with him, it would not befit me to descant upon his characteristics, or to recall a succession of incidents connected with our constant intercourse —

> "What things have we seen
> Done at the —— ! heard words that have been
> So nimble, and so full of subtle flame,
> As if that every one from whence they came
> Had meant to put his whole wit in a jest,
> And had resolved to live a fool the rest
> Of his dull life!"

Mayhew will not fail to remember how he and I, as "the boys" (so called) of the party assembled round Mr. Punch's dinner-table at the Saturday gatherings, before they were confined exclusively to the staff of accredited contributors, were frequently among the last to quit the agreeable scene; and how upon taking our departure, with something like a feeling of self-reproach at having been tempted to remain beyond the hour when Prudence usually goes to bed, Douglas Jerrold has consoled us with a favorite quotation of his from Gainsborough, "Never mind. 'We are all going to heaven, and Vandyck is of the company;'"[1] and how, when dining with Jerrold at his house on the following day, and reminding him of some of the flashes which his wit had sent forth, the latter has exclaimed, laughingly and half-incredulously, "No! did I say that?" But I will refrain from putting to the test Horace Mayhew's remembrance of the "things we have seen," lest the retrospect should bring with it the reflection that they and the actors in them have too long passed away; and moreover I might, peradventure, advert to subjects on which his impressions might not entirely harmonize with my own. I cannot, however, let this opportunity pass without recording my unfeigned sense of his kindly and affectionate nature, and of the esteem in which he is held by all who know him. In proof of his friendly disposition, I will here quote from a letter which I received from him on the occasion of that happy event of my life which has already been mentioned here: —

"I have sent to your house two little presents for Agnes — if she will be kind enough to accept them. Assure her they are sent with the strongest wishes for her future happiness.

[1] An exclamation made by Gainsborough on his death-bed, when he was visited by Sir Joshua Reynolds.

"She must look upon the lamp [a very handsome specimen of the 'moderator'] as an emblem of the light and cheerfulness that she will shed (with proper *trimming*, of course) around you; and the little Punch and Judy figures she must take up kindly in her arms as pretty images of affection from

"Her sincere friend."

The Mayhew Family.

I think this may be regarded as a fitting opportunity for the introduction of the names of three other members of the Mayhew family — Edward, Julius, and Augustus; and I may here at once state that of the four brothers to whom I have now alluded, those who have appeared before the public under the designation of "The Brothers Mayhew," are Henry and Augustus, who were the joint authors of "The Good Genius that turned Everything into Gold," "The Magic of Kindness," "The Greatest Plague of Life," "The Adventures of a Young Monkey," etc. Edward, the eldest of the four, who in the early part of his career achieved many successes by his dramatic productions and by his general contributions to periodical literature, was for some time the "Fine Arts" critic of the "Morning Post," and was in other ways associated with journalism. Finding, however, that the pursuit of letters was not calculated to secure him that permanent position for public usefulness to which he aspired, he formed the manly resolution, at the age of thirty-five, to study the profession of a veterinary surgeon, and in the course of an almost incredibly short space of time, he obtained a professorship at the college. Having thus acquired a new experience, and having still retained his literary taste, he published a little work on the "Management of the Dog," which soon became a practical text-book. In process of time he brought his newly-acquired knowledge to bear upon the treatment of the horse; and issued an elaborate work, called "The Illustrated Horse-Doctor," which was followed by a kindred production, under the title of "The Illustrated Stable Management." Both these books proved him to be a most valuable authority upon the habits, diseases, and characteristics of horses; and it is not a little remarkable that during the time he was preparing them, and for some years afterwards, he was confined to his room by a paralytic affection which rendered it impossible for him to walk; but his energy and perseverance never forsook him, and so well had he stored his mind with all that was essential to him in the task he had undertaken, that he supplied the great majority of the illustrations, as well as the letter-press. It happened, by the purest accident, that "The Illustrated Stable Management" came into my hands for review in a morning newspaper, and Edward Mayhew, learning from one of his brothers that the notice of the book was written by me, addressed me a letter, in which he said —

"I know how much I am indebted to your good feeling for the sentiments you have expressed concerning my book, and as an acknowledgment of the obligation, which, believe me, I am sincerely alive to, will you allow me to offer you the inclosed note?[1] I should not have imposed on you the trouble which it necessitates; but being absent from London, circumstances compel me to trespass on your good-nature. I feel, while making this offer, I am presenting you with that which must be of small value to you; but will you kindly accept the gift as an emblem of gratitude?

. . . .

"I have a pretty place down here, in a pretty spot.[2] Trains run cheap during the autumn. Should you ever feel disposed for a week of cool, moist atmosphere, pray remember that both I and Mrs. Mayhew will endeavor to make you comfortable."

Poor Edward Mayhew! His physical strength was originally proportionate to his mental power; but for a period of fifteen years he was compelled to fight the battle of life with brains alone; and this he did with such success that he has

[1] To Messrs. Allen, the publishers, requesting them to hand me a copy of the work.

[2] The neighborhood of Torquay.

gained for himself an enduring name. The circumstances of his death were such as to show that it indeed behooves us "to bear the ills we have" with philosophic resignation. As already observed, Edward Mayhew was deprived of the use of his limbs for fifteen years. At the expiration of that time he suddenly rose from his chair, the wheels of which had afforded him the only means of locomotion, — and walked! The effect upon the nervous system was apparently too powerful for a constitution weakened by the very severe trial to which it had been subjected; and in the course of ten days he ceased to be!

In the designs for an improved form of stables, several of which are included in the "Illustrated Stable Management," Edward Mayhew was ably assisted by his brother Julius, who, being educated for an architect, and having always cultivated a taste for art, especially in regard to those principles which demand a perfect knowledge of perspective, was essentially qualified for the task; and a reference to the book will at once testify that, although never assuming the dignity of a professed artist, he skillfully and effectually carried out the views and intentions of the author. As, however, he has never aspired to be a "public character," I forbear to give to his name a prominence which I know he would immediately repel; and yet I must allude, for one instant only, to the pleasure I have many a time derived from his society on certain "tramping' expeditions with him and his brother Augustus, when, in our walks through the country, we have left the cares of the world behind us, and have made ourselves the happiest of mortals, by appreciating to the full the humblest means of enjoyment.

As to Augustus Mayhew (always familiarly called "Gus"), the youngest branch of the tree, one would suppose that he never knew what care was, so jocund and light-hearted is he invariably found to be in the midst of his friends. He *can* be serious, very serious, when any strong sense of injury, either to himself or to an esteemed companion, or to any social cause which he has warmly espoused, has taken firm possession of him; but his unbounded good-humor and world-defying friendliness have inevitably pointed him out as a man to whom Fortune's buffets and rewards would seem to be alike indifferent. As an artist, he is little known, though in his delineations of every-day scenes and characters he has betrayed much graphic and perceptive power, but as a writer he has abundantly shown, in his "Faces for Fortunes," his "Finest Girl in Bloomsbury," and "Paved with Gold" (commenced in the form of a serial, in conjunction with his brother Henry, who, however, retired from it after the publication of the first two or three numbers), that he unites the elements of a graceful fancy and a broad sense of the ludicrous in a manner which is not often seen. But it is in society rather than in books that his light shines brightest (as has been said of many men of literary distinction), for in the task of writing he is necessarily under some restraint, lest ideas should find their way to the public eye which are only adapted to the private ear; whereas in conversation he is not compelled to "weigh his words before he gives them breath;" and hence he is enabled to indulge those peculiar modes of thought and expression which are amusing from their reckless originality, as well as from the keen insight they display into the follies and impostures of society. The fertility of his invention in the use of adjectives and similes, to give breadth and color to a daring conception, is conspicuously seen in his account of a prize-fight in "Paved with Gold," which contains a sufficient number of suggestions to enable a writer in "Bell's Life" to improve and strengthen his eccentric vocabulary. As an example of the grotesque roughness of his humor I may mention an incident which has often been alluded to by those who witnessed it, as affording a remarkable specimen of his peculiar characteristics. An altercation had occurred between Augustus's friends and an insolent, domineering sort of fellow, who had threatened personal chastisement to his opponent, and seemed inclined to put his resolve into execution; whereupon the stalwart Mayhew, advancing towards him with clenched fist and distending his capacious form to its fullest proportions, exclaimed,

"By gad, sir! dare to lay one finger upon my friend, and in five minutes your wife and children shall not know you!" Whether or not the individual whose facial outlines were thus vehemently menaced was blessed with a wife and children it did not appear, nor was it a question which entered for one moment into Augustus's consideration, but the magnanimous character of the phrase had the desired effect, for the lion immediately ceased roaring, and the object of his wrath went away with a whole skin.

Before quitting this part of my recollections I should state, if it be not already understood, that to Henry Mayhew I am indebted for my first introduction to the society of men of letters; and that long since I became known to him, a change has come over his literary aspirations; for the ability he then displayed, as a writer of farces, and as a contributor to comic periodicals, he subsequently diverted into a widely different channel. This change has been exemplified in a series of lectures, called "What to Teach, and How to Teach it," and in his two valuable books, "London Labor and the London Poor," and "The Great World of London" — works which have rendered more lasting service to the community and to himself than could possibly be achieved by any exercise of fun or fiction, even from the most fertile brain.

I am sure I need offer no apology for the allusions I have made to the Mayhew family (a family better known to fame than many writers of loftier pretensions), for they are well aware of the kindly spirit in which every word is intended; and this volume, however imperfect it may be, would be infinitely more so were I to omit all mention of such intimate allies and friends.

It is interesting to note, in following the gradations of time, what singular transitions have taken place in the minds of men devoted to literary pursuits. When Douglas Jerrold wrote "Black-eyed Susan," it would have been difficult to believe that he would ever become the editor of a popular journal, such as "Lloyd's Weekly Newspaper" (a position which he occupied for five years, to the period of his death);

or when Thackeray penned "The Yellow-plush Correspondence" in "Fraser's Magazine," that he would in after-days "witch the world" as the writer of "Esmond," and "The Newcomes;" or when Henry Mayhew produced his farce of "The Wandering Minstrel," that he would eventually make himself known as an authority on social statistics, as he has done in his "London Labor and the London Poor."

JOHN LEECH.

Valuable contributors to the amusements of the table, as they were to the pages of "Punch," were John Leech, Albert Smith, and Kenny Meadows — the two former having been on terms of intimacy long before that work was established; but my desire is not so much to speak of them in reference to their doings for "Punch," as to indicate what manner of men they were in relation to the "small sweet courtesies" of life. It was through John Leech's friendly intercession that I first became a contributor to "Bentley's Miscellany" (in the year 1848), to which publication he was then a fixed adherent. I had written a little story, and on my submitting it to Leech's opinion, he was kind enough to tell the authorities, with the utmost earnestness, that, if the paper should be accepted, he would gladly illustrate it. The result was that it was published, with an admirable etching by Leech, and was followed the next month by another, which also was touched by his artistic hand. Leech's friendliness and good-fellowship were well known to those who understood his reserved, unostentatious nature; and having adduced one proof of those qualities in him, I may fitly mention another, though I honestly wish it had reference to somebody other than my perpetually recurring self. In the illustrations to a little book, called "Sketches of Life and Character, taken at the Police Court, Bow Street," he rendered me most essential service by the exercise of his inimitable pencil; and I know that, in like manner, he lent a "helping hand" (in more than one sense of the term) to many a young aspirant in whom he felt an interest, and who appreciated the importance of securing the aid of his valuable name.

In the "Punch" times to which I have adverted, it was the habit of Albert Smith to call him familiarly and brusquely "Jack," while his still more intimate friend, Percival Leigh, addressed him as "John," or "Leech," and this was so repugnant to Jerrold's taste and feelings, that at length he exploded with the following pertinent query: "Leech, how long is it necessary for a man to know you before he may call you *Jack?*" No reply; but if my recollection serves me, "Jack" was sounded in our ears much less frequently on subsequent occasions.

Among the many little domestic gatherings to which the meetings of the "Punch" contributors gave rise, none were more agreeable or more memorable than the dinner-parties at John Leech's house — first at Powis Place, and afterwards at Notting Hill and Kensington. In one notable instance within my recollection, Leech had invited some ten or more gentlemen, consisting chiefly of his fellow-laborers in the establishment of Mr. Punch, to dine with him in Powis Place, and he had engaged for the occasion the services of an extra attendant, whose ordinary occupation was not that of the traditional "greengrocer," but that of a parish clerk. The guests were assembled in the drawing-room, *selon le reglè*, preparatory to the banquet; and it was at length observed that there was an unusual delay in announcing the dinner. This was all the more noticeable, because John Leech's household arrangements were generally conducted upon the best principles of order and regularity; and the guests were one and all in such high intellectual vigor, and so well prepared to enjoy "the feast of reason and the flow of soul," that they began to fear they should exhaust their stock of mental ammunition in a succession of skirmishes before the evening's war began. Whether the parish clerk had disconcerted the cook by the solemnity of his presence, or whether the latter, being of a serious turn of mind, was afflicted with a tender sensation which upset her culinary calculations, it was never clearly ascertained; but there could be little doubt that there was something not quite right between the kitchen and the dining-room. After a somewhat significant pause, however, a solemn figure, attired in black, and wearing a white neckerchief of most orthodox character and proportions (in a clerical point of view), appeared in the room, and in a style of elocution which would have well befitted his calling in the church, gave the welcome announcement, "The dinner is on the table!" "Amen!" cried the assembled guests, with corresponding solemnity; and one and all descended to the dining-room, tittering at the comically doleful manner in which so important a preliminary to an enlivening entertainment had been carried into effect.

John Leech possessed among his many excellent qualities, that of a fine bass voice; and the gentlemen of the "Punch" conclave will remember how often, in the midst of their rejoicings, he diverted their thoughts from the humorous to matters of more serious moment, by singing Barry Cornwall's song, "King Death was a rare old fellow." On one occasion, when he had sung this song with even more than his usual vigor, Douglas Jerrold exclaimed, "I say, Leech, if you had the same opportunity of exercising your voicc as you have of using your pencil, how it would *draw!*"

Sir Henry Webb.

John Leech used to tell an amusing anecdote of Sir Henry Webb, whose tall military figure and aristocratic head were at one time as familiar in the stalls of the theatre, especially on "first nights," as were the rubicund countenances of Lord Adolphus Fitzclarence and the late Sir George Wombwell in the omnibus-box at the Italian Opera House in the Haymarket. Some one had informed Sir Henry that a terrible murder had just taken place in the metropolis, and that the culprit had not yet been apprehended. Sir Henry appeared, or affected to be, deeply interested in the matter; and at once proceeded to make inquiries, his deep, heavy voice giving due solemnity to the questions he put. "Dear me! another murder!" he exclaimed; "and what sort of murder?" Answer—"A poor girl shot by her sweetheart. "Dear me! dear me!" said the distressed gentleman. "Girl shot by her sweetheart! Dreadful! dreadful! And when did it take place?" Answer — "Yesterday morning." Sir Henry — "God bless me! Yesterday morning! Is it possible!" Answer — "True; the girl was murdered yesterday morning, and by a fellow who was supposed to be her lover." Sir Henry — "Dear me! dear me! very shocking, indeed! And at what time yesterday morning?" Answer — "Between six and seven o'clock." Sir Henry — "Gracious goodness! Between six and seven o'clock! What an early hour! Very awful! very awful! And what was the cause of the murder?' Answer — "Jealousy." Sir Henry — "Jealousy! Heaven defend us! Horrible indeed! Jealousy! And what was the girl's name?" Answer — "Martha Jones." Sir Henry — "Dear me! dear me! Martha Jones! More and more shocking! And the murderer, what was his name?" Answer — "Philip Brown." Sir Henry — "Philip Brown! God bless me! Philip Brown! this is bad indeed! Well, well, well! Martha Jones shot by Philip Brown! And where was the murder committed?" Answer — "In Rosamond Street, Clerkenwell." Sir Henry — "Great Heavens! In Rosamond Street, Clerkenwell! How very extraordinary! God bless me! In Rosamond Street, Clerkenwell! *Then we must bear it as well as we can!*" The locality was too much for his weak nerves; but Sir Henry partook of a grand supper immediately afterwards, and on the following morning he had forgotten all about poor Martha Jones and Rosamond Street, Clerkenwell.

ALBERT SMITH.

Albert Smith's connection with "Punch" arose from the fact of his being known as a successful writer in a comic periodical, called the "Cosmorama," then in course of publication under the auspices of Mr. Last, the printer; and his first contributions to the new work consisted of "The Physiology of the London Medical Student" (which, however, had already been written, in brief, by Paul Prendergast, in "The Heads of the People"). He continued for a long time to be a zealous and valuable member of the literary staff, and certainly wrote many of the most entertaining descriptions of English social life which appeared in "Punch's" columns at a period when the contents were better adapted to the million than they have been in later days. But it was more particularly in regard to the "Illuminated Magazine" and "Bentley's Miscellany" that I came in contact with Albert Smith, and he was always found to be a writer on whose promises editors and publishers could implicitly rely. He was a most frank and agreeable companion among those whose idiosyncrasies he relished; and the following letters will show that he could be as kind and friendly as he was frank and cheerful. The first refers to the period when I was about to visit Paris at the time of the revolution, and Albert Smith had promised to get me a letter of introduction from Charles Kenney to Jules Janin, the dramatic *feuilletoniste* of the "Journal des Débats;" the second is an answer to a note I had sent him, asking him to contribute an article to, I think, the "Illuminated Magazine," upon the subject of Chamouni, which then occupied a great deal of his time; and the ostensible object of the third (addressed to me when I was at Boulogne) was to express his regret that he could not give me an opportunity of supplying one of the papers to "Gavarni in London," an ephemeral affair, of which he was the editor.

"MY DEAR GEORGE, — In case I do not see you, I inclose Kenney's letter of introduction (for you) to Jules Janin. I think the number is 20 [Rue Vaugirard], but if not, any one in the neighborhood will tell you. It is close to the Odéon, and near my old home, '*en étudiant*.' Now to my own business. I have put in a letter for Markwell,[1] which you will perhaps be good enough to give him; and also a copy of 'Tadpole;' and a letter I will thank you very much to deliver. The family live at Capecure, just over the bridge. You cross the bridge, turn to the right, and then it is the second house

[1] William Markwell, a much respected wine merchant, and formerly well known for the interest he took in dramatic literature.

to your left. Altogether it is not five minutes from the Hôtel du Nord. I hope the book will not cumber your carpet-bag. If they *should* say anything at the Douane (which they will not), show them the writing on the title-page, and say it is not a new one — that will be enough. I hope you will have a jolly time, singing 'Mourir pour la Patrie.'

"Yours always,

"ALBERT SMITH."

"Your letter about Chamouni followed me to all sorts of places. I was, however, too much occupied with collecting matter for my 'Mont Blanc' book, to undertake anything else.

"We had great fun, and the inundation caused much excitement. I suppose you saw Russell's account of it in the 'Times.' In a hurry, yours always,

"ALBERT SMITH."

"I wish we had been nearer to one another, as I could today have put one of the Gavarni papers into your hands. But the next number winds up the work; and he is such a queer customer that I never know until the last minute what subjects he has fixed upon, and then everything has to be scrambled up by whoever I can put my hand upon. I shall be heartily glad to wash my hands of it. We somewhat envy you at Boulogne. London is miserably dull just now, and everything flat as ditch-water, including, I am sorry to say, books. I have kept back my next 'Act' till December, things were selling so badly.

"I have a slight notion of going into farming!! Don't laugh — and with Joe!!![1] Don't laugh again — not believing in literature as a permanency. We think of renting a cheap slip of Jane C——'s land, at —— Hill Park, and building pigstyes, keeping fowls, etc. I don't mean, of course, to give up London, or rush into any heavy agricultural speculations, but I think we shall be able to turn a few coppers in the course of

[1] Joseph Robins, the now popular comedian, but in those days a gentleman enjoying more leisure than employment.

the year at a small risk. I would sooner make a pound by selling a porker than write a page of 'Bentley.'

"Last night I met Thackeray at the Cyder Cellars, and we stayed there until three in the morning. He is a very jolly fellow, and no 'High Art' about him.

"Old Brough has bought the 'Man in the Moon' of Ingram; and Angus[1] has a serial out on the 1st — a heavy, melodramatic, go-ahead story. Horace Mayhew is in the agonies of the 'Almanack,'[2] in which I have been helping him. It is an open opposition to 'Punch's Pocket-Book.' I wish they could get it out first.

"Let us have a line now and then, when you have a chance; and believe me, with best regards to all friends." . . . .

In one of the above letters it will be seen that Albert Smith speaks of "envying me at Boulogne;" and I am thus reminded that some of my most agreeable reminiscences of him revert to a time when he and his brother Arthur, and Joseph Robins, were enjoying together a few weeks' stay in that town. Being by good luck on a visit there myself at the same moment, I saw Smith and his two companions daily; and rather than mingle with the noise and confusion of that restless watering-place, we preferred an exclusive diversion of our own. This consisted in our meeting on the sands in the morning, and paddling to one of the little villages which lie along that part of the coast. This was Albert Smith's favorite enjoyment at Boulogne; and the many pleasant illustrations he gave us of the "whims and oddities" of life, as seen in his own experience, were ably seconded by the practical humor of Joe Robins, who already indicated the possession of that innate sense of drollery which has since been successfully developed on the stage. So warmly attached was Albert

[1] Angus B. Reach — one of the foremost contributors to the periodical literature of that time. The serial referred to was a romance, called *Clement Lorimer, or the Book with the Iron Clasps.*

[2] George Cruikshank's *Comic Almanack.* H. M. was also associated with a publication called The *Almanack of the Month,* a clever little serial, nominally edited by Gilbert à Beckett, but suggested and put together by the former.

to Boulogne before he became thoroughly imbued with that Alpine spirit which led him constantly to Chamouni, and ultimately to the summit of Mont Blanc, that in one of his fugitive pieces he wrote a tribute to its merits and attractions, from which I give the following extract as a characteristic specimen of his style : —

"In contradistinction to the imaginary enjoyment of other watering-places, let us take the pleasant, careless Boulogne. It has been customary to deride this new key-hole to the Continent; to joke about the mobs who fly there, like the ships, for a harbor of refuge; to allude to stags and sharpers, and broken incomes — in fact, to throw every possible slur upon it and its inhabitants. And yet there is no place in the world where really pleasant relaxation can be so readily procured, and at such a cheap rate. You will be told by its enemies that Boulogne is now quite an English town. Don't believe them. What is there English in its gay, lively port, and lines of smart hotels — its thorough continental Rue Neuve Chaussée and *moyen-âge* Upper Town — its *poissarde* population, with their short red petticoats and naked legs or blue stockings — its hundreds of glittering white caps in the *Place* on market-day? Walk a mile away from it in any direction, towards Wimereux, Wimille, or Portel, and you will see as much of France as though you had been right across it from Boulogne to Besançon. Where will you show us such a glorious stroll as that along the cliffs to Ambleteuse, with the sea and the picturesque rocks and Martello towers so far below you, and literally in sight of home all the way, if the day be but moderately clear?

"There is no *ennui* at Boulogne, because there is no conventional observance of rules of deportment. Everybody does what he likes, not what he thinks he ought to like. And if you wish it, there is a charming private society. In fact, Boulogne is fining down to exceeding respectability; for it has become a trifle too expensive for the outlawed tribes, and they have emigrated, many, we believe, to Calais."

Apropos of Albert Smith's ascent of Mont Blanc, and the

deservedly popular entertainment which sprang from it, I shall here introduce a burlesque form of invitation sent by him to his friends on the occasion of opening or reopening what he boldly called "the show." This may possibly have been published before; but if so, I cannot very justly be charged with "piracy," for I have never yet seen it except in its original form; and as it was addressed to me personally, I hope I may be allowed to deal with it according to my own inclination. In the first place, however, let me state that I chanced to dine in Albert Smith's company at the Cheshire Cheese, in Fleet Street, on the evening before he started from London on his journey to Chamouni. His animal spirits were tuned to a high key, and he spoke in rapturous terms of his intended visit; but I had not the least idea that he proposed to do more than spend a few weeks at his favorite resort.

"Off to-morrow morning!" he exclaimed; "and I shall make the ascent of Mont Blanc in a day or two."

"Bold thing to do," I said, "for a man who has not been in training, and you are rather heavy for a mountain climber."

"Never mind," he replied. "Pluck will serve me instead of training; and I have n't the slightest fear."

When I afterwards shook hands with him I cordially wished hin a "*bon voyage*," and the next time I saw him he had written his story of Mont Blanc, and was preparing his entertainment.

The following is a literal transcript of the document just referred to: —

"We, Albert Smith, one of Her Britannic Majesty's representatives on the summit of Mont Blanc, Knight of the most noble order of the Grands Mulets, Baron Galignani of Piccadilly, Knight of the Grand Crossing from Burlington Arcade to the Egyptian Hall, Member of the Society for the Confusion of Useless Knowledge, Secretary for his own Affairs, etc., etc., etc.

"Request and require in the name of His Majesty the Monarch of Mountains all those whom it may concern, more especially the Police on the Piccadilly Frontier, to allow George Hodder to pass freely in at the street-door of the Egyptian Hall, and up-stairs to the Mont Blanc Room, on the evening of Saturday, Dec. 1, 1855, at 8 P. M., and to afford him every assistance in the way of oysters, stout, champagne, soda and brandy, and other aid of which he may stand in need.

"Given at the Box-office, Piccadilly, 28th day of November, 1855. ALBERT SMITH.

"God Save the Queen!

"*Vu au bureau de la Salle. Bon pour entrer Piccadilly, par l'Arcade de Burlington.* TRUEFITT.

"SAMEDI, *1st December*, 1855.

"*Viséed* for the Garrick and Fielding Clubs, the Vaults below the Houses of Parliament, Truefitt's Hair-cutting Saloon, the Glacier de Gunter, Jullien's, Laurent's, the Café de l'Europe, Pratt's, Limmer's, and all other places on the Rhine, between Rule's Marine Museum, or Appetizing Aquarium, and the Jolly Grenadier public-house, No. 1, Ellison Square, Pall Mall, South Sebastopol. RULE.

"*Notice.* — By the recent police enactments regulating large assemblies in the neighborhood of Piccadilly, this passport must be considered as available *for one person only*, and does not include the 'friend' who has always been dining with the bearer."

Albert Smith made few enemies, but many friends, and his name is invariably alluded to amongst them in terms which sufficiently show that his loss, as a quick-witted, lively companion, still continues to be felt. Indeed it may be said that apart from his merit as a pleasant and humorous writer, he occupied a position as a public "entertainer" which has never yet been worthily filled.

Kenny Meadows.

Of Kenny Meadows I had much experience in his domestic life; and in that position he was invariably as communicative as he was cordial, ready at all times to repeat anecdotes of great men whom he had known familiarly, and to relate many of the interesting vicissitudes of his own checkered career. William Godwin, the author of "Caleb Williams," he had met as a social companion; and "Tom Moore" he had seen in the poet's own drawing-room, practicing a song at the pianoforte; and he was particularly struck with the bright, dapper, *unpoetic* look of the little man, as he sat there *en déshabillé*, and he was much gratified at the very polite manner in which he received him.

Meadows's written, but not published, account of this interview was to the effect that he had been requested by the Messrs. Longmans, of Paternoster Row, to wait upon Moore — then living in Duke Street, St. James's — with a letter, which he was enjoined to place in his own hands, and not to come away without doing so. The poet was from home when the artist first knocked at his door; and hence the latter, pursuant to the instructions he had received, "wandered about to kill time" (to use his own words). On his presenting himself at the house a second time, the servant informed him that Mr. Moore had just come in, and he was ushered up-stairs. "The little exquisite" had pulled off his boots, and, to Meadows's astonishment, he displayed flesh-colored silk stockings — a piece of vanity which would excite much less surprise, now that the biography of the poet has become known. He politely handed a chair to his visitor, and begged him to be seated while he wrote a reply to the note the latter had delivered to him. This task accomplished, Moore made some complimentary allusion to certain illustrations Meadows had recently published; "but," says the latter, in describing the interview, "if I could have looked into the seeds of time and have known the poet's subsequent criticism upon my drawing of 'The Peri,' I would have damaged his curly black head for him."

Meadows was essentially valuable to "Punch" for the thoughtfulness of his designs — as exemplified, for instance, in "Punch's Letters to his Son," "Punch's Complete Letter Writer," and many of the "cartoons," which were intended to portray something more than a burlesque view of a current event or a popular abuse. The quiet, unostentatious way in which he worked at his art, too often under the most adverse and discouraging circumstances, and the pride he displayed when he felt that he had made a "happy hit," was somewhat like the enthusiasm of a youth who had just attained the honor of a prize. As a draughtsman, he never cared to be guided by those practical laws which regulate the academic exercise of the pictorial art; for he contended that too strict an adherence to Nature only trammeled him, and he preferred relying upon the thought conveyed in his illustrations, rather than upon the mechanical correctness of his outline or perspective. Among the many ideas on which he congratulated himself, he often alluded to his design illustrating the blessings of peace, which he typified by placing a butterfly at the mouth of a cannon. This he rejoiced to think had preceded Sir Edwin Landseer's picture of "Peace," in which the distinguished royal academician represented a lamb in the same position that Meadows had given to the butterfly. It is hardly to be supposed that Sir Edwin Landseer borrowed his notion from that of Kenny Meadows; but the latter, not unnaturally, considered there was presumptive evidence in favor of the supposition.

Meadows was very fond of a quiet stroll into the country — as far as Hampstead or Highgate; both of which places had from long custom more charms for him than he could see in any other accessible spot within a short distance of the metropolis. Highgate, with its picturesque rural neighborhood, was especially full of interesting associations for him; and he would frequently stop short at the entrance to some snug-looking residence — notably, for example, that of Mr. Gillman, once famous as the home of the poet Coleridge — and expatiate upon the public virtues and private characters of its former inmates, and upon events which had occurred therein during his own experience. In speaking of the Gillmans, he said the only reward they received for their hospitable conduct —(but it was a great one, added Meadows)—"was that of an immortality, for who would ever have heard of them but for their connection with the great poet?" Meadows, in these our pleasant perambulations, was wont to speak of an old lady who kept the Lion and Sun hotel in that neighborhood. This was a favorite resort of Coleridge, and the communicative landlady used to remark that he was a great talker, and "when he began there was no stopping him." Whenever she returned to the room, she said, after leaving it for a short time, he would still be "going on," and sometimes he made such a noise that she wished him further. Innocent grandam! Little she dreamt that in after time his "talk" would be treasured by the world as amongst the choicest fruits of genius!

Indeed, an afternoon's walk with Kenny Meadows from Camden Town, where he long resided, to Highgate, and an hour's rest at the Gate House, formed a most healthful recreation to me; for the benefit I derived from listening to my old friend on one of those pleasant rambles seemed to bring back a link from the past, so amply stored was his mind with the recollection of events which had happened within his experience. But Meadows was not always the mentor or mere cicerone on these occasions; for he would sometimes be in a jocular mood, and not disposed to take a serious and retrospective view of things which he brought under my notice. I had told him that a few evenings previously I had visited a friend of his at Kentish Town, and that when the door was opened the whole of his family, numbering about twelve, stood in the passage! At once perceiving that there was something extremely ludicrous in the picture, Meadows turned it to account by observing that he pitied poor ———, for his children were so numerous you could n't shut the street-door for them!

At the time of "Punch's" original gatherings Kenny Meadows was the Nestor of the party; and at this present writing he is, I have reason to believe, in a condition of health very little impaired by his advanced age, but is enjoying, at the close of a life in which he has seen too much that was bitter, the sweets of a Government pension, bestowed upon him by Lord Palmerston, for his poetical illustrations to "Tyas's Shakespeare."

George Cruikshank.

By a natural association of ideas, the name of George Cruikshank seems to connect itself with that of Kenny Meadows, for there is not much difference in their ages, and both have spent the greater part of a long life in illustrating popular works by the exercise of an imaginative power which has always added strength and grace to the subject-matter they have undertaken to embody. It would be idle to remark that there is a great deal that is not common between them; but each has oftentimes given pictorial expression to an idea which the other would have been proud to conceive. There was a time when anecdotes were rife concerning George Cruikshank's *bonhomie* before he signed the teetotaler's pledge; but in the long lapse of years they have almost faded from the memory, and he is now as familiarly known as the enthusiastic apostle of temperance, as he is for the moral lessons he has taught in his designs.

"Now, this won't do!" he will exclaim if he meets an intimate friend who he can plainly perceive has *not* limited his libations entirely to cold water for the last few hours. "Do you see that house there?" "Yes." "Ah," continues Cruikshank, "he was a worthy fellow who once lived there; but drink, sir, drink settled him, as it has done many a man." "Well, but *in moderation*," replies the individual thus admonished. "Moderation!" cries George; "don't talk to me about moderation; there's no such thing in regard to drink. Give it up entirely, as I have done, or it will give *you* up." "Well, but you see"— "See!" rejoins the mentor, interrupting him. "Why, look at me. What do you think of that for an arm at seventy odd years of age" (extending his right arm and displaying it, as if about to strike a blow). "Where 's the drinker who could show such an arm at the same age ?" I once mentioned this fact to Kenny Meadows, after it had been told me by the person to whom it had occurred, and Meadows observed, laughingly, "Well, I have drunk my share in my time, and I am older than Cruikshank, and find nothing to complain of in my muscular power." But no one could, for a moment, gainsay the zeal and honesty with which George Cruikshank has devoted himself to the cause of teetotalism; and there cannot be a doubt that he has effected considerable good by his precept and example. Of the various public occasions on which I have seen Cruikshank in the exercise of his function as a disciple of total abstinence, I call to mind one instance, as quite sufficient to exemplify the pains he has taken to inculcate the virtue, despite the severe test to which his patience has often been exposed. Some years since, when Henry Mayhew, in the progress of his work, "London Labor and the London Poor," had made himself familiar with the costermongers of London, that earnest writer presided at a supper given to the fraternity in a remote part of the East end. The only drink to be consumed was to consist of water and ginger-beer; and amongst the company at the principal table was George Cruikshank, who looked on with delight at the exemplary conduct of a body of men whom he had always been taught to suppose were the very opposite of teetotalers.

In the course of the evening a speech was delivered by the treasurer of the Costermongers' Society (the exact name of which I forget), and, on hearing this, the honest-hearted George began to think that it was time the costers were ranked among the public teachers, instead of being classed with the pariahs of society. Unfortunately, the ginger-beer bottles were convenient vessels for carrying something more potent than water; and there were certain individuals, seated in close proximity to the chairman and his redoubtable supporter, George Cruikshank, who had taken an opportunity of smuggling into the room, by means of one of the said bottles, an alcoholic decoction of the same color as *aqua pura*. This was of course entirely unknown either to the chairman or to

Cruikshank, and when the latter, in addressing the polite assembly, congratulated them upon the happiness they were enjoying, "with nothing before them in the shape of drink stronger than water," great was his horror, just as he pronounced the last word in the sentence, at hearing a voice exclaim, "How deuced weak!" The traitor was drinking gin under the very nostrils of teetotalism! The imperturbable Cruikshank said nothing, but the *look* he gave was intended to throw poison into the spirit! As to the eloquent treasurer, his connection with the society was not calculated to render much service to the cause, for it soon afterwards transpired that he had embezzled the funds intrusted to his keeping!

In the works of George Cruikshank there is a curious instance in proof of the fact that artists have often produced their finest effects by pure accident, when every attempt to attain the desired object by toil and care has failed. When the great George brought forth his remarkable figure of Fagin in the condemned cell, where the Jew malefactor is represented biting his finger-nails in the tortures of remorse and chagrin, Horace Mayhew took an opportunity of asking him by what mental process he had conceived such an extraordinary idea; and his answer was that he had been laboring at the subject for several days, but had not succeeded in getting the effect he desired. At length, beginning to think the task was almost hopeless, he was sitting up in bed one morning, with his hand covering his chin, and the tips of his fingers between his lips, the whole attitude expressive of disappointment and despair, when he saw his face in a cheval glass which stood on the floor opposite to him. "That's it!" he involuntarily exclaimed; "that's just the expression I want!" and by this accidental process the picture was formed in his mind. The practical filling-up of the design was soon carried into effect, and the result is too well known among the masterpieces of Cruikshank's pencil to need any description from my humble pen.

A Lover of Autographs.

My connection with the Sanatorium brought me in contact with a gentleman well known in the city for his urbanity and mercantile intelligence, and for his liberal doings in matters of a charitable nature, such as those which came under his control as a member of the committee of management. Holding a responsible office in his establishment was an ambitious gentleman who had published a volume of poems, and who had a great desire to possess autograph-letters of eminent men. This latter fact I allude to because I had reason to believe it was the cause of his introducing me to an eminent writer, whose works I had read with an appreciation beyond that which is ordinarily commanded by contemporary authors, and whom I could not have supposed I should ever have the privilege of meeting in friendly intercourse. In my capacity of secretary to the Sanatorium, I had been called upon to address a letter to the late Thomas Hood, requesting him to act as a steward on the occasion of a public dinner then about to take place in aid of the funds of that institution, and I immediately received, in answer to my application, a letter which the great humorist well knew would be read aloud to the company assembled at the banquet, and in which, therefore, he had contrived to embody those characteristics of drollery and pathos so peculiarly belonging to him. The effect of the letter was that the writer regretted that, "although a married man, and well tended," and receiving those domestic comforts which should help to enable him to bear the buffets of fortune, he could not, on account of impaired health, accept the honor sought to be conferred upon him. The dinner took place, and the letter was read out as Mr. Hood anticipated. Among the guests was the autograph-seeking gentleman before alluded to; and in the course of the evening he came to me to express the unbounded interest he felt in the letter as a valuable illustration of Hood's peculiar humor. I fully appreciated the incontestible remark, and *kept* the letter — for which, by the way, I was afterwards offered a high price in specie, but disdained to accept it, feeling assured that I possessed a treasure which must be regarded as a literary curiosity of more than ordinary interest.

Leigh Hunt.

In the course of a week or two from the date of the festive gathering, I received a pressing invitation from the poetaster in question, to dine with him at his house at Peckham, "to meet Leigh Hunt and his daughters," and begging me to take with me the letter of Thomas Hood, as Mrs. ——— (his wife) was most anxious to see it. Here was an honor so entirely unsought and unexpected, that I could only consider it in the light of "greatness thrust upon me;" and alarmed though I was at the idea of meeting the intimate associate of two such world-renowned men as Byron and Shelley, and who had suffered imprisonment for the bold expression of his opinions as a journalist, I very naturally availed myself of the opportunity. The evening arrived, and the party consisted, besides the host and hostess, of Mr. Leigh Hunt and his two daughters, Julia and Jacintha (I trust I am betrayed into no error as to the names of the fair ladies), Mr. Augustus Dickens, youngest brother of Mr. Charles Dickens, and who then held a clerkship in the same merchant's office as the host, and myself. Mr. Hunt sat opposite to me, and it must be confessed that my respect for the viands before me was much weakened by the reflection that I was in presence of a poet, whose "Story of Rimini" had attracted the notice and gained the commendation of Lord Byron, and who had often been alluded to by Shelley in his prose writings as among his choicest companions.

To be seated at the same table with Leigh Hunt was, I thought, like seeing Byron and Shelley by a reflected light; and I could not but watch, with a curiosity amounting almost to awe, every movement of his face, and every word that fell from his lips. True, I soon discovered that, after all, he was but mortal man, and that, despite the history of his past career, he talked and acted as a being of ordinary instincts rather than as one who might be supposed to have wings to fly with. Still I was constantly reminded of the indisputable fact that Leigh Hunt was "somebody," and that I was assuredly complimented in being brought into such close companionship with him.

I hardly dare venture to describe his personal appearance, further than to say he *looked* the man of that refined intellectual power which had given him his place in the literature of his time; that his complexion seemed strangely to harmonize with his hair (for he wore no whiskers, and moustaches at that time had not found their way to this country), in one uniform tint of iron gray; and that his shirt-collar ascended from his neck in a *négligé* manner, which might be considered slovenly, but which was picturesquely effective in its loose luxuriance. There was, moreover, a sort of valetudinarian air about him, and he appeared extremely particular as to what he ate and drank, preferring, he said, the mildest form of nutriment, such as he was accustomed to at home — "just the wing of a chicken," and "only a moderate quantity of sherry and water" being especially demanded.

Dinner over, the company were ushered into the drawing-room, which communicated with the *salle-à-manger*, and there the host and hostess very wisely suggested "a little music." Accordingly the Misses Hunt most kindly indulged the company with a specimen of their taste and skill in pianoforte-playing; and at length our host prevailed upon his distinguished visitor himself to "favor us with a tune" — a knowledge of music being known to be one of Mr. Hunt's accomplishments. With this request he most readily complied, and good-humoredly observed, "I will give you a favorite *barcarolle* which I was in the habit of playing to Birron and Shelley in Italy" (he pronounced the first name as if it were spelt as I have written it — with two "rr's" and the "i" short).

He executed the task with a spirit and delicacy which could hardly have been expected from an amateur who had passed the greater part of his days in the cultivation of literature — "walled in by books," to use his own phrase; but if he had caused the instrument to speak or to roar, instead of making it "discourse most eloquent music," I think I should gladly have lent my aid to secure an *encore*. Indeed, the performance suggested a combination of three great names, whose metrical sounds had long rung in the ears of admiring Englishmen; and I could not help thinking how greatly many of Mr. Hunt's compeers must have envied him the power and opportunity of entertaining two such renowned geniuses as Lord Byron and Percy Bysshe Shelley.

In the course of the evening our host took pains to remind me of his wife's high appreciation of the autographic letters of eminent men, and he assured me that she would be "so much obliged to me" if I would *lend* her, for a few days, the interesting epistle I had in my possession from Tom Hood. Full of gratitude for the honor I had received at his hands, I immediately consented; and — as may well be imagined — I never saw the letter afterwards. Thus was I made to sacrifice a treasure which had come to me from Tom Hood for the pleasure and privilege of an introduction to Leigh Hunt; and it is in no revengeful spirit that I mention the climax to the story, when I state that the master of the feast was afterwards dismissed from the office he held in the city for the trifling error of paying more regard to his own pocket than to the interests of his employers.

Mr. Hunt had engaged a fly for the evening (in those days cabs had not asserted their all-prevailing sway in the streets of the metropolis); and as he lived at Kensington, and I dwelt on the road thither, he very graciously offered me a seat — an act of courtesy on his part, which I, of course, cheerfully accepted; so that I now found myself one of four in the same carriage with a world-renowned character whom I had previously been proud to encounter in the same room. In the course of a most agreeable conversation (during which I particularly observed that Mr. Hunt never strove to assert the superiority which he possessed), I could not resist the opportunity of telling him that, like himself, I had been educated at Christ's Hospital; whereupon he playfully observed that he was there *a little* before my time,[1] and that Coleridge and Charles Lamb were somewhat before *his* time. Here again I was rendered deeply sensible of the good fortune which had befallen me; for I had not only been in close companionship with the friend of Byron and Shelley, but was now riding from one extreme of London to another with one who had sat under the same masters as Coleridge and Charles Lamb. Byron and Shelley, Coleridge and Lamb! Four bright and penetrating examples of the literary character of this century — so potent in their moral and intellectual influence, that it is difficult to avoid the impression that, however unsuccessfully we may draw our conclusions respecting their mental or physical *calibre*, one seems to have been brought, as it were, into familiar communion with them, in having enjoyed the society of their accomplished friend, Leigh Hunt. He most kindly invited me to his "quiet suburban abode;" but alas! I let the happy chance slip by me!

Not long after the memorable little dinner at Peckham, a weekly periodical was started, under the experienced editorship of Mr. Hunt, and called "Leigh Hunt's London Journal." Thinking that a favorable chance was here afforded me of coming in contact with Mr. Hunt under more practical circumstances than I had yet done, I forwarded to him a contribution to the journal, and received a gratifying note in return, accepting it. Unfortunately, however, the periodical did not prove a permanent success; and when the final number made its appearance, the article in question had not been permitted to see the light. Many good-natured friends stated at the time that it was in consequence of its being known to the inquiring readers that they were threatened with a contribution of mine that the publication came to an untimely end! Without stopping to inquire into the truth or cynicism of this allegation, it is melancholy to relate that the MS. has been lost to a disappointed posterity. Hoping to redeem it, I wrote a

1 Leigh Hunt was at that time sixty years of age, as, in fact, he told me during our ride; and (not to be too particular) I was less than a quarter of a century younger than I am now.

respectful letter to Mr. Hunt, and in order that he might extend to me a little more indulgence than is generally shown by editors to casual contributors, I reminded him of the flattering circumstances under which I had met him some time previously, and of the friendly feeling he had then displayed towards me. In answer to my communication I received the following letter from his son, Vincent Leigh Hunt, dated —

"*April* 16, 1851.

"DEAR SIR, — I hold the pen for my father, whose state of health obliges him, at present, to write as little as possible.

"The address of Mr. Stores Smith, the projector and proprietor of the late journal, is No. 1, Edith Villas, North End, Fulham. With regard to the MS. it is believed to be at Messrs. Stewart and Murray's, printers (of the Journal), Green Arbor Court, Old Bailey, but if you do not find it there, and will let my father know as much, he will cause further search to be made.

"My father, who has a very agreeable recollection of you, is duly sensible of your kind expressions."

I applied to the printers as directed, but with no satisfactory result; and it was not very probable that I should ever trouble Mr. Hunt to "cause further search to be made." As to the "Journal," its existence was not prolonged beyond six months — sufficient time to bring into life the contents of one volume.

It is, of course, beyond my province to express any opinion in regard to Leigh Hunt's valuable contributions to the literature of his time. Full justice has been rendered him in this respect by Mr. Edmund Ollier in an interesting memoir of the poet and essayist. It will be sufficient for me to confine myself in this, as in most other cases, to the wholesome practice of "speaking of a man as we find him;" and I certainly found in Leigh Hunt a man who appeared the very opposite of one who could be capable of disparaging either a living prince or a dead poet. The monument which has recently been erected to his memory, by subscription, may at least be taken as a proof that he lived to be regarded as a gentle-hearted, kindly-disposed man ; and that, notwithstanding the errors into which he was betrayed in his earlier years, he won the respect and good-will of those who knew him best, and whose opinion he would wish to be recorded on his tomb.

JAMES SHERIDAN KNOWLES.

It will not, I think, be out of place here to mention that I once met James Sheridan Knowles (the author of a play which, if he had written no other, would have made his name immortal in the annals of dramatic literature — " Virginius ") under circumstances of singular interest. I had entered the coffee-room of a tavern in the neighborhood of Covent Garden, where a large number of actors and others connected with the theatrical profession were, as usual, assembled ; and I found that the company, instead of indulging in that freedom of speech, and that audible interchange of opinion which was their wont, seemed to be under some kind of restraint ; for those who did venture to say anything, spoke

> " In a bondman's key,
> With bated breath, and whispering humbleness."

This extraordinary reticence surprised me greatly ; and on looking round the room, in some perplexity, I perceived Sheridan Knowles (who was then in the zenith of his fame) seated in a far corner, taking no part in any conversation, and apparently not quite at his ease. " There 's Sheridan Knowles ! " whispered more than one gentleman of the party, as I advanced to find a seat for myself ; and, as I immediately perceived, it was the fact of the great dramatic author being present which had exercised a species of awe over an assembly of players ! In the course of a few minutes he rose to take his departure ; and I was much interested in observing that every man in the room rose in obeisance to him. This was a tribute to genius which made a deep impression upon me at the time, and I have often thought since that it did much honor to those who, in offering it, played a part so worthy of the theatrical profession.

Sheridan Knowles was singularly remarkable, as is well known, for an ingenuous simplicity of speech, together with an absence of mind, which it was difficult to conceive in a man of such eminence; and many anecdotes are told of him which prove the correctness of this statement. As I have never seen any of these in print, though they may possibly have appeared, I shall offer no excuse for introducing in this place a few instances, which were communicated to me by the persons to whom they relate.

Jerrold once asked Knowles to explain the meaning of a particular incident in the plot of "The Hunchback," which had always appeared to him to involve an improbability unworthy of so excellent a production. "My dear boy!" said Knowles, "upon my word I can't tell you. Plots write themselves." The same fellow-dramatist, having on another occasion made some observation to Knowles on a scene in Shakespeare which had much impressed him, was anxious to test his friend's opinion upon the subject (thinking, of course, that he would prove himself a great authority in reference to such a question); but the moment Jerrold pronounced the name "Shakespeare," Knowles exclaimed, "'Pon my honor, I never read Shakespeare. I leave him for my old age!"

When a version of "Frankenstein" was being performed nightly at two metropolitan theatres, the hero being represented at the one by O. Smith, and at the other by T. P. Cooke — Knowles, on meeting the former one day in the street, stopped him, and cried, "Faith! I met your namesake yesterday — Mr. T. P. Cooke!"

The names of Mark Lemon and Leman Rede used to puzzle him severely: and as both were, at the period I speak of, frequently before the public as writers for the stage, Knowles could never bring himself to understand which of the two was the subject of congratulation when a dramatic success had been achieved by either of them. At length he met Leman Rede and Mark Lemon walking arm-in-arm. "Ah!" said Knowles, the moment he was close enough to accost them, "now I'm bothered entirely! Which of you is the other?"

Of Knowles's ability as an actor I will not attempt to express an opinion, further than to say it was very far below his powers as an author ; and I will venture to relate a trifling incident, which I witnessed, in order to show that he could not be relied upon as a master of all the resources and conventionalities of the stage. He was playing the Duke of Buckingham, in "King Henry VIII.," at Covent Garden Theatre, and in one of the early scenes it was his task to deliver several important speeches, all requiring the most careful and vigorous declamation, and leaving very small chance for an adroit escape in the event of the memory proving treacherous. In these he was evidently somewhat at a loss, and indeed gave no little confirmation of his own statement that he had "never read Shakespeare." At length he came to a passage which brought him to a complete stand-still, and instead of looking to the prompter for assistance, or getting out of the difficulty by some dexterous *ruse*, as a more "knowing" artist would have done, he remained in front of the foot-lights, and thumped his forehead several times with his hand ; but the words would not come ! The gesture was one which is, of course, well understood in private life, but which could not be otherwise than ludicrous when seen upon the stage, as in the instance now recorded. There was an unavoidable titter amongst the audience, but respect for the author and sympathy with the actor prevented it from rising into absolute laughter.

INDEX.

CRITICAL NOTICES.

From the Christian Union.

"To all lovers of literary anecdote, and of gossip whose whispers are the murmurs of fame, the book will prove a refreshment in many a tired mood."

From the Boston Post.

"No more refreshing volume could be carried into the country or to the sea-shore, to fill in the niches of time which intervene between the pleasures of the summer holidays."

From the N. Y. World.

"We undertake to say that no one will feel the fatigue even of a long day's journey, if, in a Pullman car, he will undertake to satisfy himself with a 'Bric-a-Brac.'"

From the Congregationalist.

"It is of handy size, and with the pleasant tint of its paper, agreeable face of its type, and cover of odd device, has a generally 'natty' look which will make friends for it at once."

From the N. Y. Daily Times.

"One of the most compact, fresh, and entertaining volumes of literary and artistic *ana* that has lately been offered a public always eager for this precise variety of entertainment . . . . The editor has used his material with such admirable tact and skill that the reader glides insensibly from one paragraph into another, now amused, now instructed, but never wearied."

From the Boston Journal.

"A pleasanter volume than this, it has not been our fortune to happen upon for a long time. It is thoroughly delightful in style and manner, as it is unique in method."

From the N. Y. Evening Post.

"Mr. Stoddard's work appears to be done well-nigh perfectly. There is not a dull page in the book."

From the Worcester Gazette.

"We commend the book to the summer tourist who can be content with anything better than a novel, and will condescend to be amused."

From the Providence Press.

"The new 'Bric-a-Brac Series;' something unique and beautiful, both in design and execution . . . . If this first volume is a fair specimen of his judgment and skill, the series will prove first-class and popular, among lovers of pure literature."

From the Springfield Union.

"If we do not allow ourselves the luxury of quotation, it is because of a veritable *embarras de richesse* with such a collection of titbits to pick from. The get-up of the Bric-a-Brac Series is something quite unique and gorgeous."

From the Philadelphia Age.

"These reminiscences are highly interesting, as they not only give an insight into the every-day life of the individuals themselves (Chorley, Planché, and Young), but teem with anecdotes of the distinguished men and women with whom they associated or came in contact."

From the Buffalo Courier.

"Judging from the volume before us, none of these will be disappointed, for it is in reality a feast calculated to pique the dullest literary appetite, and spread in the daintiest possible way to boot. . . . . 'Infinite riches in a little room,' is the motto Mr. Stoddard has taken, and its spirit is faithfully kept in the sample of the series now given to the public."

A New Narrative Poem

BY

Dr. J. G. HOLLAND.

THE

MISTRESS OF THE MANSE.

By DR. J. G. HOLLAND,

Author of "Bitter-Sweet," "Kathrina," "Arthur Bonnicastle," "Titcomb's Letters," &c., &c.

One Vol., 12mo, Cloth, ... $1.50.

THIS is the first narrative poem written by DR. HOLLAND since the appearance of "KATHRINA," and it is sure to take its place at once beside that and "BITTER-SWEET." The scene of the "MISTRESS OF THE MANSE" is laid on the banks of the Hudson. It is a love-story beginning where so many leave off, at marriage; it abounds in striking pictures of natural scenery; it is full of the philosophy of life which comes from a pure experience; and it is distinguished by all that comprehension of the poetic in every-day life, and all that impulse and vitality which have from the beginning characterized the writings of its author. This is the first long poem by DR. HOLLAND written in rhyme instead of blank verse, the stanza chosen being the same as that used by him in the introduction to "BITTER-SWEET."

DR. HOLLAND'S WORKS.

Each in One Volume 12mo.

ARTHUR BONNICASTLE. One vol. 12mo, $1.75.

*BITTER-SWEET; a Poem,	$1 50
*KATHRINA; a Poem,	1 50
*LETTERS TO YOUNG PEOPLE,	1 50
GOLD FOIL, hammered from Popular Proverbs,	1 75
*LESSONS IN LIFE,	1 75
*PLAIN TALKS on Familiar Subjects,	1 75
*LETTERS TO THE JONESES,	1 75
MISS GILBERT'S CAREER,	$2 00
BAY PATH,	2 00
THE MARBLE PROPHECY, and other Poems,	1 50
GARNERED SHEAVES, Complete Poetical Works, "Bitter-Sweet," "Kathrina," "Marble Prophecy," red line edition, beautifully illustrated,	4 00

* These six volumes are issued in Cabinet size (16mo), "Brightwood Edition," at he same prices as above.

www.ingramcontent.com/pod-product-compliance
Lightning Source LLC
LaVergne TN
LVHW010210110826
845151LV00002B/652

* 9 7 8 1 4 2 5 5 3 4 7 9 0 *